EDUCATION IN NAZI GERMANY

EDUCATION IN NAZI GERMANY

Lisa Pine

Oxford • New York

English edition
First published in 2010 by
Berg
Editorial offices:
First Floor, Angel Court, 81 St Clements Street, Oxford OX4 1AW, UK
175 Fifth Avenue, New York, NY 10010, USA

Berg is the imprint of Oxford International Publishers Ltd.

Library of Congress Cataloging-in-Publication Data

Pine, Lisa.
    Education in Nazi Germany / Lisa Pine. — English ed.
        p. cm.
    Includes bibliographical references and index.
    ISBN 978-1-84520-265-1 (pbk.) — ISBN 978-1-84520-264-4 (cloth)
    1. Education—Germany—History—20th century. 2. Education and state—
Germany—History—20th century. 3. Education—Political aspects—Germany—
History—20th century. 4. National socialism and education—Germany.
5. National socialism and youth—Germany. I. Title.
    LA721.8.P56 2010
    370.942'09043—dc22

                                                            2010037203

British Library Cataloguing-in-Publication Data

A catalogue record for this book is available from the British Library.

ISBN   978 1 84520 264 4 (Cloth)
        978 1 84520 265 1 (Paper)
e-ISBN 978 1 84788 765 8 (Institutional)
        978 1 84788 764 1 (Individual)

Typeset by JS Typesetting Ltd, Porthcawl, Mid Glamorgan.
Printed in the UK by the MPG Books Group.

www.bergpublishers.com

For my parents

CONTENTS

Acknowledgements   ix

Introduction   1

1   The Historical Context   7

2   Nazi Education Policy   13

3   The Curriculum and School Textbooks   41

4   The Nazi Elite Schools   71

5   The Hitler Youth   95

6   The League of German Girls   117

Conclusion   137

Glossary of Abbreviations and Terms   141

Bibliography   143

Index   153

ACKNOWLEDGEMENTS

It is a pleasure to be able to thank the many people who have helped me in the process of researching and writing this book. I am grateful to the staff of the Bundesarchiv in Berlin, the Institut für Zeitgeschichte in Munich, the Georg Eckert Institute in Brunswick, as well as staff at the British Library, the British Newspaper Library, the Wiener Library and the German Historical Institute in London, for their assistance.

I should like to thank the British Academy for a Small Research Grant awarded to me in 2008 for archival research in Berlin. I am grateful to the SPUR Institute and the Research Opportunities Fund at London South Bank University for their generous funding of my research over the last few years.

I should like to thank my very capable and efficient research assistants, Manuel Siebert, Anna Heizmann and Anna Keller for all their hard work. I am very grateful to Stephanie Salzmann and Ulrich Schlie for their wonderful and kind hospitality in Berlin. I should like to express my appreciation to Hans Hahn and Laurence Marlow for reading the manuscript and suggesting improvements. My thanks are also due to my editor, Julia Hall, for her enthusiasm for the project, her patience and her help, and to my copy-editor, Julene Knox, for her hard work.

My acknowledgements would be incomplete without a note of personal thanks to my wonderful family, who have supported me throughout the writing of this book. My husband, Andrew Fields, who always has faith in my endeavours, and my children, Gabrielle and Sasha Fields, who have consistently encouraged me to write this book and have been very patient in allowing me to do so.

INTRODUCTION

In my great educative work, I am beginning with the young. We older ones are used up. Yes, we are old already. We are rotten to the marrow. We have no unrestrained instincts left. We are bearing the burden of a humiliating past, and have in our blood the dull recollection of serfdom and servility. But my magnificent youngsters! Are there finer ones anywhere in the world? Look at these young men and boys! What material! With them I can make a new world.

Adolf Hitler*

The main objective of this book is to provide a re-evaluation of education and the so-cialization of youth in the Third Reich in the light of new knowledge, theories and debates about the nature of the Nazi state. This will be achieved by analysing three main areas: education policy, the Nazi elite schools and the Nazi youth groups. Education is fundamental to our entire macro-view of the Third Reich, as the process of shaping the minds of the future generation was such a significant aspect of the Nazi regime. This book addresses a number of important questions, many of which have not been adequately treated in the secondary literature on the Third Reich: What were the aims of Nazi education policy? Was the regime successful in achieving these objectives? Who made Nazi education policy? What changes were made to the education system and to the school curriculum? How did the Nazi regime use school textbooks as propaganda instruments? What was the role and significance of the Nazi elite schools in the Third Reich? How was youth socialization achieved in the Nazi youth groups?

The Nazi regime sought to win over young people by means of both the schools and the youth groups. Indeed, some Nazi pedagogues believed that schools should play a secondary role to youth groups. This book links the schools and youth groups together conceptually, demonstrating how the Nazi regime utilized both, in order to achieve a 'total education' of German youth. In particular, the Nazi regime used education and socialization to create identity. Whilst recent works have considered the role played by propaganda, the SS, the Nazi women's organizations and other Party formations in the creation of identity, the part played by schools and youth groups together requires more detailed analysis. Education and socialization in Nazi Germany were fundamental to the shaping and forging of national identity, as well as self-perception and the percep-tion of 'others'. This was bound up with the wider issue of inclusion in and exclusion from the *Volksgemeinschaft* (national community). Education under National Socialism was directed at creating a new awareness, changing the way people thought and eroding traditional loyalties. Propaganda, underpinned by the threat and use of terror, was another integral part of this process. The Hitler regime employed a combination of policies designed to create consensus, as well as censorship, aiming to ensure that access to other sources of information or ways of thought was unavailable. Hence, the specific area of study of education and youth socialization is central to our understanding of the National Socialist state. The shaping of culture and stamping of identity in line with the Nazi *Weltanschauung* (world view) and the education and socialization of youth to become the ideal future generation of Germans are fundamental to our wider comprehension of the Third Reich.

The existing literature consists of books that deal with various aspects of education and others that treat the youth groups. The historiography of Nazi education is vast and complex, but much of it also rather dated, having been written between the 1960s and 1980s. Eilers was the pioneer in this field, publishing in 1963 the first post-war account of education under National Socialism.[1] This book was followed by a number of significant works on schools, education and the curriculum in the Nazi era published in the 1970s and 1980s.[2] Since then, a handful of works on education appeared in the 1990s, but even these are now over a decade old.[3] Important research on Nazi youth groups published in the 1980s and 1990s highlighted the significance of youth groups to Nazi education.[4] It is now time to move the subject forward with a fresh approach and to offer a perspective on Nazi education policy that encompasses both schools and youth groups. Indeed, Nazi educationalists believed that 'teachers and HJ leaders are equal partners in the education of German youth'.[5]

Recent debates about the nature of National Socialism necessitate a re-examination of a number of angles and perspectives. Firstly, it is important to consider the continuities and discontinuities in education policy between the *Kaiserreich* (Second German Empire), the Weimar Republic and the Third Reich. In this way, it will become possible to evaluate the extent to which Nazi policy was novel. Education policy in the *Kaiserreich* was already falling under the influence of a move towards greater militarization and nationalism in society as a whole. It has been suggested that modern Germany took a *Sonderweg* (special path) in the nineteenth century that distinguished her development from that of democratic Western European states.[6] This view asserts that the modern German state developed its own 'peculiar' national character, which was nationalist and authoritarian. Was this the case? Was Nazi policy distinctive from that of earlier administrations or the culmination of this 'special path'? There is much evidence to suggest strong similarities to the educational policies of previous governments. In many ways, the Nazi regime built upon existing foundations – yet it often added a more radical slant or direction to educational policy. For example, elite educational institutions had existed throughout previous centuries, but under National Socialism they took on a different ideological mantle.

Secondly, historical debates surrounding the nature of the Nazi state and system of rule itself can be applied to the area of education policy, in order to establish which theoretical approach is the most valid. For example, the 'intentionalist–structuralist' debate has been applied to certain aspects of Nazi policy, most notably foreign policy and anti-Semitic policy, in order to evaluate the extent of Hitler's own role in policy-making. It is necessary to consider this in regard to educational policy too. The evidence suggests that Hitler's ideology and views on education provided a backdrop to education policy. However, Hitler did not take an active role in its evolution. Policy emerged from other initiatives and centres of power. Furthermore, it is necessary to assess the extent to which there was a central focus or command for the making of educational policy.

Was the Ministry of Education necessarily the focal point of policy-making in this sphere? In fact, the primacy of Bernhard Rust's position as Minister of Education in policy-making was not unchallenged by other individuals and agencies. Competing protagonists and organizations struggled over areas of responsibility in educational policy-making.

Thirdly, a consideration of how educational policy fits into the overall debate on 'modernity versus reaction' in the Third Reich is important. Was Hitler's policy towards education 'modernizing' (as it claimed to be) or not? Herf has conceptualized the Weimar Republic and the National Socialist eras together as exemplars of 'reactionary modernism'.[7] This highlights the tensions between the embrace of modern technology and the atavistic ideological principles that existed in both the Weimar and the Nazi years. Certainly, the Nazis excoriated the big cities and idealized the countryside. The Nazi *Blut und Boden* (blood and soil) mythology and its yearning for a return to a pre-industrial idyll conflicted with the reality of advances such as the building of motorways and the impact of mass tourism on German society. Similarly, there were aspects of both modernization and anti-modernism in Nazi educational policy, which were inconsistent in this regard. As was the case in many other areas of social policy, in particular policy towards women and the family, ambiguities abounded. Certain aspects of educational policy appeared modernizing, whilst others were not. For example, the Nazi government rationalized the secondary school system, yet educational standards declined. This was partly because Nazi ideological tenets conflicted with practical considerations, particularly in the wartime period.

Despite inconsistencies and internal conflicts in policy-making, the Nazi regime aimed at a 'total education' of youth that corresponded with Hitler's fundamental ideas on education. Hitler had strong views on the role of the state in education. In the Third Reich, the emphasis of education moved away from the individual to the requirements of the state and the 'national community'. Education through the 'experience of community' was an essential concept, because individuals were not regarded as autonomous, but as part of the entire organism of the *Volk*. This was bound up with the issues of belonging and identity as well. Individuals functioned as members of the 'national community' and as guarantors of its development and strength. Everyday life was conceived of as part of a perpetual struggle for the national cause and against the 'enemies' of the state. The mobilization of youth in this way, as well as the creation of a sense of conformity and uniformity, formed an integral part of the Nazis' overall design.

It is important to consider why youth was so important to the Hitler regime. Nazi leaders viewed the German youth as a catalyst for change away from what they regarded as the decadent political system of the Weimar Republic towards the new 'national community' of the future. The Nazi education theorist Ernst Krieck described the youth as the bearer of the principle of the German (National Socialist) revolution, from which would develop 'a new nation, a new form of humanity and a new order of living space'.[8] In order to achieve this, the regime's 'total' education and socialization programme encompassed both schools and youth groups. 'Youth organization is to be seen by schools as a linear expansion and deepening of the work of schools'.[9]

Nazi 'total education' removed youth from the usual frames of social reference, such as the family, trying to encompass the entire experience of youth. It immersed young people in a completely organized network. It made huge incursions into leisure time and took up the majority of their waking hours. Furthermore, Hitler was keen to place the function of socialization firmly within youth groups and schools, removing it from the family as much as possible. Moreover, Hitler's contempt for intellectual endeavour and his cynicism towards schoolteachers further enhanced the position of youth groups within the Nazi state. This is a large part of the reason why youth groups in the Third Reich had such a significant role designated to them. Schools' and parents' roles were partly undermined by Hitler's idea that 'youth must be educated by youth', a concept taken from the German youth movement.

Before embarking upon an examination of Nazi education policy, it is important to place the subject within its proper historical context. Hence, this book begins with a short chapter that considers the background to education in the Third Reich by looking at trends in education in the preceding eras. The second chapter analyses the impact of the Nazi *Machtergreifung* on German education. What were Hitler's views on education and how did they shape Nazi education policy? This chapter goes on to examine the role of the *NS-Lehrerbund* (NSLB) or National Socialist Teachers' Association in education. It explores educational policy and decision-making. It examines the role of the Ministry of Education and the influence of competing agencies and individuals upon its work. Furthermore, it analyses the changes made by the National Socialist regime to the German education system at all levels – from kindergarten to university.

The third chapter examines the school curriculum during the Third Reich and the impact of Nazism in the classroom. Many subjects within the school curriculum were used to expound Nazi ideology, most notably biology, physics, chemistry, history, geography, mathematics and German. This chapter analyses the use of school textbooks to disseminate Nazi ideology. In particular, it focuses on political socialization in schools, including the key themes of anti-Bolshevism, the creation of Nazi myths and heroes, as well as the forging of the 'national community'. Furthermore, it considers the introduction of racial science into the school curriculum and anti-Semitism into the classroom. This created a culture of racial hatred and provided an ideological pretext for the Nazis' mass murder of the Jews. In addition, this chapter examines the Nazi emphasis on physical education. This aspect of education was close to Hitler's heart and a subject upon which he had strong views.

Chapter 4 examines the role of elite education in the Third Reich. Nazi elite educational institutions performed a special function within Nazi education and socialization processes as a whole. The purpose of elite education in Nazi Germany was to train a leadership cadre for the next generation. The Nazi regime established three main types of educational institutions to train the future elite of German society: the *Nationalpolitische Erziehungsanstalten* (National Political Educational Institutions or Napolas), the *Adolf Hitler Schulen* (Adolf Hitler Schools or AHS) and the *Ordensburgen* (Order Castles). These institutions were a microcosm of the Nazi *Weltanschauung*. They fostered the leadership principle (*Führerprinzip*), promoted competitiveness and emphasized life as a struggle and as survival of the 'fittest'. They encouraged physical prowess. They excoriated the 'enemies of the Reich', in particular, Jews, Communists and Socialists. They emphasized racial purity, glorified war and fostered militarism. They underlined the necessity for *Lebensraum* (living space) and had a role to play in the achievement of a 'greater German empire'.

The next two chapters deal with the Nazi youth groups. Chapter 5 discusses the *Hitlerjugend* (HJ) or Hitler Youth and Chapter 6 treats its female counterpart, the *Bund Deutscher Mädel* (BDM) or League of German Girls. There was an established tradition of youth groups and movements in modern Germany that long pre-dated the Third Reich. The aim of these two chapters is to determine what was distinctive about the nature and purpose of the Nazi youth groups. How did youth identity manifest itself before the Nazi era and how did this change after 1933? The Nazi regime used its youth groups to foster within their members a sense of self-identity and identification with the aims of National Socialism. In addition, the separate youth groups for boys and girls signified distinctive gender roles and expectations.

Chapter 5 analyses the aims of the Hitler Youth and their implementation. What activities did its members undertake? How were they socialized? Clearly, in the HJ, as in other Nazi formations, the individual was subordinated to the group. Conformity to the organizational norm was designed to create true believers in the National Socialist system. HJ members were bound to the community of the organization, and above and beyond that, to the 'national community'. The role of youth in National Socialism was to struggle against old traditions and against the enemies of the regime. This chapter examines discipline and training in the HJ, designed to prepare for this fight. It considers a variety of aspects including physical fitness, hygiene and dress codes, as well as education in National Socialist principles.

Chapter 6 examines the role of the League of German Girls as an organization for the regimentation and socialization of German girls. What tasks were its members engaged in? What was the impact of the League of German Girls upon its members? This chapter shows how girls were socialized differently from boys. It examines the training and education given to girls, activities and duties of BDM girls before and during the war, as well as attitudes towards sexual behaviour. It illustrates how the BDM formed an intrinsic part of the process of socializing German girls, as part of a blood-binding community, whose members were obligated to serve their 'national community' in any way required of them by the Nazi state. An examination of all these aspects of education and socialization, by evaluating the aims of Nazi 'total education', will enhance our understanding of the Third Reich.

NOTES

* H. Rauschning, *Hitler Speaks: A Series of Political Conversations with Adolf Hitler on his Real Aims* (London, 1939), p. 246.

1. R. Eilers, *Die nationalsozialistische Schulpolitik. Eine Studie zur Funktion der Erziehung im totalitären Staat* (Cologne, 1963).
2. K.-I. Flessau, *Schule der Diktatur. Lehrpläne und Schulbücher des Nationalsozialismus* (Frankfurt am Main, 1979); M. Heinemann (ed.), *Erziehung und Schulung im Dritten Reich* (Stuttgart, 1980); H. Kanz (ed.), *Der Nationalsozialismus als pädagogisches Problem: Deutsche Erziehungsgeschichte 1933–1945* (Frankfurt am Main, 1984); K.-I. Flessau *et al.* (eds), *Erziehung im Nationalsozialismus* (Cologne, 1987); R. Dithmar (ed.), *Schule und Unterricht im Dritten Reich* (Neuwied, 1989).
3. B. Ortmeyer, *Schulzeit unterm Hitlerbild* (Frankfurt am Main, 1996); W. Keim, *Erziehung unter der Nazi-Diktatur* (Darmstadt, 1997); H. Sünker and H.-U. Otto (eds), *Education and Fascism: Political Identity and Social Education in Nazi Germany* (London, 1997).
4. M. Klaus, *Mädchen in der Hitlerjugend. Die Erziehung zur 'deutschen Frau'* (Cologne, 1980); H. Boberach, *Jugend unter Hitler* (Dusseldorf, 1982); K. Huber, *Jugend unterm Hakenkreuz* (Berlin, 1982); A. Klönne, *Jugend im Dritten Reich: Die Hitler-Jugend und Ihre Gegner* (Cologne, 1982); M. Klaus, *Mädchen im Dritten Reich. Der Bund Deutscher Mädel (BDM)* (Cologne, 1983); D. Reese, *'Straff, aber nicht Stramm – Herb, aber nicht Derb'. Zur Vergesellschaftung der Mädchen durch den Bund Deutscher Mädel im Sozialkulturellen Vergleich zweier Milieus* (Weinheim, 1989); G. Kinz, *Der Bund Deutscher Mädel: Ein Beitrag zur Außerschulischen Mädchenerziehung im Nationalsozialismus* (Frankfurt am Main, 1990); B. Jürgens, *Zur Geschichte des BDM (Bund Deutscher Mädel) von 1923 bis 1939* (Frankfurt am Main, 1994).
5. BA NS 12/1196, 'Die Schulungsarbeit des Amtes für Erzieher (NSLB)', 19 Sept. 1935, p. 2.
6. On the *Sonderweg* argument, see J. Kocka, 'German History before Hitler: The Debate about the German *Sonderweg*', *Journal of Contemporary History*, Vol. 23 (1988), pp. 3–16.
7. J. Herf, *Reactionary Modernism: Technology, Culture and Politics in Weimar and the Third Reich* (Cambridge, 1984), p. 220.
8. E. Krieck, *Nationalpolitische Erziehung* (Leipzig, 1941), p. 48.
9. BA NS 12/819, 'Bekanntmachung des Staatsministeriums'.

1 THE HISTORICAL CONTEXT

There was a close relationship between pedagogy and politics in modern German history, and the education system was bound up with the development of the dominant political culture. The *Volksschule* (elementary school) was intended as part of a comprehensive educational system, without reference to social class or background. The German *Gymnasium*, inspired by Wilhelm von Humboldt (1767–1835), was founded as an institution to prepare pupils for higher education. Its syllabus centred on three spheres of education: gymnastics, aesthetics and didactics. Didactics, which included languages, history, mathematics and science, became the most important of the three areas in terms of preparing pupils for university. The *Abitur* (school-leaving certificate), which had first been introduced in 1788 in Prussia, became the prerequisite for entry to German universities in the 1830s. The *Gymnasium* created a new dominant role for the middle classes – whose political culture was important in this era – based upon educational ideals.

The concept of *Volksbildung* (national education) of the whole nation, as a foundation for national culture, promoted by important German educationalists, such as Adolf Diesterweg, at first had liberal connotations. Social integration was central to developments and reforms in school education. However, in 1854, the Stiehl Ordinance standardized the curriculum, pedagogic forms and the training of teachers. It stymied the attempts of educational reformers, and because of it the state played a much larger role in the content of mass education than in previous decades. Hard work and discipline formed the ethos of schools as educators of subjects, rather than citizens. As Hahn points out: 'By 1870 the term *Volksbildung* had completely changed its ethos; it had lost its national, liberal and democratic spirit and had become institutionalised as a force for inculcating in the common people an attitude of submission to authority and to the state'.[1] The education system that developed was unable to establish democratic structures or genuine socialization.

However, there were still pedagogues who sought to put into place measures in education in response to the economic, social and demographic changes brought about by Germany's unification and industrialization. The educational philosophy of Johann Friedrich Herbart (1776–1841) was pertinent to these changes in German society, both giving a professional ethos to elementary education and calling for a greater emphasis on science and a broader curriculum than Humboldt had envisaged in the secondary school system.[2] Vocational education became more significant in this period too. Georg Kerschensteiner (1854–1932) founded the *Arbeitsschule* and influenced a new form of vocational training. He introduced a dual system of vocational education. Male apprentices were to receive technical training as well as a broad general education in subjects such as German, civics, law and commerce. Girls' education was a preparation for motherhood and family life. Whilst Kerschensteiner's system raised the status of crafts and trade in Germany, this separate emphasis on boys' and girls' education did nothing to help moves towards female emancipation. There was also an authoritarian aspect to his method, with its subordination of the individual to state power. In these aspects, we can see elements of an educational philosophy later picked up by National Socialism.

The liberal ethos that characterized the German bourgeoisie was replaced by a conservative nationalism. Bismarck's *Realpolitik* had already begun the move away from concepts of liberalism, but the Humboldtian concept of *Bildung* suffered its most serious crisis after the unification of Germany in 1871 and the establishment of the *Kaiserreich*. The newly unified nation had different priorities and values. The educational system became more reactionary and nationalist, and less liberal and democratic towards the end of the nineteenth century. The true needs of the new German state were deemed to be based upon military and political success. Policy in Germany moved in a different direction from the general western European trend towards greater liberalism and democracy. Wehler suggests that the absence in Germany of the revolutions experienced by Britain, France and America in the seventeenth and eighteenth centuries contributed to the *Sonderweg* (special path) of modern German history. He emphasizes the absence of bourgeois liberalism in the *Kaiserreich*.[3] The militarization of everyday life in the *Kaiserreich* created an emphasis on hierarchy and obedience to authority. German educators became more nationalistic and defensive, as well as, simultaneously, imperialistic and chauvinistic. The works of nationalist writers such as Paul de Lagarde and Julius Langbehn gained currency. Langbehn urged Germans to liberate themselves from foreign values in order to raise the stature of German cultural life.

During this period, irrationalism left its mark upon concepts of education and society. Educationalists regarded themselves as upholders of the nation's culture. A new discipline of *Kulturkunde* found its way into the school curriculum. This subject integrated German language, literature, history, geography, religion and civics.[4] The Reich School Conferences of 1890 and 1900 saw the adaptation of the education system to meet the requirements of the jingoism of the ruling class. Furthermore, the German Youth Movement, which sought a re-evaluation of 'Germanness', contributed to this rising nationalism. Traditional humanist culture found itself struggling against this strong tide of nationalism and *Realpolitik*. Kaiser Wilhelm II became engaged in the *Schulstreit* (school dispute) in 1890. He called for more 'character building' and physical education in *Gymnasium* education, as well as a greater emphasis upon the nation's heritage, history and geography. The traditional focus on education in the classics in the *Gymnasium* decreased in significance. The result of the school dispute was a considerable expansion of the secondary school system with changes to the *Realgymnasium* and the introduction of a new type of school – the *Oberrealschule*. These schools favoured a more technological education than the *Gymnasium*, which was considered to overburden its pupils' minds and to lack practical relevance. These schools fulfilled the real demands of technology and industry. By 1900, the status of the *Realgymnasium* and the *Oberrealschule* achieved parity with that of the *Gymnasium*, although Latin was still needed for university entrance. The *Gymnasium* came under attack and suffered a decline in status.[5] Friedrich Lange was typical in his assault upon the 'excessive humanism' of the *Gymnasium*, as well as its education in 'aesthetic idealism'.[6] He asserted the aims of patriotism, duty and 'the idea of Germanhood'. He questioned what the models of classical antiquity could provide in education that Germany's own history could not.

It is significant to note that there were organizations that demanded female emancipation in education in this period.[7] The *Allgemeiner Deutscher Frauenverein* (General German Women's Association, founded in 1865) called for entry for women into vocational work and higher education. Helene Lange (1848–1930) and Gertrud Bäumer (1873–1954) were influential figures in pushing for reforms in girls' education and admission to higher education. Curricular expansion in girls' *Lyzeum* schools that enabled them to take the *Abitur* was achieved by 1908. There was co-education at secondary level in some states, but the overall ratio of women to men at this level was still approximately one to three.[8]

As the First World War approached, 'the ideas of 1914' were chauvinistic, militaristic and bellicose in nature. This development went hand in hand with a victory of nationalist ideas over party politics with the call for a *Burgfriede* – a truce between political parties for the duration of the war. The impact of the First World War and of the Treaty of Versailles led many German academics and educationalists to seek spiritual renewal and to struggle against Germany's loss of status. They opposed the Weimar Republic and adopted a reactionary position.

However, during the Weimar era, modernism made its mark on education as it did on other areas of social and cultural life. Progress and reform were the watchwords of the republican era with a rejection of *völkisch* and authoritarian trends among reformers. Lamberti argues: 'the Weimar years were a time of exuberant pedagogical innovation and optimistic plans to reform the stratified educational system in the name of democracy and social justice'.[9] Modernism in education policy 'sought to extend compulsory schooling, develop a co-educational system, support the more technically orientated schools and broaden access to higher education'.[10] Thuringia and Saxony led the way in attempting to achieve these aims. Bremen and Hamburg also endeavoured to carry out extensive changes to the education system. Elementary school reform included the abolition of voluntary religious education, the introduction of a collegiate system for teachers, and the establishment of teachers' councils. The most progressive were the 'community schools' in Hamburg, such as the Lichtwark School.[11] Fritz Karsen established a new secondary school in Berlin-Neukölln, which enrolled youths from working-class families.[12]

Although such new schools courted controversy, Karsen believed that there was support for modern and experimental pedagogy in Berlin.

The League of Radical School Reformers, established in 1919 by Paul Oestreich, a schoolteacher from Berlin, also had some influence during the Weimar era. Oestreich called for a move away from the stifling values of the past, towards democratic reform in education. The League of Radical School Reformers was concerned with 'creative education'. It argued that 'our schools merely transmit knowledge in an authoritarian and dogmatic manner and in the framework of a thoroughly militaristic organisation'. It called instead for a system that would help a pupil towards 'the full development of his own particular nature'.[13] It rejected designs to improve the schools within the existing system, calling for a more co-operative and communal approach to achieving its educational ideals. The League of Radical School Reformers also called for reform of the extremely nationalistic and militaristic textbooks of the *Kaiserreich*. Whilst a small amount of headway was made here, the majority of school textbooks, especially in history and geography, continued in the trend of the former era.

This link between the *Kaiserreich* and the Weimar Republic was significant in terms of personalities and educational trends too. Otto Boelitz, the Prussian Minister of Education between 1921 and 1925, although not crudely nationalistic, nevertheless asserted that the most important educational task was the renewal of national power and unity.[14] Carl Becker, who succeeded him in this role between 1925 and 1930, took a similar stance. Both had been reared in a nationalist tradition from which they found it difficult to move away. Prince Max von Baden took a conservative, counter-revolutionary stance on education. He founded a school at Salem near Lake Constance in 1920, which reflected his political and social views.[15] During his opening speech, his themes were authoritarian and militaristic. He asserted the need for spiritual renewal, expressing a reverence for the countryside and a disdain for the cities. Prince Max von Baden aimed at a national rebirth led by the traditional military elite.

Nevertheless, the Weimar Constitution guaranteed a number of fundamental educational rights, including equal access to education, equality between men and women and free education for eight years. It also advocated compulsory school attendance for the first four years of elementary school and entrance to secondary school based upon merit. It set down the principle of a standardization of teachers' education, in which all teachers had to have a university education and were given civil servant status. The new subject areas *Staatsbürgerkunde* (civics) and *Arbeitsunterricht* (work instruction) became compulsory. Private preparatory schools were to be abolished. The 1920 School Conference was the high point of the reform plans. There was considerable reluctance in some quarters to implement all these new reforms, and several initiatives were shelved. Indeed, elections in 1920 removed the Majority Social Democratic Party (MSPD) – the party that had spearheaded these educational reforms – from power. In the main, any ideas of removing education from Church control failed to be implemented. The Catholic Centre Party, which succeeded the MSPD, aimed to maintain and extend religious influence over education. Naturally, the Protestant Church accorded with these aims, and both churches rallied against the evils of socialism. As Hahn points out, by the end of the Weimar Republic, 'some 80 per cent of elementary education remained denominational'.[16]

In secondary education, the *Mittelschule*, which provided a route into the higher level of secondary education, was expanded. The *Deutsche Oberschule* was established in 1922. This provided another route to the *Abitur* and entrance to university education. As well as requirements to study French and English, this school concentrated on German language and German culture. From 1923, the *Oberlyzeum* for girls allowed entry to university education through the modern languages route, but without Latin. Similar routes to higher education were made available for girls as for boys. By 1930, almost half of the female pupils in secondary education were in the *Oberlyzeum*.

A significant shortcoming of Weimar secondary education reforms, as Hahn demonstrates, was that 'the proliferation of different schools prevented any attempt to integrate the various social strata' within German society.[17] In particular, the four types of secondary schools with their different syllabuses highlighted social divisions. The *Gymnasien* education centred on the classics, the *Realgymnasien* on European civilization, the *Deutsche Oberschulen* on German culture, and the *Oberrealschulen* on natural sciences. German culture was taught in all these schools, with a particular emphasis on history, geography, civics and religion. The Nazi regime was later able to build upon this strong nationalist, cultural perspective. There was, furthermore, a backlash against emancipation in female education in certain quarters. The *Frauenschulen*, which sought to teach girls about their 'special tasks' as mothers and homemakers, provided the answer to such concerns and again were a vehicle the Nazi government later used to promote its ideological imperatives in regard to women's position and role in society.

The Weimar Republic existed for just fourteen years. In terms of educational reforms, this time span was not long enough to bring about a vast amount of progress, especially taking into account the economic and financial problems that beset the Weimar governments. Nevertheless, as Lamberti observes: 'the opening of experimental public schools in many cities and the introduction of the new pedagogy in the urban schools placed Weimar Germany in the forefront of the progressive education movement'.[18] The most progressive period of the Weimar Republic in educational terms were its first two years.

Educational reformers faced an array of hostile anti-modernist groups and organizations. After a small amount of headway in progressive education had been made by 1920, the combination of this reactionary opposition with economic and financial problems impeded a great deal of further progress. Nevertheless, as Lamberti emphasizes: 'In the midst of economic distress and suffering and in the face of powerful adversaries, the progressivist pedagogues fought to realise their ideal of ... a more open and democratic educational system. The slowing down of the momentum of reform in the later years of the republic should not diminish the significance of what was achieved.'[19] In the early 1930s, Nazi ideologues and propagandists capitalized on the resentment of reactionaries and traditionalists who disliked the progressive nature of Weimar educational reforms and experimentation.

It is noteworthy that some of the trends in educational progress brought about during the Weimar years continued from those of the *Kaiserreich*. There was already some progress, for example, as we have seen, in female education, during the *Kaiserreich*. However, among some German educationalist circles, there was also a great deal of reaction during the Weimar years, with a continuation of the extreme nationalism that characterized the *Kaiserreich*. For example, the Prussian State Boarding Schools, housed in the former Cadet Institutions, were an expression of ardent nationalism and militarism. Hence, education during the Weimar era spanned the entire gamut from radical left-wing reformism across more moderate ground to authoritarian and nationalist viewpoints. The existence of strong anti-democratic and reactionary elements at work in education during the Weimar Republic meant that the Nazi 'seizure of power' in January 1933 did not mark a sudden, wholesale change. It is important to acknowledge the links that existed between educational developments not only between the *Kaiserreich* and the Weimar Republic, but also between the Weimar Republic and the Third Reich. It is to educational policies in the Nazi era that we now turn in Chapter 2.

NOTES

1. H.-J. Hahn, *Education and Society in Germany* (Oxford, 1998), p. 17.
2. Ibid., pp. 30–31.
3. H. Wehler, *Aus der Geschichte Lernen?* (Munich, 1988), p. 38.
4. Hahn, *Education and Society*, p. 30.
5. On changes in secondary education, see J. Albisetti, *Secondary School Reform in Imperial Germany* (Princeton, 1983).
6. F. Lange, *Reines Deutschtum* (Berlin, 1898).
7. On this, see J. Albisetti, *Schooling German Girls and Women: Secondary and Higher Education in the Nineteenth Century* (Princeton, 1988).
8. Hahn, *Education and Society*, p. 35.
9. M. Lamberti, *The Politics of Education: Teachers and School Reform in Weimar Germany* (New York and Oxford, 2002), p. 1.
10. Hahn, *Education and Society*, p. 50.
11. R. Samuel and R. Hinton Thomas, *Education and Society in Modern Germany* (London, 1949), p. 12.
12. Lamberti, *The Politics of Education*, p. 119.
13. Samuel and Hinton Thomas, *Education and Society*, p. 32.
14. See O. Boelitz, *Der Aufbau des preussischen Bildungswesens nach der Staatsumwälzung* (Berlin, 1925).
15. On this, see Samuel and Hinton Thomas, *Education and Society*, pp. 13–14.
16. Hahn, *Education and Society*, p. 56.
17. Ibid., p. 57.
18. Lamberti, *The Politics of Education*, p. 246.
19. Ibid., p. 245.

2 NAZI EDUCATION POLICY

HITLER AND EDUCATION

Hitler's views on education were clearly concerned with a reshaping of values, the creation of national identity and racial awareness. He was contemptuous of intellectual endeavour and scholarly education. This is evidenced by his statement that 'the whole method of instruction in secondary and higher schools is just so much nonsense. Instead of receiving a sound basic education, the student finds his head filled with a mass of useless learning, and in the end is still ill-equipped to face life'.[1] Hitler associated intellectualism with Judaism and decadence. Instead of intellectualism, he called for a greater emphasis upon physical education. In addition, Hitler believed that education and training had to be so ordered as to give the young German 'national comrade' the conviction of 'absolute superiority' to others.[2] Hitler spoke of the need for self-confidence and national pride to be inculcated in German youth: 'The curriculum must be systematically built up … so that when a young man leaves school he is not a half-pacifist, democrat or something else, but a whole German.'[3]

Hitler's hatred of intellectualism is clear from his statement: 'Put young men in the army, whence they will return refreshed and cleansed of eight years of scholastic slime'.[4] Hitler's contempt for schoolteachers was equally great; he claimed: 'I cannot endure schoolmasters'.[5] He dismissed his own schoolteachers with much disdain, describing his foreign languages teacher as 'a congenital idiot' and asserting that he 'could not bear the sight of him'.[6] He continued: 'our teachers were absolute tyrants. They had no sympathy with youth; their one object was to stuff our brains and to turn us into erudite apes like themselves'. Hitler claimed: 'When I recall my masters at school, I realise that half of them were abnormal; and the greater the distance from which I look back on them, the stronger is my conviction that I am quite right.'[7] It is unsurprising, therefore, that he sought to produce a different breed of teachers in the Third Reich and to train them in accordance with his own educational imperatives for German society. The organization entrusted with this task was the *Nationalsozialistischer Lehrerbund* (NSLB) or National Socialist Teachers' League.

THE NSLB

The NSLB was established on 21 April 1929. It actively recruited new members in the years before the Nazi *Machtergreifung*. The majority of the NSLB membership at this time was made up of young radicalized teachers, aged between 20 and 40, who felt estranged from the associational life of the teaching profession and disillusioned with the Weimar Republic. Lamberti notes that 'enthusiasm for National Socialism among the students training for the profession in the early 1930s was especially striking'.[8] Nazism's appeal was apparent among low-salaried assistant teachers without permanent positions. However, the NSLB did attract a number of older teachers as well. Approximately one-third of its members recruited before 1933 had entered the teaching profession during the *Kaiserreich*.[9] Whilst the NSLB capitalized on the low morale within the teaching profession at this time, particularly relating to the issue of salaries, its main propaganda themes were 'cultural politics and national pride rather than material interests'.[10] The NSLB promised a change in the image of teachers towards 'a new and more positive perception of themselves as forward-looking activists serving big national goals'.[11]

Hans Schemm, the leader of the NSLB, was one of the old guard of the NSDAP, whose ideas were conservative and *völkisch*.[12] Born on 18 October 1891 in Bayreuth, the son of a manual worker, Schemm was fascinated by German cultural traditions and was deeply influenced by the thinking of Johann Fichte, Richard Wagner, Friedrich Nietzsche and Houston Stewart Chamberlain, whom he often quoted in his speeches.[13] In a speech to educators in Bremen on 15 December 1933, Schemm stated: 'in our schools, we must build, mould and educate. Nothing foreign, nothing external, as Fichte said, shall stop us in this task'.[14]

The statutes of the NSLB laid down its duties. The first and most significant was 'education of its members as exemplary National Socialists' so that they could be equipped to carry out their special tasks and obligations inside the 'national community'.[15] The NSLB was to support the national leadership of the NSDAP and its chief educational office. It was to supply proposals and guidelines regarding all questions of education and pedagogy. Its duties further comprised control and surveillance of all German published texts, especially those published for a youth audience, and participation in Party youth and welfare organizations. The NSLB was to provide facilities for further ideological and professional training. The structure of the NSLB was organized along the same lines as the NSDAP, with divisions into *Gau*, *Kreis* and *Ort* groups.[16] Before 1933 the NSLB prided itself upon its struggle against parents' councils and other teachers' organizations.[17]

After the Nazi *Machtergreifung*, the membership of the NSLB grew rapidly to 12,000 in March 1933.[18] Many of the teachers that flocked to join after that were largely motivated by opportunism rather than ideological conviction. They joined because they did not wish to lose their positions or because they saw membership as a way of progressing their careers, once it became clear that *Gleichschaltung* (streamlining) was an inevitable part of the Nazi scheme. As a result, Schemm transformed the multitude of teachers' organizations and the mass of unorganized teachers into one community and integrated them into the NSLB. There were early calls to eliminate 'Marxists and freemasons' from educational posts.[19] Nazi pedagogues believed that 'only a strict clampdown against the red enemies' of National Socialism could make a difference to the future of German education.[20] Jewish and 'unreliable' teachers were purged from the profession within a few months of Hitler's accession to power. By 1936, there was also a ban on 'double membership' of the NSLB and a confessional teachers' association.[21] By 1937, the NSLB comprised 320,000 teachers (97 per cent of all teachers). Hence, the NSLB played a significant role in the regime's initial process of *Gleichschaltung* to homogenize the teaching profession.[22]

The NSLB had two main functions. The first was to provide reports on the political reliability of teachers for appointments and promotions. The second task of the NSLB was to ensure the ideological indoctrination of teachers. The organization saw its purpose as the creation of 'the new German educator in the spirit of National Socialism'.[23] It ran courses for teachers and set up special teacher training camps for this purpose. Teachers were trained in racial knowledge, for example about the supremacy of the 'Nordic race' and the 'pollution' of its purity by 'racial miscegenation'. They were taught about the characteristics of the 'Jewish race'. They were instructed about genetics and hereditary health, as well as the concepts of 'blood and soil', 'living space' and the requirement for German expansion eastwards.[24] Lectures on German prehistory, history and racial ancestry formed part of NSLB teacher training. 'The National Socialist teacher will only be able to live up to the National Socialist future if the idea of National Socialism burns within him'.[25]

In addition, NSLB 'exchange camps' focused training on the 'border zone' issue.[26] During the school holidays, teachers were sent to particular areas, such as Silesia or Saxony, in order to take a two-week-long course on the history and racial history of the region. The teachers had to pay for the accommodation and travel to the training camps, although there were reduced rail fares for this purpose. If they could not afford the cost, there was a possibility of some transfer of funds to enable them to attend the training camps.[27] Such camps were designed to bring teachers from different regions together in the spirit of National Socialism.[28] For example, NSLB teacher training in the district of Silesia was intended to strengthen the 'border-consciousness' of Silesian teachers by fostering and nurturing the connection to the homeland and the love of the German nation.[29] It aimed to emphasize 'Silesia's location within the pan-German east', covering themes such as the Silesian man and his work in the past and the present and the belonging of Silesians to the German nation. Tasks and training materials presented Silesia as part of the collective land of the German people. Furthermore, in the summer term, there were 'homeland hikes', and in the winter term, workshops and general meetings on specific questions.[30] Teachers were to get to know their homeland under expert guidance through hiking. They used geological maps to introduce the geological history of the area and to consider its contemporary natural landscape.[31] They learned about the history of towns and villages on their hikes. In study groups and workshops they examined the whole of the Silesian region, its family names and demographic circumstances. Once teachers were trained in these subject areas, they could teach them in their schools. They could teach history, geography and biology with reference to the specific training they had acquired about Silesia on these courses.[32]

A report on an NSLB training camp in Silesia in 1936 stated that the training aimed to 'adjust all the teachers to the common foundation of the National Socialist world view'.[33] At the camps, participants worked through *Mein Kampf,* even if they were already familiar with it, in order to understand its essential points and eliminate any misunderstandings. Group work was used to correct, complete, deepen and encourage an understanding of *Mein Kampf.* The report stated that 'the educators approached the work with eagerness and interest and have attempted to penetrate the spirit of National Socialism in lively conversations'.[34] The camp-supervisor explained the tenets of Nazi ideology and created a sense of community in which 'we' was more important than 'I'. A special emphasis was placed on the 'borderland' issue. Teachers were instilled with the sense that they played an important part in the future of Germany. 'They recognize the overwhelming greatness of the deeds of the Führer and his followers, the enormous work that has been done and still needs to be done. They have to realize that everyone, in particular the German teacher, has a long way to go before work is completed'.[35] The report admitted that 'not everyone who has taken part in the camp left as convinced National Socialists', but 'of the large majority of educators it can be said that they wholeheartedly support the Führer and are prepared to undertake additional work for the movement and the *Volk*'.[36] Apart from the 'ideological training work', the camp activities also included compulsory physical training for teachers under the age of 50, an early morning run, gymnastics, flag-raising, recreational time, visits to places of local interest, hikes and marches, visits by Party officials and speeches.[37]

By 1939, some two-thirds of the teaching profession had attended NSLB camps, whose fundamental objective was to imbue their participants with the Nazi *Weltanschauung.* The aim was to develop a 'way of life which was completely opposed to the liberal teacher conferences and congresses' of the Weimar period.[38] The camps were designed to create a sense of unity and homogeneity among teachers and to remove barriers between them, in particular in relation to status. Participants in these training camps were constantly monitored. The observers and camp-trainers kept personal files on all participants, containing information about their characters, in order to be able to select 'the best National Socialists' from their ranks. These files were used as the basis upon which promotions and requests for school changes were decided.[39] The NSLB called for an exemplary way of life for educators and teachers in the Nazi state.

A participant in one of the ten-day NSLB teacher training camps described his experiences. He talked of the spirit of camaraderie among the camp-participants: 'a communal life began for all of us, in this community … in order to find what was to become an adventure for all of us'.[40] He stated that the comradeship and general mood in the camp was 'exemplary'. The camp-participants comprised one camp-leader, four group leaders and sixty-five course participants, aged between 23 and 54. The purpose of the camp was 'to turn educators of different occupational classes and different age groups into one combat community – a community in which all dividing walls are torn down by collective existence and experience'. He described waking up every morning 'cheerfully'. The camp began each day with sports. He recounted how 'a true fighting spirit overcame all who have come to make their body younger not just mentally but also physically'. After washing, tidying up and making beds ('the making of the bed, which at home is done by the beloved wife, had to be done by one's own hand here'), the flag-raising and day's tasks began. Cross-country running was an integral part of the training as it created physical agility and ability, toughness, strength of will, determination and discipline. Such characteristics would endow participants with a readiness to serve and make sacrifices for the nation and educate them to be 'National Socialist fighters'.[41] The participant told of another attendee, who had been disabled in the war and so was unable to do all the exercises; the camp-leader's response was that 'what is important here is not that one or the other exercise is completed successfully but that everyone gives their best and experiences the spirit in this camp, takes it home and carries it on'.[42] The participant stated that 'not being overfed with lectures was important', yet he listed nine lectures, an average of one per day, including the themes of 'The German Space and Defence Problem', 'Racial Fundaments of the Jewish Question', 'Race and Culture', 'The National Socialist Perception of History' and 'Freemasonry and Jewry'. This last lecture in particular made an impression on him. It 'opened the eyes of all participants in a deep and thorough way to how the German people before, during and after the war ... was lied to and betrayed', until Hitler 'freed the German people from a scourge of mankind'. He left the camp steeped in National Socialist ideology, with a true belief in the *Führer* and a determination to carry out his part in the national task of educating youth. It is difficult to know how typical his enthusiasm was, but certainly his record is a useful first-hand account of participation in a camp, which correlates quite closely with the professed intentions of the NSLB in its aims and claims.

An activity report for a two-week camp for female teachers aged 23 to 55 from different school backgrounds also described how 'differences were overcome with the happy and sincere comradeship which prevailed'. This camp included one or two daily ideological lectures, with ceremonies, music and song to forge community spirit, as well as visits and a variety of physical training.[43] Camaraderie was also noted in a report from a training camp for female teachers in Parchim: 'From the beginning a comradely feeling of belonging together prevailed, since we knew that all of us were the bearers of one great idea and wanted to help our Führer to realize the great idea of the national community'.[44] Political and ideological training as well as physical education were the main aspects of the camp. The reporter comments that 'the training camp was a great success and has brought awareness of the community deep into our hearts'.[45]

The aim of the NSLB's teacher training was to transform all German teachers into 'National Socialist *Volkserzieher*' (people's educators).[46] The ideological training was intended to transform those participating 'totally and in every aspect of their lives'.[47] Ideological training was central to the work of the NSLB. The NSLB's Department of Press and Propaganda played an important role in this regard. It had to eliminate any liberal, ideological hangover from the Weimar era and ensure that all teachers stood together 'in National Socialist solidarity'. Furthermore, by means of propaganda, 'enemies of National Socialism' were identified and challenged.[48] Propaganda outlined the struggle between National Socialist, Nordic and Judaeo-Christian values. In this struggle, 'National Socialism cannot give up its claim of totality unless it wants to bury itself'.[49] The regime noted that participation in the teacher training camps needed to be encouraged through rallies and propaganda at the regional and local levels. 'The camps have to be places which mould fighters, prepared to show complete commitment to the National Socialist world view.'[50] NSLB members who demonstrated any deviance from this were excluded from acting as speakers at these camps.

The fifty-seven rural teachers who took part in a camp at Herberg from 21 July to 27 July 1935 were expected to play their part in the 'correct education of the German people to a true national community'.[51] 'The teachers are a combat unit for the realization of this aim; the training camp is their training school.'[52] One participant explained his joy upon receiving the letter inviting him to the camp: 'Probably no one sensed what a unique community these strangers, who came from all parts of our fatherland, would become during the one-week camp'.[53] The lectures gave participants an understanding of their homeland. The main success of 'the perfect camp-activities' was that 'all of us would hold each other together'. Other participants commented on this 'comradeship'.[54] A great sense of camaraderie was achieved, underpinned by the ideology of 'blood and soil' and sense of community.[55] This was considered to be especially important for teachers in rural areas, as they were isolated in their villages and so this type of camp gave them a sense of their common purpose and an understanding of what their part was in the building of Hitler's 'national community'.[56]

However, not all teachers had such a favourable view of the teacher training camps. The following two examples illustrate this. In the first, participants were offended by the anti-Christian sentiments of the camp-leader. In the second, inadequate organization was identified as a problem.

In December 1934, German evangelical female teachers wrote to the Minister of Education, Bernhard Rust, about the camp they had attended in Kettwig. They took exception to the trainer, Mr Friedrich, who was anti-Christian in his sentiments. Friedrich told them that 'participants believing in the doctrine of Christian theology in the Old and New Testament had to accept the blasphemy of their Christian belief'. He allowed for no discussion or opportunity for appeal against these attacks on Christian belief. Although they claimed their general allegiance to Nazism, they appealed to Rust 'to protect Christian teachers against such affronts'.[57] An investigation into the complaint, by school inspector Huhnhäuser, suggested that Friedrich indeed gave a lecture at this training camp, without the inspector's knowledge. The report suggested that 'Friedrich must have talked ruggedly, especially in terms of the church, so that a number of Catholic female teachers had to leave crying'.[58] Rust's own response to the teachers was that 'similar situations will not occur again'. He circulated an order to his subordinates that 'a recurrence of such tactlessness' should be avoided.[59]

The second example of a problematic experience was the tent camp of the NSLB at Heringsdorf in Gau Pomerania in June–July 1935. This was described by one participant as an unmitigated 'disaster', with 'inadequate organization' and much confusion.[60] The report on the Heringsdorf camp described the untidiness, problems with distribution of food and drinks, and unhygienic latrine sites. It stated that many participants behaved badly and got drunk. The speeches and evening party were described as 'enjoyable' despite the unfavourable circumstances in the camp. The official response to this report was one of outrage, although it was impossible to deny all the problems that were raised.[61] The idea of the tent camp was designed to 'pull educators out of old habits and to wake them up'. Despite the problems, the NSLB considered it to be 'a great event for the majority of Pomeranian educators'.[62]

The content of the schedule for a teacher training camp from 5 to 13 August 1935 was rather typical of NSLB training camps as a whole. Lectures were given on key aspects of Nazi ideology and policy, entitled 'People and State in the Third Reich', 'The Tasks of the NSV in Germany', 'The Woman in the National Socialist State', 'The Goal and Path of the DAF', 'The German Peasantry as the Bearer of the German Population', 'National Socialist Foreign Policy', 'Race: A Central Concept of the National Socialist World View' and 'Education to the National Community'.[63] Such topics were standard fare among teacher training schedules. Furthermore, there was special training for the teaching of biology under National Socialism, for example an NSLB training course on this subject was held in Tübingen from 11 to 17 October 1936. This covered a variety of topics including 'The Reproduction Battle', medicinal plants, 'Ancestral Biology and Breeding Lore' and 'Biology and the World View', as well as practical exercises and visits.[64] Additionally, there were training courses for 'racial lore', covering topics such as 'Race and Space', 'Race and Language', 'Race and Fairy Tales', 'Race and Art' and 'Race and Musical Education'.[65] This type of 'racial political work' was energetically promoted by the NSLB.

Clearly, the role of the camp-leader was very significant in these camps, and leaders were chosen with care. Camp-leaders had to have 'a strong personality' and to act in an exemplary manner.[66] The camp-leader had to rally the participants 'to nurture comradeship and forget all class differences'. Through the experience of the camp, the leader was to create 'an inseparable team and common destiny that lasts much longer than the days in the training camp'.[67] Their influence would enable teachers to go back to their schools ready to imbue their pupils with the spirit of National Socialism.

Schemm called upon teachers to 'stand in front of their boys with a German soul, transparent like glass, keeping no secret from them ... The boys shall look to their teachers as leaders and comrades'.[68] He passionately maintained: 'the highest ideal for the German teacher must be his awareness of his fortune to be in this position. This joy and fulfilment must come over him everyday on entering the school.'[69]

Fritz Waechtler took over the leadership of the NSLB, after Schemm was killed in an accident on 5 March 1935.[70] He was not an engaging successor to Schemm, and the fortunes of the NSLB went into decline. Although it still regarded its role as being at the forefront of the ideological training and indoctrination of all teachers, by this time the NSLB was expending a considerable amount of effort in justifying its continued existence and underlining its own importance. It appears that it was not succeeding in this aim as effectively as it had hoped. It defended its position, stating that the years 1935 and 1936 were those of 'small works and individual struggle', as an excuse for its lack of public visibility at that time.[71] In its publications and its actions, the NSLB glamorized its leaders at every level in keeping with the National Socialist 'leadership principle'. Its members produced propaganda material that justified the organization's role in the National Socialist state, highlighting its struggles alongside those of the Party as a whole. From 1938, as the immediate significance of the ideological training of teachers had diminished by this time and state funds were directed towards other more pressing concerns, the NSLB was attempting to defend its role more than ever. A significant aspect of the NSLB's work at this time was its appeal to its members to help with harvesting. Waechtler emphasized the shortage of agricultural workers on the land and the urgent need for assistance with harvesting. He urged NSLB members to report for harvesting duties for a few weeks during their school holidays.[72]

During the war, the NSLB worked harder than ever to justify its position. In 1942, it produced a painstakingly detailed report on all its activities, in particular attempting to highlight its 'important' contribution to wartime measures. The NSLB suggested that its wide-ranging tasks had 'in no way decreased' in importance since the beginning of the war, but on the contrary had become increasingly significant.[73] In addition to its previous tasks, the NSLB engaged itself in an array of wartime measures, under the slogan 'All for Victory!', including the 'collection of healing herbs', the 'collection of scrap materials' and the foraging for 'food from the woods' by pupils and school classes.[74] All pupils were directed to keep war diaries. These types of activities were popular among teachers. In this regard, one of the most dangerous strengths of Nazism was its ability to exploit of apparently innocuous activities and popular sentiments for its sinister aims. Furthermore, under the slogan 'Pupils help Pupils', the NSLB encouraged German schoolchildren and teachers to make 'voluntary donations of books, teaching materials and illustrative material for the construction of a German school system in the East'.[75] The NSLB was involved in the evacuation of children from the cities to the countryside (*Kinderlandverschickung* – KLV). The NSLB maintained that it still had a crucial role to play during 'total war', particularly in terms of upholding a cohesive and calm attitude on the home front: 'There is no doubt that the German teacher with his influence over the German youth significantly influences the mood of the German people'.[76] Hence, 'particularly during critical times', the attitude of the teacher was significant in influencing the nation more broadly. The NSLB maintained that it still had duties and responsibilities that were 'decisive for the outcome of the war'.[77] Despite its protestations, the NSLB was closed down in 1943.[78] Having examined the specific role of the NSLB, the next section considers the making of educational policy more broadly.

NAZI EDUCATIONAL POLICY-MAKING

The broad educational aim of the Nazi state was 'to ensure that a rundown, morally contaminated public ... robbed of its ethical principles' was 'again made a community of people ... aware of their inner values, their skills, their duties, their being!'[79] 'At the hour of the new state's birth, a new class was also born: the class of people's educators.'[80] 'People's educators' were more than simply 'teachers'. They formed 'an indispensable pillar of the state'. They were entrusted with the task of producing an unbreakable 'national community', without class, denominational, educational or regional distinctions. This was the educational goal of the new state and teachers were to set an example to the nation by creating their own microcosm of this community throughout the teaching profession.[81]

Bernhard Rust was a former schoolteacher. He had been an early member of the NSDAP, joining in 1922, and had become *Gauleiter* of Southern Hanover-Brunswick in 1925. Rust was appointed Prussian Minister for Education on 4 February 1933 and Reich Minister for Education and Science on 30 April 1934. In August 1937, Rust's Ministry established centralized control over the appointment of all teachers. In 1939, Rust set up a Reich Examination Office to deal with all educational examinations.

However, Rust was engaged in a constant struggle to keep control over his sphere of influence. As was the case in so many other areas of policy-making, with no clear policy guidelines from Hitler, different individuals and agencies tried to take the initiative. Rust attempted to prevent incursions into his remit from Josef Goebbels's Ministry of Propaganda, among other competing agencies. In particular, the Ministry of Education found itself in an increasingly defensive position as several branches of the NSDAP tried to extend their influence into school organization and education after 1933. The two main reasons for conflict from the viewpoint of the Ministry of Education were the desire of the Party to lower academic standards in secondary schools and the incursions into schools by the HJ and other Party organizations. Internal quarrels took a considerable amount of time to resolve and they seriously obstructed the work of the Ministry of Education.[82] Rust encountered intervention and challenges to his authority from a number of Nazi leaders, notably Baldur von Schirach, Martin Bormann, Robert Ley, Alfred Rosenberg, Philip Bouhler and Heinrich Himmler. Even civil servants from his own Ministry flouted his authority. Furthermore, the Head of the Party Chancellery read every significant decree by the Ministry of Education before it was issued. This process meant that the Party's standpoint was always included and it also slowed down the work of the Ministry and countered its effectiveness.[83] There was also conflict between the Ministry of Education and the HJ leadership. For example, the HJ leadership proposed to reward those pupils who actively participated in the HJ with good grades. This was one of the most significant and ongoing conflicts between the Ministry of Education and the HJ leadership throughout the Nazi era.[84] In practice, the Ministry of Education had only marginal influence on decision-making on the issue of youth participation in the war effort, although, theoretically, it was entitled to coordinate these efforts. In this sphere, Rust came up against the influence of the HJ leadership.[85] In addition, Rust's position came under continual threat from the Party as a whole.

Party leaders despised the traditional educational system, viewing it as a relic of the earlier times that Nazism had struggled to overcome.[86] They regarded a long-term school policy as undesirable and believed an ad hoc approach to be more desirable. Their chief concerns lay with issues such as the Four Year Plan, rearmament and the preparations for war. It was against these attitudes that Rust had to struggle. Not surprisingly, the Party favoured educational institutions of its own – the HJ, the Labour Service, the NSV and the Party Schools. The Party's own institutions were trusted and respected by Party branches and leaders. Until the end, the Party's own schools, for example, received financial support and had access to the full range of the Party's propaganda apparatus, in a way that the state's institutions under the Ministry of Education did not. Whilst the NSLB as the professional teachers' organization and the official Party organization for school education might have served the Ministry of Education by steering the NSDAP onto a more favourable course with regard to schooling, it was unable to do this, mainly due to the lack of an enthusiastic and able leadership. Hence, the policies of the NSLB undermined the position of the Ministry of Education even further.[87] Hitler was not impressed with Rust's character and achievements. He stated on 29 August 1942: 'we have made progress in the field of education, in spite of having a pedant at the head of the Educational Department. With another in control, progress would have been more rapid'.[88]

The influence on National Socialist ideology of thinkers such as Heinrich von Treitschke, Oswald Spengler, Julius Langbehn and Paul de Lagarde was significant. Moreover, a clear rejection of the Enlightenment and rationalism influenced cultural life and filtered into the work of Nazi pedagogues, which instead incorporated anti-liberalism, fanatical nationalism and racism. In May 1933, Wilhelm Frick, the Minister of the Interior, attacked liberal values in education, stating that 'the individualistic concept of education has been the main contributor to the destruction of national life within society and state and above all in its unrestrained application in the post-war era has shown its total inadequacy as a guiding principle for German education'.[89] In order to reverse this trend of Weimar education, the aim of Nazi education was to underpin the rebuilding of national life based upon National Socialist principles. Schnurr has conceptualized a change from the Weimar 'welfare state' into the National Socialist 'training state'.[90] The Nazi 'pedagogization of all areas of life' was an attempt at complete social control.[91] The pedagogue Eduard Spranger embraced the 'events of 1933' and the importance of 'a sense of the nobility of blood and of the bond of blood' as well as the need for 'a conscious cultivation of the health of the people'.[92] The aim of schools in the Third Reich was to train and educate the politically aware young German pupil, who 'in all thoughts and actions is rooted in the service to and sacrifice for his *Volk* and whose history and destiny is completely and inseparably bound to that of his state'.[93] Under National Socialism, 'the Humboldtian concept of education was criticised for its individualism and its emphasis on intellectual aspirations, which were perceived as factors weakening the *völkisch* community spirit'.[94]

CHANGES TO THE EDUCATIONAL SYSTEM
KINDERGARTENS

Before examining the changes made by the National Socialist state to schools, it is important to briefly consider the impact of the Nazi regime upon kindergartens. The kindergarten movement, which cared for preschool children between the ages of 3 and 6, had grown since the mid-nineteenth century so that working mothers were able to leave their children in a safe environment whilst they were at work. Friedrich Froebel (1782–1852), an eminent German educationalist and founder of the *Kindergarten*, considered infancy to be the most important period for education. He believed that children could grasp the concepts of harmony, unity and order at a very young age and that they benefited from a sense of community with fellow pupils as well as their family members. By the Weimar era, kindergartens had become part of the wider, nascent welfare programme that was designed to lower infant mortality, to increase the birth rate and to provide recuperation for mothers and household help for pregnant and *kinderreich* mothers.[95] Despite considerable debate about the issue of making public kindergartens freely available to all mothers who wanted them, during the Weimar years there was no large-scale expansion of kindergarten provision. Many working mothers were still in the position of having to find a relative, neighbour or friend to look after their children. Those who called for an expansion of kindergarten provision argued that this was important for the 'recovery and reconstruction' of the life of the nation. Kindergarten teachers believed that putting children in protected, supervised environments would ameliorate their conditions, in particular their physical health and their safety. In the kindergartens, they would help to raise 'a new generation' of German citizens.[96] Acknowledging the advantages of the kindergartens, a number of private companies and organizations, such as Siemens, ran their own. Apart from these, many municipal authorities, as well as the Protestant and Catholic Churches, ran kindergartens. The Weimar government established guidelines, sometimes providing financial assistance. The state required that doctors visited regularly to check up on the health of the children. Such moves were part of the Weimar concern to improve the welfare of mothers and children. Kindergarten teachers visited children at home to meet their parents and check their home environments. Government officials were pleased that the kindergartens benefited the children of working mothers and offered the possibility of checking up regularly upon children's health, and many mothers were pleased to have the advice and support of kindergarten teachers in bringing up their children. However, tensions did sometimes occur, in cases in which mothers felt there was too much observation and intervention on the part of teachers and the state.[97]

Under National Socialism, the nature of kindergarten education changed. The Nazi government utilized kindergartens as a space in which it could further its own aims whilst helping to alleviate mothers' burdens, in line with its rhetoric. Of course, the position of kindergartens under National Socialism was inherently contradictory, as the regime's ideology called for women to be stay-at-home mothers. Pragmatically, however, the Nazis could see the benefits of the kindergartens, both as a means of enabling mothers to work when the state required them to, and as an opportunity to raise young children in the spirit of National Socialism. The Nazi state introduced standardized guidelines for kindergartens. They were to be uniform in appearance and organization. A picture of Hitler was to be hung in a prominent position, the swastika flag was to be raised and the Hitler greeting was to be used. Children had to be 'racially pure' and had to undergo a medical examination and to present a certificate of health before attending kindergartens.[98] Compliance with these norms was expected of all kindergartens, including those affiliated to the Catholic Church. However, as Mouton notes, 'the degree to which the Nazis succeeded in imposing uniform standards on kindergartens varied according to local conditions, party leaders, kindergarten teachers, and the local population's acceptance of the changes'.[99] Those kindergartens that worked in the Froebel tradition or that were affiliated to the Churches were less easy for the regime to homogenize.[100]

Rather than taking over church kindergartens, the Nazi state allowed them to continue to exist, but placed increasingly stringent guidelines and financial restrictions upon them, in particular by reducing government subsidies, in order to encourage them to fall into line with state policy. The Nazi state also opened its own kindergartens under the aegis of the *NS-Volkswohlfahrt* (NSV) or National Socialist People's Welfare organization, to compete with the church-run kindergartens, although many parents still chose to keep using the latter. Nevertheless, by 1941, many Protestant and Catholic kindergartens had 'coordinated' themselves with the NSV.

The Nazi regime also used kindergartens for political expediency. For example, they set up NSV kindergartens in areas in which they felt the population was 'distant from National Socialism' and in rural areas, where previously none had been available, hence creating a sense of benevolence among the people and gratitude to National Socialism for making this provision (see below for more on so-called 'harvest kindergartens').[101] The

National Socialist regime used kindergartens as a means of intervening in families and imbuing young children with Nazi ideals. Furthermore, all kindergarten teachers had to pass a state examination which tested their knowledge of and commitment to National Socialist ideology, in particular with regard to racial purity. Kindergarten teachers were also expected to acknowledge the need for different socialization for girls and boys.

The NSV kindergartens were clean, bright, spacious and airy, creating a 'healthy environment' for the children. Every day, on arrival, the children washed and cleaned their teeth. They were then separated into different age groups and supervised by nurses and welfare workers as they played, exercised, ate, sang and slept. The 'Guidelines for Day Nurseries' in 1936 set out the following among its tasks: to sponsor the physical, mental and spiritual development of the children, to educate them in National Socialism and service to the 'national community', and to instil a sense of care for the German nation and morality. Hence, the kindergartens clearly socialized preschool children in the spirit of National Socialism. NSV kindergartens were considered to be 'essential bases ... for the education of young German people'.[102] The number of NSV kindergartens grew from approximately 1,000 in 1935 to 15,000 in 1941.[103]

Furthermore, the Nazi regime established 'harvest kindergartens' in rural areas in order to free agricultural women from their family responsibilities during the day so that they could carry out their harvesting. The 'harvest kindergartens' were regarded as necessary due to the lack of available, satisfactory supervision for children during harvest time. Care for children during the harvest period provided by the most elderly and frail villagers was considered to be inadequate and unsuitable. 'Harvest kindergartens' were first set up in the summer of 1934 to supervise children in rural areas from the age of 2 upwards. They consisted of one or two rooms, simply furnished with tables, benches and chairs, wash basins and a play area outside – either a garden or a sandpit. The kindergartens provided pillows, blankets, toothbrushes and hand towels for the children, but plates, beakers and spoons had to be provided by the parents. Milk was supplied by local farmers. The harvest kindergartens were run by trained kindergarten workers, with the assistance of older schoolgirls and BDM girls, provided that they were not needed for harvest work.[104] The children were medically examined and a health questionnaire was filled out for each child. Oral hygiene and general health were regularly monitored. Children with lice or any infectious diseases were not allowed to attend the kindergartens until they were better. The number of 'harvest kindergartens' rose from 600 in 1934 to 8,700 in 1941 and to 11,000 in 1943.[105] Their duties included the following: to promote the physical, mental and spiritual development of the children, to educate them in the ideas of National Socialism and to maintain contact with the parental home.[106] Hence, parents' evenings were introduced. In the harvest kindergartens, educational work corresponded with the reality of agricultural life. Children were taught to be 'productive'. The significance of the ideological concept of 'blood and soil' was promoted. The Nazis' thoroughgoing socialization of young children thus began in the kindergartens and harvest kindergartens, even before children reached school-going age.

SCHOOLS

At first, the Nazi government initiated a number of ad hoc, yet significant changes to the German school system. A report on the school system in Hamburg suggested changes to the education system and its reorganization to meet the aims of the National Socialist state.[107] It stated that during the Weimar era, the school system in Hamburg had come heavily 'under the influence of the Marxist spirit' and it outlined the setbacks associated with changes undertaken during the period 1918–33. As we have seen, the National Socialist state saw questions of schooling and education as an integral part of the whole organic state and 'national community'. It was the school's duty to communicate German culture to its pupils and to develop them as 'German human beings'. Furthermore, the National Socialist state aimed to prevent the 'Marxist' way of thinking from permeating the countryside. The Nazi state believed that families in rural areas had to show commitment and make sacrifices in regard to their children's education, not to leave it entirely to the state. The rural schools were to be state schools and community schools at the same time. In an organic state, the rural school was linked to both the state and the community.[108] Indeed, the Nazi regime attached such significance to rural schools in their relationship to German 'blood and soil' that it established a number of model Party elementary schools in rural areas: the 'Hans-Schemm-Schools'.[109]

In an organic state, each part was obliged to evolve to its own maximum perfection and play its part in the whole. The education system was an integral part of this entity and had a duty to serve the state to achieve its maximum perfection. It was the obligation of the educational system, under guidance from the state, 'to choose and judge and harvest from the produce and goods of culture: to favour what complies with the authoritative values and goals and to suppress what is perturbing and perverse for education and culture and what could be poisonous for the public body'.[110] Moreover, it was the duty of the educational system under National Socialism to prepare, implement and present these goods in order to develop a positive educative force. This included the production of teaching materials and educational plans. There was a further demand for those in the upper echelons of education, in particular school inspectors, to undergo a thorough selection process for the highest positions within this area. In this way, 'the organ of education can flourish to its maximum potential and the basic questions of the entire educational system can be worked on more thoroughly than ever'.[111] There was a sense that existing school inspectors did not have the correct skills, training and attitude to accomplish this. School inspectors were to be appointed on the basis of character and merit. They were not to be burdened with administrative duties that prevented them from carrying out their most salient tasks.

Between 1933 and 1937, the Nazi government was concerned with consolidating its power and imbuing the German population with its ideology. In terms of educational policy, this entailed a number of initiatives. In April 1933, all teachers were given civil service status. The Law for the Restoration of the Professional Civil Service (7 April

1933), with its 'Aryan' clause, provided for the legal removal of Jewish and 'undesirable' teachers from the profession. A law of January 1934 removed the autonomy of the *Länder* (states) in order to achieve centralized state control over education. The collegiate system among teachers was abolished, and the introduction of the 'leadership principle' in schools meant that all powers in schools accrued to the headteachers.[112] There was a call for the elimination of self-administration practiced by the teachers, the parents' council, the headmaster and the school inspectors in the Weimar Republic. Self-administration was based upon the principle of equality. Nazism considered that this approach lacked the necessary leadership over the entire educational work of a school: 'There cannot be any space for this kind of formal-democratic self-administration in the National Socialist state.'[113] Instead the primacy of the headmaster's authority in a school was to be reinstated. The Nazis rejected the democratic nature of the parents' councils in schools and these were eliminated in 1934. They introduced instead the School Community, consisting of parents, teachers and an HJ representative. This new system gave the impression of continuity with the previous arrangements, but did not interfere with the headmaster's role as 'leader'.

Plans for reforms towards creating the school of the German 'national community' were drafted by Nazi educationalist Weischedel in May 1934. Weischedel had already been engaged with the pedagogic literature on National Socialism and had worked as a teacher and headteacher. National Socialist school reform was 'not about the correction of some detrimental elements' but the arrival at 'a meaningful overall solution'.[114] Weischedel rejected any quick reforms and claimed that organic change was needed: 'National Socialist school reform is a lengthy, continuing process of transformation'.[115] It had to be carried out taking into account the pupils, the family and the transformation of the state and its culture. The Nazi educational programme had to comprise clear guiding principles which were in line with the fundamental ideas of National Socialism. The whole educational system was to undertake a uniform task permeated by the spirit of National Socialism.

In contrast to these ad hoc adjustments, the most sustained efforts and significant changes in education under National Socialism were carried out between 1938 and 1942. This was the period in which the Nazi regime was at its peak. By 1938, it was ready to make more notable steps in educational reorganization and during the first years of the war, before it became bogged down in its battle against the Soviet Union, the Nazi regime continued to put a significant amount of effort and resources into the 'education' of the *Volk*. After 1942, the demands of the Nazi war effort and the focus on the execution of the 'Final Solution' became so all-encompassing that other aspects of policy, educational policy among them, were overshadowed.

In particular, the National Socialists wanted to pare down the number of different types of schools that they had inherited from the Weimar era and to separate education for boys and girls. The secondary school system was reorganized and secondary education was shortened by one year.[116] The aim of secondary education was to educate 'the German man in all his strengths' and to prepare him for university and for practical life.[117] The *Aufbauschule* (feeder school), initiated in the Weimar Republic, was expanded, giving children from rural areas access to secondary education. These schools fed into the *Oberschule*, giving pupils the opportunity to join the last stage of *Oberschule* education. The Nazi government reduced the number of existing secondary schools to the *Gymnasium* and two types of *Oberschulen*, in which boys and girls were educated separately. The last three years in the *Oberschulen* were divided into a science/mathematics stream or a modern language stream in the boys' schools. School leavers with modern language qualifications also found it hard to gain access to university, as they had not studied Latin, which was an entry requirement for many university courses. The girls' schools offered a choice of domestic science or modern languages. The course in domestic science, popularly termed the 'pudding matriculation', did not qualify girls for university entrance. The 'special task' of the girls' schools was to prepare their pupils for the specific requirements of being 'a German woman and mother in family, home, workplace and national community'.[118] Certainly, this accorded with Hitler's view that 'The goal of female education must invariably be the future mother'.[119]

Girls were harshly discriminated against in the Nazi education system, as entry to the *Gymnasium* was for male pupils only and it was the only place where classics could be studied. Such policies led to a severe reduction in the number of women in higher education. In 1933, the Nazi government placed a cap on the number of female students who could be enrolled in German universities, setting the maximum at 10 per cent. By 1939, only 6,342 women were registered at German universities. During the war, the Nazis overhauled this policy, partly because young men were conscripted into military service and so university places were freed up. In 1942, approximately 42,000 women were enrolled at university, making up 64 per cent of the student population. Practical considerations had prompted a change in policy away from the reactionary Nazi ideology, which held that women should be discouraged from entering higher education.

The Nazi regime, with its claims of creating a classless, ideologically comprehensive educational system, placed increasing restrictions on private schools. The Weimar constitution had permitted the existence of private elementary schools run by the Churches, as well as private schools for physically disabled children. The National Socialist government took steps to eliminate private schools altogether, mainly aiming to eradicate separate denominational schools, which stood in the way of building the 'national community'.[120] The *Reichsschulpflichtgesetz* (National School Law) abolished private preparatory schools.[121] It made attendance at the state *Volksschule* (elementary school) compulsory, with exceptional cases made for children with mental or physical disabilities. The aim of the *Volksschule* was to provide education for all German children who belonged to the 'national community', regardless of class or denomination.[122] The *Volksschule* carried out its educational tasks based on the strength of German *Volkstum* (national traditions). The aim was to homogenize the composition of German elementary schools. There was considerable concern among Nazi educational leaders that Protestant and Catholic children had been separated in denominational schools. In the Nazi state 'such a division – separation into different schools according to religious belief – cannot continue … Children should be together in order to understand and appreciate the further unity of the community, our *Volk*'.[123] Not surprisingly, these steps led to concerns on the part of the Churches. Rust received letters of petition from Church representatives against these measures. For example, correspondence to Rust expressed 'great concern about the creation of non-denominational schools'.[124] These appeals to preserve the denominational schools met with no success.

The abolition of confessional or denominational schools under National Socialism breached Hitler's Concordat with the Vatican (20 July 1933), in which Hitler had promised that Catholic schools would be allowed to continue to exist. By mid-1939, all denominational schools in Germany had been replaced with non-religious 'community schools' and all private Church-run schools had been shut down. This was achieved mainly by arranging 'elections' by parents in favour of or against the schools, of which the purported results, claimed by Nazi local party leaders, were that parents favoured their closure. In this way, denominational schools were shut down without the need for a formal order of abolition.

Furthermore, there was a drastic reduction in the amount of religious instruction given in state schools. Stories of the forefathers from the Old Testament were regarded as 'unnecessary', and even Christian education was expressed in terms of the path and culture of 'the Nordic man'.[125] Religious education in schools had to conform to state requirements. In reality, this meant that religious instruction was either eliminated from the curriculum entirely or severely curtailed. Religious symbols and images, such as crucifixes, were banned from schools.[126] Nevertheless, the NSDAP had concerns about the efficacy of these measures, particularly in rural areas. One report from 1938 stated: 'It is shocking to look into the situation of the rural areas, which still seem to be in the firm grip of the black teachers [Catholics]. Bible quotes and church songs are what the pupils know best, while some of the 10-year-olds do not even know the name of the Führer, let alone how to spell it.'[127]

The Nazi leadership believed there was a superfluity of private 'special schools' for mentally and physically disabled children. It sought to reduce the amount of educational resources for 'abnormal people' through its eugenics programme: 'By eugenic measures and the sterilization law, we hope to decrease the education of abnormal people to a minimum'.[128] The regime hoped to achieve the 'purification' of the *Volk* by regulating the education of 'abnormal people'. Whilst the primary aim was to educate healthy German children with full mental faculties, the Nazi state also believed it had a duty to prevent 'the creation of abnormal people'. It was considered 'an economic waste' to spend time and money on 'the education and upbringing of feeble-minded children'.[129]

The Nazis had claimed that they would modernize education, with free universal education, streamlining of the school system, provision for talented children from low-income families and a university-level teachers' training programme. The reality, however, was that fewer children from disadvantaged backgrounds benefited from education under National Socialism than had done so during the Weimar era. From 1933, *Hochschulen für Lehrerbildung* were established with the aim of uniform vocational and practical training of teachers to a higher standard.[130] However, by 1941, these were closed down and as a result poorly qualified teachers were able to enter the profession. Most teachers' training remained below university level. Indeed, the status and image of the teaching profession had declined markedly under National Socialism and Party reports noted these problems.[131]

At first, the Nazi regime had maintained the Prussian colleges for training teachers and extended the system, for example to Bavaria and Württemberg, which had not changed teacher training during the Weimar era. However, it became clear that more radical changes were needed and that a shortage of elementary schoolteachers loomed. In 1938/9, in particular, there was a sharp drop in the number of full-time, male elementary schoolteachers. Hitler ordered in 1940 that a different type of institution should be established. This was the *Lehrerbildungsanstalt* (teacher training institute), which paid greater attention to political socialization. The new scheme was designed to increase the supply of teachers and to bring their training under Party organization. These new institutions had a much more political character. By 1942 there were 233 of them in the German Reich.[132] However, even these did not succeed in making up for the shortage of elementary schoolteachers, and the regime became dependent upon 'school helpers'. School helpers were aged between 19 and 30, having been educated to intermediate school level and then taken a three-month course followed by practical experience. In the end, despite all the training and plans for educational reforms, the Nazi regime demoralized teachers and brought about a decline in standards.

Regarding the Nazis' overall racial aims, it is noteworthy that education in German schools was intended only for 'racially pure' German children. On 25 April 1933, the Law against the Overcrowding of German Schools and Universities placed a ceiling of 1.5 per cent on the number of Jewish pupils permitted within any German educational institution. In November 1938, this law was amended to exclude Jewish children from the German state school system altogether. After that, Jewish children were only permitted to attend separate Jewish schools, at the expense of the Jewish community.[133] They were not part of the 'national community' and were therefore excluded from German schools. In 1942, the Jewish schools were closed down.[134] 'Gypsy' children were also discriminated against in the German school system and various ad hoc attempts were made to prevent them from attending school. On 22 March 1941, the Ministry of Education finally passed a decree that prohibited 'Gypsy' children from attendance at state schools altogether.[135]

In 1941, Hitler called for the introduction of the *Deutsche Heimschulen* (German State Boarding Schools). These were mainly intended for children whose fathers were in the armed forces or had died in military action or whose homes had been disrupted by the war or destroyed by air raids.[136] In addition to these schools, there were two *Musische*

Gymnasien (Musical Grammar Schools), one in Leipzig and one in Frankfurt.[137] These were boarding schools for children with exceptional musical talents. The curriculum was similar to that of the *Deutsche Oberschule*, but with the distinction that ten periods per week were given to the study of music and art. Admission to these schools was strict and privileged. Prospective pupils of these schools had to demonstrate their 'pure' German blood and good character, as well as their outstanding musical or artistic talents.

During the war, a programme of *Kinderlandverschickung* (KLV) was put in place. Children from the cities were sent to the countryside to be removed from the dangers posed by the Allied bombing campaigns. The KLV camps provided an ideal opportunity for the regime to imbue its youth with its ideology, as children were removed from their parental homes. There were approximately 5,500 KLV camps established by 1943. Entire classes and schools moved to KLV camps as schools in the cities were closed down.[138] Many parents reluctantly agreed to send their children away, and there were concerns that the regime was deliberately removing children from their parents in order to take the function of socialization away from the family. At the KLV camps, the children took part in drills and marches. They had to wear a KLV uniform and were educated to be true and valuable members of the 'national community'. They were used for agricultural work and harvesting. By the spring of 1944, they were engaged in pre-military training, run by the HJ, the army or the SS.

Nazi changes to education were implemented in the name of 'modernizing' the school system and making it more efficient. However, the true objective of Nazi policies was to ensure centralized state control over education, in particular to eliminate ecclesiastical influence. Although the status of the *Gymnasium* was actively diminished by the regime, it attracted even more middle-class pupils than before. Hence, Nazi claims to have made the system more egalitarian were unfounded. Furthermore, the carefully designed infiltration by Party influence of the state system was a hallmark of Nazi education policy. In reality, these policies did more to damage the existing educational system than to improve it. Although the Third Reich lasted only twelve years, its policies had a huge impact. It claimed that previous school reforms, which 'evolved from the daily life of urban, Marxist liberalism', signified the 'disintegration and dissolution' of the German educational system.[139] Yet Nazi educational policies did not bring about any improvements in elementary and secondary school education in comparison to those of the Weimar Republic. The next section of this chapter turns to the universities, to examine the impact of National Socialism upon higher education.

UNIVERSITIES

Whilst some universities in Germany, such as the University of Heidelberg (1386), were established in medieval times and the development of the universities progressed through the patronage of the territorial princes over several centuries, the modern period of German university development was marked by the creation of the University of Berlin

(1810). Wilhelm von Humboldt played a most important part in the development of the University of Berlin, which was steeped in the humanist tradition, and which served as a model for other German universities. He was concerned that the university should not be too narrow in its purpose. Prussia needed visionary and strong leaders and this consideration marked the character of the university. Humboldt was clear that the humanist tradition should be adhered to. The University of Berlin was defined as a 'privileged corporation' with self-government rights.

One significant aspect of the modern German universities was academic self-government. This was exercised by the faculty professors and elected dean, in faculty boards, which recommended nominations for professorial appointments and gave prospective lecturers the right to teach. A second characteristic was freedom of teaching. Professors and lecturers could teach freely, without political restraints or other limitations. They could choose the subjects they taught. The third salient feature was freedom of study. As there was no fixed syllabus, students could attend lectures of their preference and even move between universities. This system was aimed at developing the initiative and sense of responsibility for learning in students themselves.

As many of the German universities had developed in close association with the territorial princes, universities were dependent on the state in financial matters. This sometimes led to pressures to submit to state influence, especially as professors were state officials and their salaries were paid by the state. Professors came from a particular level in society and there existed a social snobbishness among them – a 'professorial class' (*Gelehrtenstand*). A mutual relationship existed between the holders of political power and the professors, who became the intellectual bodyguard of the *Kaiserreich* in return for the privilege, prestige and status associated with their position. Some professors, such as Heinrich von Treitschke, used their freedom to teach extreme nationalism that seemed to negate the purpose of the concept. Nationalism was a key trend in the German universities in the last third of the nineteenth century. Nationalist associations such as the Pan German League and the Navy League, established in the 1890s, were closely associated with university professors, many of whom chose to throw in their lot with the nationalist and imperial ambitions of the era. They became known as the *Flottenprofessoren* (navy professors).[140]

Turning to the students, at the beginning of the nineteenth century, there were two main types of students' fraternities: the *Landsmannschaften*, which were made up of students from a particular region, and the *Studentenorden*, which had associations with freemasonry. Duelling and drinking played an important part in the life of both these types of student organizations. In 1815, a new type of organization – the *Burschenschaft* – was set up at Jena. In 1817, at the Wartburg meeting, the *Burschenschaften* of the various universities came together in a general association. At the same time, the *Landsmannschaften* renamed themselves the 'Corps'. The 'Corps' members were aristocratic, whilst the *Burschenschaften* members were middle class. The *Burschenschaften* were closely associated with movements for liberalism and national unity at this time. They also aimed to put an end to the excessive duelling in the universities and to encourage students to live a more moral lifestyle. By the mid-nineteenth century, this trend waned as the *Burschenschaften* members continued to drink and duel. In the *Landsmannschaften* and the *Burschenschaften*, students' individuality was stifled. Student groups became increasingly conservative and anti-democratic by the end of the nineteenth century.[141]

In 1919, in the new Weimar Republic, the *Deutsche Studentenschaft* was founded to represent students' interests and to organize welfare. This was politically nationalist in its leanings. The *Deutsche Gildenschaft*, established in the same year, was even more extremely nationalist and racist. There were also anti-Republican students' groups including the *Stahlhelm-Studentenring-Langemarck* and the *NS-Deutscher Studentenbund* (National Socialist German Students' Association). On the other side of the political spectrum, there were the Republican Students' Group, the German Students' League (*Deutscher Studentenbund*) and the Socialist students' associations, all of which supported the Republic. Yet the voices of the nationalist and anti-democratic students' groups became very influential, particularly with the economic problems that beset Germany in the early 1930s. The National Socialist German Students' Association came to have a very large influence within the student movement overall.

The new social and political circumstances of the fledgling democracy required reforms in the universities. Criticism from left-wing circles called for the universities to expand their socially narrow student base. Carl Heinrich Becker, the Prussian Minister of Education between 1925 and 1930, noted that the universities were in need of reform, yet at the same time described them as 'fundamentally sound'.[142] Although he wrote on the subject of university reform, he vacillated in terms of policy-making.[143] University teaching in Germany tended to attract those from the upper echelons of society. The system was not designed for giving democratic rights to lecturers in terms of how the universities were run and administered. During the Weimar era, some steps were taken to give lecturers a small amount of representation on the faculty boards. However, all this changed again as the Nazi era approached, and authoritarian and nationalist voices came to the fore.[144]

In the realm of higher education, the Nazi government attempted to clamp down on academic freedom. Its task was made easier by the activities of radical students who had taken over representative student bodies in the majority of German universities eighteen months before the Nazi *Machtergreifung*. The National Socialist German Students' Association had been formed in 1926, under the leadership of Wilhelm Tempel, a law student. In 1929, Baldur von Schirach had succeeded Tempel as its leader. Schirach claimed that the National Socialist German Students' Association had three main tasks: to promote the study of National Socialist ideas, to spread Nazi ideology in the German universities and to train leaders for the NSDAP. But its true ambition was to control the whole student population.[145] The National Socialist German Students' Association quickly and actively set to work printing and distributing posters and pamphlets. Other student groups and organizations were passive by comparison and responded in a way that suggested they did not realize how serious the Nazi student organization was about propaganda and power.

Once the Nazis came to power, students campaigned against Jewish and 'unreliable' professors and disrupted their lectures. Students organized and participated in book-burning demonstrations on 10 May 1933 in university towns across Germany. This was a public act 'against the un-German spirit'. Students seized 'un-German' books, including those of Marx and Freud, from the libraries and consigned them to flames, whilst shouting out slogans against their authors. Goebbels described the public book burning as a strong, great and symbolic act. The students were clear about their ideological 'enemies' and the National Socialist German Students' Association planned the event carefully in advance so that the actions of 10 May 1933 were coordinated in university towns across the country. Elected students' committees were abolished and students' societies, the Corps and *Burschenschaften* either dissolved themselves or were closed down in the process of *Gleichschaltung*. The student body certainly recognized its role in the renovation of the scholastic community and participated with eagerness at this time although, as Giles has pointed out, student apathy was a problem for the National Socialist Students' Association later in the Nazi era.[146] From 1936, the National Socialist German Students' Association acquired a new leader, Gustav Adolf Scheel. He held the title *Reichsstudentenführer*.

The Rectors that ran the universities were checked for reliability and compliance with the dictates of the regime. Those that were not deemed suitable were replaced. Jewish and 'liberal' professors were forced out of their posts. Martin Heidegger, Professor of Philosophy, was elected Rector at the University of Freiburg in April 1933. He claimed that academic freedom now meant service to the 'national community' and talked of 'conquering the world of educated men and scholars for the new national political spirit'. Academic autonomy in teaching and research was subordinated to the interests of the Nazi state. By 1934, approximately 1,600 out of 5,000 university teachers had been dismissed.[147] Many German academics emigrated. The sciences were particularly hard hit. The world-renowned physicist Albert Einstein was among the many scientists who left their posts at German universities to take up positions in America, Britain and elsewhere. Still, most university professors remained in their posts and many of them were supportive of the National Socialist government.

University professors and lecturers had to belong to the *NS-Dozentenbund* (National Socialist Association of University Teachers). This was initially a part of the *NS-Lehrerbund*, but it acquired a separate status in 1935. Walter Schultze, as *Reichsdozentenführer*, ran the *NS-Dozentenbund*. Its main aim was to ensure that university activities conformed to the requirements of the NSDAP. Schultze stated that its main task was 'to make the universities truly National Socialist' and that education needed 'to participate in the National Socialist regeneration of our people's spiritual unity and community'. He continued by claiming that: 'The Association takes into its ranks all the forces at a university whose character and ideology attest to their unconditional loyalty and readiness to serve...', aiming 'to give the mission of the German scholar, researcher and teacher the prestige that is expected by National Socialism in the Party and in the state and, last but not least, by the people united by National Socialism'.[148]

As in the case of schools, with the creation of the Reich Ministry of Education in 1934, there was centralized control of the universities. In April 1935, regulations were passed that established the leadership principle in the universities. The Rectors were no longer elected representatives, but nominees of the Reich government. The powers of the Rectors were significant. The senate and faculty boards no longer had any say in the running of the universities and their function was reduced to that of merely advising. In this way, the rights of the universities to academic self-government were abolished. The concept of freedom of teaching was also eliminated.[149]

In 1933, the Nazis had imposed a *numerus clausus* on university entrance admission. Even without this, student numbers dropped considerably, not least because of the derision the Nazis had for academic pursuits and values. In fact, the number of students enrolled at German universities dropped from 95,807 in 1931 to 48,558 in 1936, and fell further to 39,236 in 1939.[150] By this time it was becoming clear to the Nazi leadership that whatever their view was of academia, in practical terms, there was a dearth of academically trained individuals. After 1938, the regime made alterations to university admission requirements in order to try to attract students. For example, after September 1938, it became possible for an adult aged between 25 and 40 to enter university without an *Abitur*, by taking a special 'examination for great talent' (*Hochbegabtenprüfung*). A 'special maturity examination' award from a technical school also counted as an entry qualification to university in certain subjects. In 1934, the Nazis had also introduced 'Langemarck Scholarships' to encourage pupils from lower-class backgrounds to study at university. The NSDAP selected prospective candidates carefully and they attended special courses. In 1940, 800 students were accepted to this particular scholarship of whom 36 per cent were from working-class backgrounds. Nevertheless, these various attempts to raise student numbers did not succeed. The war itself disrupted university life even more drastically and student numbers continued to decline. Rüdiger vom Bruch shows that National Socialism 'severely damaged the German university, its reputation, and its self-understanding'.[151] It 'destroyed the German university as a self-administering corporate body and an independent research community with a functioning system of rules'.[152] Under National Socialism academic independence and autonomy in the universities were renounced.

National Socialism brought about a root and branch re-engineering of the education system at all levels – from kindergartens, through schools, to universities. At all stages, Nazi education was characterized by its anti-liberalism, anti-intellectualism and irrationalism. The loftier ideals of the *Volk* took precedence over true scholarship and knowledge. Education policy was underpinned by a desire to disseminate National Socialist ideology as much as possible and in this context other educational aims were subordinated. The next chapter examines this in a more detailed consideration of the curriculum and an investigation of the impact of Nazism on school textbooks.

NOTES

1. *Hitler's Table Talk 1941–1944: His Private Conversations*, with an introduction by H. R. Trevor-Roper (New York, 1976), p. 547.
2. A. Hitler, *Mein Kampf*, translated by R. Mannheim, with an introduction by D. C. Watt (London, 1992), p. 374.
3. Ibid., p. 387.
4. *Hitler's Table Talk*, p. 548.
5. Ibid., p. 139.
6. Ibid., p. 567.
7. Ibid., pp. 547–8.
8. M. Lamberti, 'German Schoolteachers, National Socialism, and the Politics of Culture at the End of the Weimar Republic', *Central European History*, Vol. 34, No. 1 (2001), p. 63.
9. Ibid., p. 80.
10. Ibid., p. 74.
11. Ibid., p. 64. See also W. Feiten, *Der Nationalsozialistische Lehrerbund. Entwicklung und Organisation* (Weinheim and Basel, 1981), pp. 46–50.
12. On Schemm, see F. Kühnel, *Hans Schemm. Gauleiter und Kultusminister (1891–1935)* (Nuremberg, 1985).
13. Feiten, *Der Nationalsozialistische Lehrerbund*, pp. 40–41.
14. BA NS 12/967, 'Der Erzieher', Nr. 1, 1934, p. 7.
15. BA NS 12/263, 'Satzung des Nationalsozialistischen Lehrerbundes', p. 1.
16. BA NS 12/263, 'Satzung des Nationalsozialistischen Lehrerbundes', p. 3. On organization, see also Feiten, *Der Nationalsozialistische Lehrerbund*, pp. 76–132.
17. BA NS 12/1404, 'Der Nationalsozialistische Erzieher', Nr. 9, 1937, pp. 4–5.
18. On this, see BA NS 12/967, 'Der NSLB – seine Geschichte, seiner organisatorische Entwicklung und die daraus resultierende Stellungnahme zur gegenwärtigen organisatorischen Lage'.
19. For example, see BA NS 12/641, 'Denkschrift über die Misstände im Schulwesen Ostpreussens', 10 March 1933, p. 1.
20. Ibid.
21. BA NS 12/600, 'Rundschreiben. Betrifft: Verbot der Doppelmitgliedschaft im NSLB und in konfessionellen Erzieherverbanden', 17 December 1936.
22. Feiten, *Der Nationalsozialistische Lehrerbund*, p. 55.
23. ibid., p. 19.
24. BA NS 12/1401, Rundschreiben Nr. 11/33, 'Schulungsplan für den NSLB Untergau Oberschlesien'.
25. BA NS 12/1401, 'Bericht über die Durchführung der A-Schulungslager des NSLB – Gau Schlesien 1936', p. 1.
26. J. Schiedeck and M. Stahlmann, 'Totalizing of Experience: Educational Camps', in H. Sünker and H.-U. Otto (eds), *Education and Fascism: Political Identity and Social Education in Nazi Society* (London, 1997), p. 63.
27. See BA R 4901-1/4607, 'Der Preußische Finanzminister an Herrn Oberpräsidenten für höheres Schulwesen', 31 May 1934.
28. G. Pieper, 'Austauschlager: Ihr Sinn und ihre Gestaltung', *Nationalpolitische Erziehung* (1937), p. 293. Cited in Schiedeck and Stahlmann, 'Totalizing of Experience', p. 63.

29. BA NS 12/1401, 'Schulungsbrief der Gauhauptstelle Erziehung und Unterricht'.

30. Ibid., p. 1.

31. Ibid., p. 2.

32. ibid., pp. 8–10.

33. BA NS 12/1401, 'Bericht über die Durchführung der A-Schulungslager des NSLB – Gau Schlesien 1936'.

34. Ibid., p. 1.

35. Ibid., p. 3.

36. Ibid., p. 2.

37. Ibid., pp. 4–7.

38. BA NS 12/1402, 'Denkschrift über das Junglehrer Schulungslager in Hassitz bei Glatz, 2. bis 21. Oktober 1933'.

39. BA NS 12/1196, 'Die Schulungsarbeit des Amtes für Erzieher (NSLB)', 19 Sept. 1935, p. 5.

40. On what follows see BA NS 12/41, 'Tagebuch Pappelhof', p. 386.

41. Ibid., p. 387.

42. Ibid., p. 388.

43. BA NS 12/41, 'Tätigkeitsbericht'.

44. BA NS 12/41, 'Bericht über das Schulungslager für Erzieherinnen in Parchim'.

45. Ibid.

46. BA NS 12/1196, 'Die Schulungsarbeit des Amtes für Erzieher (NSLB)', 19 Sept. 1935, p. 1.

47. Ibid., p. 3.

48. BA NS 12/1406, 'Abteilung Presse und Propaganda'.

49. BA NS 12/1400, 'Bericht über Kreiswaltertagung'.

50. Ibid.

51. BA NS 12/41, 'Landlehrer im Lager'.

52. Ibid.

53. Ibid.

54. BA NS 12/41, 'Als Sachse im Schulungslager Hamberge'.

55. BA NS 12/41, 'Acht Tage Schulungslager des NS-Lehrerbundes'.

56. BA NS 12/41, 'Landlehrer im Lager'.

57. BA R 4901-1/4607, 'Verein Deutscher Evangelischer Lehrerinnen e.V.', 4 December 1934.

58. BA R 4901-1/4607, 'Betrifft: Beschwerde des Vereins deutsch. ev. Lehrerinnen in Barmen', 25 January 1935.

59. BA R 4901-1/4607, 'An den Herrn Oberpräsidenten (Abt. für höheres Schulwesen)', 22 February 1935.

60. BA R 4901-1/4607, 'Abschrift. Zeltlager des NS-Lehrerbundes, Gau Pommern', p. 1.

61. BA R 4901-1/4607, 'Abschrift. Bericht über das 1. Zeltlager des NS-Lehrerbundes Gau Pommern vom 26. Juni bis 1. Juli 1935 in Heringsdorf'.

62. Ibid.

63. BA NS 12/41, 'Arbeitsfolge für das Schullager der anhaltischen Lehrer aler Schularten vom 5 bis 13 August 1935'.

64. BA NS 12/606, 'Sachgebiet Biologie. Schulungslehrgang des NSLB in Tübingen vom 11.–17. Oktober 1936'.

65. BA NS 12/628, Rundschreiben, 'Betrifft: Reichslehrgang für Rassenkunde', 13 October 1937. See also BA NS 12/628, Rundschreiben, 'Betr.: Jahresarbeit 1938', 16 February 1938, pp. 1–2, which highlights work and achievements on teaching racial lore.

66. BA NS 12/41, 'Acht Tage Schulungslager des NS-Lehrerbundes'.

67. Ibid.

68. BA NS 12/967, 'Der Erzieher', Nr. 1, 1934, p. 8.
69. Ibid., p. 11.
70. Feiten, *Der Nationalsozialistische Lehrerbund*, p. 148.
71. BA NS 12/1404, 'Der Nationalsozialistische Erzieher', Nr. 9, 1937, p. 9.
72. BA NS 12/600, 'Rundschreiben. Betrifft: Erntehilfe der deutschen Erzieher', 29 June 1938.
73. BA NS 12/1438, 'Aufgaben und Leistungen des NS-Lehrerbundes im Kriege', p. 1.
74. BA NS 12/1438, 'Aufgaben und Leistungen des NS-Lehrerbundes im Kriege', p. 2. On the NSLB and the 'homefront', see also Feiten, *Der Nationalsozialistische Lehrerbund*, pp. 188–91.
75. BA NS 12/1438, 'Aufgaben und Leistungen des NS-Lehrerbundes im Kriege', p. 2.
76. BA NS 12/567, 'Stillegung des NSLB'.
77. Ibid.
78. On this, see Feiten, *Der Nationalsozialistische Lehrerbund*, pp. 197–200.
79. BA NS 12/641, 'Rundschreiben über das neue Erziehungsziel', p. 2.
80. Ibid.
81. Ibid., p. 4.
82. BA R 4901/708, 'Konflikte zwischen Reichserziehungsministerium und NSDAP', pp. 1–4.
83. BA R 4901/708, 'Betr.: Konflikte des Reichserziehungsministeriums mit Dienststellen der NSDAP', p. 1.
84. Ibid., pp. 8–9.
85. Ibid., p. 7.
86. On what follows, see BA R 4901/708, 'Die Schule als Streitobjekt zwischen Partei und Staat', pp. 1–2.
87. BA R 4901/708, 'Die Schule als Streitobjekt zwischen Partei und Staat', p. 3.
88. *Hitler's Table Talk*, pp. 548–9.
89. Cited in H.-G. Herrlitz *et al.*, *Deutsche Schulgeschichte von 1800 bis zum Gegenwart* (Weinheim and Munich, 1993), p. 149.
90. S. Schnurr, 'Vom Wolfahrtsstaat zum Erziehungsstaat: Sozialpolitik und soziale Arbeit in der Weimarer Republik und im Nationalsozialismus', *Widersprüche*, Vol. 8 (1988), pp. 47–64.
91. Sünker and Otto, *Education and Fascism*, p. vii.
92. Cited in Hahn, *Education and Society*, p. 75.
93. W. Frick, *Kampfziel der deutschen Schule* (Langensalza, 1933), p. 24.
94. Hahn, *Education and Society*, p. 83.
95. M. Mouton, *From Nurturing the Nation to Purifying the Volk: Weimar and Nazi Family Policy, 1918–1945* (Cambridge, 2007), pp. 164–5.
96. A. T. Allen, *Feminism and Motherhood in Germany, 1890–1914* (New Brunswick, 1991), pp. 63–5. On this, see also A. T. Allen, 'Children between Public and Private Worlds: The Kindergarten and Public Policy in Germany, 1840–Present', in R. Wollons (ed.), *Kindergartens and Cultures: The Global Diffusion of an Idea* (New Haven, 2000), pp. 16–41.
97. Mouton, *From Nurturing the Nation to Purifying the Volk*, p. 166.
98. Ibid., p. 179.
99. Ibid., p. 180.
100. On the Froebel tradition, see F. Froebel, *The Education of Man*, translated by W. Hailmann (New York, 1887) and N. Isaacs, 'Froebel's Educational Philosophy', in E. Laurence (ed.), *Friedrich Froebel and English Education* (London, 1969).
101. Mouton, *From Nurturing the Nation to Purifying the Volk*, p. 182.
102. BA R 89/5242, 'Hilfswerk Mutter und Kind und Hitler-Freiplatz-Spende 1936/37', p. 14.
103. L. Pine, *Nazi Family Policy, 1933–1945* (Oxford, 1997), p. 31.
104. BA NSD 30/25, 'Richtlinien für Erntekindergärten im Rahmen des Hilfswerkes "Mutter und Kind"', pp. 4–5.

105. H. Vorländer, *Die NSV. Darstellung und Dokumentation einer nationalsozialistischen Organisation* (Boppard, 1988), p. 70.

106. BA NSD 30/25, 'Richtlinien für Erntekindergärten im Rahmen des Hilfswerkes "Mutter und Kind"', p. 3.

107. BA NS 12/641, 'Die hamburgische Landschule im nationalsozialistischen Staate'.

108. Ibid., p. 11.

109. On this, see Samuel and Hinton Thomas, *Education and Society*, p. 39.

110. Ibid., p. 16.

111. Ibid., p. 20.

112. Hahn, *Education and Society*, p. 79.

113. BA NS 12/641, 'Die hamburgische Landschule im nationalsozialistischen Staate', p. 14.

114. BA NS 12/811, 'Die Schule der deutschen Volksgemeinschaft. Entwurf eines nationalsozial. Schulprograms von G. Weischedel', 22 May 1934, p. 1.

115. Ibid.

116. BA R 4901/1 4620/1, 'Betrifft: Neuordnung des höheren Schulwesens'.

117. BA NS 12/964, 'Errichtung von Hochschulen für Lehrerbildung und Deutsche Oberschulen in Aufbauform. Neugestaltung der Lehrerbildung in Bayern', p. 3.

118. BA R 4901/1 4620/1, 'Betrifft: Neuordnung des höheren Schulwesens', p. 35.

119. Hitler, *Mein Kampf*, p. 377.

120. BA R 4901/709, 'Private Volksschulen', pp. 1–5; BA NS 12/814, 'Aus dem NS-Lehrerbund', p. 9.

121. See BA R 4901/1 3304/1, 'Reichsschulgesetz vom Januar 1937'.

122. BA R 4901/1 3304/1, 'Entwurf eines Reichsgesetzes über die einheitliche Gestaltung der deutschen Volksschule'.

123. BA R 4901/1 3304/1, 'Begründung'.

124. BA R 4901/1 3304/1, 'General-Vikariat Trier an den Herrn Reichs- und Preußischen Minister für Wissenschaft, Erziehung und Volksbildung', 7 April 1937.

125. BA NS 12/41, 'An die Kreisschulaufsichten zur Bekanntgabe an alle Schule'.

126. On this, see L. Pine, *Hitler's 'National Community': Society and Culture in Nazi Germany* (London, 2007), p. 88.

127. BA NS 12/1196, 'Auszüge aus Berichten der Gauschulungsämter', p. 1.

128. BA NS 12/825, 'Übersteigerung der Anormalen-Erziehung – was aber jeder darüber wissen sollte'.

129. BA NS 12/825, 'Gutachten zur Übersteigerung der Anormalen-Erziehung', Wilhelm Neidhardt, 25 November 1934, pp. 1–2. See also BA NS 12/825, 'Heilerziehung und Heilerzieher im Dritten Reich'.

130. BA NS 12/964, 'Errichtung von Hochschulen für Lehrerbildung und Deutsche Oberschulen in Aufbauform. Neugestaltung der Lehrerbildung in Bayern', p. 1; BA NS 12/964, 'Organisationsplan einer Hochschule für Lehrerbildung'.

131. On this, see BA NS 12/1196, 'Auszüge aus Berichten der Gauschulungsämter', pp. 1–7.

132. Samuel and Hinton Thomas, *Education and Society*, p. 58.

133. BA R 4901/709, 'Private Volksschulen', p. 2.

134. On the history of Jewish schools under National Socialism, see J. Walk, *Jüdische Schule und Erziehung im Dritten Reich* (Frankfurt am Main, 1991).

135. M. Burleigh and W. Wippermann, *The Racial State: Germany 1933–1945* (Cambridge, 1991) pp. 214–15.

136. Samuel and Hinton Thomas, *Education and Society*, p. 53.

137. Ibid., p. 54.

138. G. Knopp, *Hitler's Children* (Stroud, 2002), p. 186.

139. BA NS 12/641, 'Die hamburgische Landschule im nationalsozialistischen Staate', p. 17.

140. Hahn, *Education and Society*, p. 28.

141. On this, see K. Jarausch, *Students, Society and Politics in Imperial Germany: The Rise of Academic Illiberalism* (Princeton, 1982).

142. Cited in Samuel and Hinton Thomas, *Education and Society*, p. 123.

143. C. H. Becker, *Vom Wesen der deutschen Universität* (Berlin, 1925).

144. On this, see A. Gallin, *Midwives to Nazism: University Professors in Weimar Germany 1925–1933* (Macon, 1986), pp. 86–7. See also F. Ringer, *The Decline of the German Mandarins: The German Academic Community, 1890–1933* (Cambridge, Mass., 1969).

145. G. Giles, 'The Rise of the National Socialist Students' Association and the Failure of Political Education in the Third Reich', in P. Stachura (ed.), *The Shaping of the Nazi State* (London, 1978), pp. 161–2.

146. G. Giles, *Students and National Socialism in Germany* (Princeton, 1985). On students under National Socialism, see also M. Grüttner, *Studenten im Dritten Reich* (Paderborn, 1995).

147. R. Evans, *The Coming of the Third Reich* (London, 2004), p. 423.

148. Cited in G. Mosse (ed.), *Nazi Culture: Intellectual, Cultural and Social Life in the Third Reich* (London, 1966), pp. 314–15. For a detailed examination of the universities during the Nazi era, see H. Heiber, *Universität unterm Hakenkreuz: Teil 1* (Munich, 1991) and H. Heiber, *Universität unterm Hakenkreuz: Teil 2* (Munich, 1992).

149. Gallin, *Midwives to Nazism*, p. 108.

150. Samuel and Hinton Thomas, *Education and Society*, p. 112.

151. R. vom Bruch, 'A Slow Farewell to Humboldt? Stages in the History of German Universities, 1810–1945', in M. Ash (ed.), *German Universities Past and Future: Crisis or Renewal?* (Oxford, 1997), p. 23.

152. Ibid., p. 24.

3 THE CURRICULUM AND SCHOOL TEXTBOOKS

This chapter examines the school curriculum and school textbooks during the Third Reich. How was Krieck's aim of 'national political education' achieved in schools?[1] In addition to the changes to the educational system discussed in the previous chapter, the main method was the transformation of the curriculum, in order to emphasize certain subject areas in which 'nation' and 'race' could be expounded, and to decrease the significance of other subject areas. For example, a Nazi directive for elementary education from 1940 stated:

> It is not the task of the elementary school to impart a multiplicity of knowledge for the personal use of the individual. It has to develop and harness all physical and mental powers of youth for the service of the people and the state. Therefore, the only subject that has any place in the school curriculum is that which is necessary to achieve this aim. All other subjects, springing from obsolete educational ideas, must be discarded.[2]

In secondary education, Nazi educationalists believed that 'German, history, geography and biology require a deeper treatment'.[3] This chapter focuses on the key subject areas promoted by National Socialism: biology, physics and chemistry, geography, history, mathematics, German, racial studies and physical education.

The introduction and use of new school textbooks assisted Nazi pedagogues in their aim of inculcating pupils with Nazi ideology. At first, there were many different textbooks in the curriculum, which displeased NSDAP ideologue, Alfred Rosenberg. He ordered Philipp Bouhler, Director of the Party Censorship Office, to examine all the textbooks in use for their ideological content. Bouhler's work demonstrated the need for a process that entailed more than a simple 'weeding out', and worked towards the creation of a uniform Reich Reader for the entire nation. The Ministry of Education began to actively implement this idea, removing old readers from the curriculum and replacing them with new ones. Ernst Krieck, a prominent Nazi educational theorist and professor at the University of Heidelberg, was involved in the educational theory behind the introduction of these readers. New editions were to include the themes of 'blood and soil', leadership, honour and loyalty, service and sacrifice, struggle and work.[4] Between 1935 and 1940, Bernhard Rust introduced new Reich Readers at different age levels. Editors selected specific reading material for them, based on the themes of 'blood and soil' and the *Volk*. They had to conform to Nazi Party censorship requirements. They included extracts from German and Nordic folklore and sagas, tailoring the selections to the ideological values of National Socialism. Rust defined the purpose of the readers as being to 'serve the ideological education of young German people, so as to develop them into fit members of the national community – members who are ready to serve and to sacrifice'.[5]

The spirit of *völkisch* ideology was conveyed through children's books. A strict censorship policy was put into place to screen all books. Josef Goebbels's 'black lists' contained the titles of all 'alien' or 'decadent' works that were to be removed from circulation. In reality, many of the textbooks from the Weimar era did propagate reactionary political and social values. They were nationalistic and militaristic in their ethos. Hence, these ideas were already clearly extant in German school textbooks before National Socialism came to power. Nevertheless, the Nazi regime aimed to achieve a completely regimented and standardized system of school textbooks. By 1941, textbook production became the exclusive preserve of *Deutscher Schulverlag*, owned by the NSDAP press *Eher Verlag*.

BIOLOGY

Biology teaching was of great significance in the Third Reich and was energetically promoted by the regime as a whole and the NSLB in particular. In no other subject area were the Nazi themes of 'blood and soil', 'race' and 'living space' so directly linked to the subject matter. Biology had the task then of instructing pupils about the living nature of German 'living space' as the basic nourishment of the German *Volk*, as well as the goal of an eternal German *Volkstum*. Laws of heredity and life, fertility, selection and blood purity were central to the teaching of the subject. Paul Brohmer was one of the leading writers of a new biology curriculum under the National Socialist regime.[6] In 1938, after the new curriculum was introduced, new textbooks appeared that took into account the changes. Brohmer utilized 'race biology' as a means of encouraging German children to struggle to maintain racial purity. He underlined the dangers of 'racial miscegenation' and justified the regime's racial, population and eugenics policies in his writings. Biology lessons became vehicles for Nazi racial doctrine, emphasizing themes such as race, heredity and the 'selection of the fittest'. Pupils were instructed in the classification of racial types and craniology. Films and slides were produced as teaching aids.[7] Visual presentations were deemed to be particularly useful in showing the distinctions between examples of 'racially pure' and 'inferior' or 'hereditarily diseased' individuals. Biology was 'assigned a central function in education' with 'two hours of teaching a week in all grades'.[8] As well as racial ideology, biology was to impart other aspects of Nazi ideology, such as love for the homeland and the 'national community', which were linked to the subject. As such, biology as a subject gained considerably in importance and prestige under National Socialism.

Furthermore, biology teaching was also carried over into other subject areas, including mathematics and German, by using biology topics in these other disciplines. Hans Schemm's statement that 'National Socialism is politically applied biology' meant that biology teaching was directed towards educating children in the laws of life and in the ideology of National Socialism.[9] Pupils were to think in both biological and national terms simultaneously. In particular, 'hereditary biology' was a significant part of 'biological thinking' under National Socialism.[10] The realization of the hereditary health of the German people was to be 'drummed into' children in school education so that it became 'second nature to them'.[11] Lore of the family, lore of race, genetics, eugenics and population policy formed the core of 'hereditary biology'. This subject purported to demonstrate that 'racial mixing' and an increase in the number of the 'hereditarily ill' damaged the integrity and value of the German population. The 'hereditary health' of the 'national community' was central to all work in this area. The promotion of 'valuable' hereditary lines and the concurrent prevention of the reproduction of the 'hereditarily ill' were emphasized.[12] Pupils were given an understanding of the need for sterilization and of Nazi eugenics laws. They were shown the power of genetic transmission from one generation to the next. The preservation of the 'Nordic character' and an understanding of racial differences were the central aims of 'hereditary biology' lessons.

Nazi pedagogues, as well as Nazi leaders, regarded 'racial miscegenation' and 'bastardization' as serious threats to the German nation. In 1938, Alfred Vogel, a biology curriculum writer and primary school headmaster in Baden, produced a series of anti-Semitic teaching charts designed as teaching aids to the new curriculum. These accompanied a teachers' book designed for the instruction of 'biology' to primary school children.[13] Vogel encouraged teachers to instruct children about the laws of nature and heredity, as well as racial consciousness and the 'blood community' of the German nation. He drew parallels between cross-breeding in plant biology and 'racial mixing' in society.[14] Vogel advocated a 'race corner' in the school grounds that could be used to carry out experiments on plants and allow pupils to see the strength of the 'pure-bred' plant over the mixed-bred one. The inferences from this were applied to human society. Vogel examined 'hidden' inherited tendencies in biology, claiming that it was not correct to judge a living thing from its outwardly visible characteristics. The implication of this was that heredity was the only important signifier of race, so that a Jew posed a danger to the German nation even if he did not look like a Jew or did not practice his religion.

Topics for biology instruction included: 'the heredity of physical characteristics', 'the heredity of mental and spiritual characteristics', 'the heredity of frailties and illnesses', 'the heredity of physical and spiritual characteristics of the German race', 'the care of racial inheritance', 'the law of selection' and 'the Jews and the German people'.[15] Vogel advocated the need to educate young Germans about 'the racial value of our people and the tireless struggle over the preservation of our racial character' and about 'the complete rejection of the Jews'.[16] His illustrated charts, including 'The Racial Composition of the Jews' and 'German Ways – Jewish Ways', were used to show the perils presented to the German nation by the 'parasitic', 'wandering Jew'. His charts stereotyped the Jews, both as stateless intruders and as financial and political dominators. He also linked Jews with Freemasons and suggested that they were engaged together in a conspiracy for world domination. Whilst biology teaching did not propose overtly the policy of the genocide of the Jews, it did provide a legitimization for this policy, as well as for the Nazi 'euthanasia' campaign.

The 'school garden' was also employed by National Socialist pedagogues as a useful addition to the curriculum.[17] The school garden was to be a true 'community garden' for the entire school, where each child participated for the benefit of the whole school community. This was a microcosm of the concept of the 'national community'. In the school garden, children developed their physical skills, as well as their sense of duty and responsibility. They also gained practical knowledge such as how to grow fruit and vegetables and how to control pests. Pupils learned about seeds, fertilization and soil usage. They undertook experiments on soil, fertilization and genetics, as part of the school garden activities. The topics were exploited to emphasize Nazi ideological imperatives. For example, links were made between particular plants and the 'German nation', the importance for the 'national community' of fruit and vegetable growing was shown, and hereditary transmission as demonstrated in the school garden was used to emphasise racial and eugenic issues.

Biology teaching in girls' schools was particularly concerned with the 'mother instinct'. It emphasized a girl's main responsibility as her role in marriage and family life. Biology teaching included topics such as breeding and rearing animals, genetics, race studies, practical studies on the care of babies and young children, care of the sick and first aid, and preparations for girls' roles as future housewives in relation to both the domestic and the national economy.

PHYSICS AND CHEMISTRY

Of the three natural sciences, biology clearly took precedence in the Nazi curriculum, as it lent itself most easily to the regime's ideological objectives. Teachers of physics and chemistry had to make more of an effort to show that their subjects were pertinent to the Nazi government and its aims. In particular, the significance of physics for warfare was emphasized, as physics teachers tried to justify their subject by relating it to military objectives.[18] A new branch of physics teaching under National Socialism – 'the physics of weapons' – was designed to awaken the ability to bear arms. Military physics increased in significance from 1936 onwards. Pupils were instructed in orientation, measurement, communications, ballistics and military engineering. A new handbook was provided for teachers on this subject.[19] Physics under National Socialism, according to its author,

Erich Günther, had the purpose 'of awakening not only the ability to bear arms but also the will to do so, and, beyond that, to show the ways and technical means to carry out the decision to bear arms'. Gauging of distance, sighting the line of fire and working out military objectives were all a fundamental part of this.

The importance of physics as a 'decisive practical factor' for weapons training and defence against enemy attack was underlined as follows:

> We need excellent engineers not only for peace work but also just as much for building fighting and defence equipment of every kind, be it firearms or range finders, be it submarines, airplanes or combat vehicles. We need officers with thorough education in technology and natural sciences, who understand how to take charge of these war materials properly, and it hardly needs mentioning how diverse the knowledge of physics and the abilities are that are necessary for instance to command firing the heaviest artillery or a submarine.[20]

Hence, physics was envisaged as a subject to be used for training engineers and military personnel. Physics instruction centred on ballistics, optics and aeronautics. Physics pedagogues fell into line with Nazi requirements in these areas. Willy Göllnitz, a secondary school teacher in Chemnitz, very clearly stated the need and rationale for practical weapons training: 'Present-day weapon technology requires that the most important concepts of internal and external ballistics be taught particularly to pupils in higher schools, who are destined later to fill leading positions in the army. But fortunately the times of blackboard physics are over'.[21] Practical shooting experiments, including how to determine projectile trajectories and time of flight, were deemed to be 'the only way to arouse the necessary scientific interest in pupils alongside the natural pleasure in shooting'.[22] Optics, including the use of prisms, mirrors, lenses, cameras and telescopes, was another area of physics that had importance in terms of military preparation. Artur Friedrich, a secondary school teacher in Chemnitz, argued for the need to equip pupils with a practical knowledge of these subjects so that they would be 'fit for defence' and able to carry out their future 'duties as soldiers with more understanding and interest'.[23]

Physics teaching in the Third Reich was aimed at creating an understanding of the importance of technology, defence and the military in the life of the nation. Physics channelled the National Socialist world view. Physics teachers were to instruct pupils in problem solving and provide them with knowledge and practical skills only within the remit and requirements of Nazi educational policy. Furthermore, education in physics in the Third Reich particularly emphasized aviation, and the regime asked its educators to create an enthusiasm for flying among pupils. The objective was to prepare young people for service in the air force. New textbooks on aeronautical physics were produced for this purpose. Aeronautical physics, including topics such as propeller operation and flight dynamics, was deemed an important subject in the preparation of young boys for the air force. Instruction in this area was aimed both at imparting technical and scientific knowledge and at encouraging enthusiasm for flying and for the air force. By 1938, aviation and defence physics formed a significant part of the science curriculum.[24]

Physics was also employed to teach pupils the achievements of German physicists and the contributions of German research to scientific knowledge. This was intended to enhance national pride and underline the significance of the National Socialist 'Aryan' world view. The work of Jewish physicists was excluded in line with Nazi racial ideology. As the 'racial heredity' of a person directly influenced his work, only the 'Aryan' scientist could be seen to truly achieve and create. Most significantly, this meant that Albert Einstein's name was erased in the physics textbooks of the Nazi era. Einstein's theory of relativity was rejected on the grounds that it was 'theoretical magic' and a 'great world-wide Jewish bluff'. 'Aryan' physicists, in contrast, such as Philipp Lenard and Johannes Stark, flourished under the political system of National Socialism. Their 'Aryan' physics aimed to preserve the 'national community' and express the life of the nation. Stark, in particular, called for there to be 'no Jewish propaganda' in German physics textbooks.[25]

Physics teaching under National Socialism had 'to contribute to national political instruction and forming willpower'. Furthermore, 'knowledge of the natural conditions and requirements of the national community in the German living space, the ability and the will to do further work on the questions of physics research and technology in this connection, and also teaching to think realistically, which is so important for forming National Socialist willpower, can only be fostered organically on the basis of the pupils' horizon which schools should help to expand gradually'.[26] Although topics such as classical mechanics and electromagnetism continued to be taught, much of the practical emphasis took the form of instruction in physics related to military topics for boys and domestic topics for girls. In the girls' schools in which sciences were taught, over the course of three years, the physics curriculum contained the following subjects: mechanics, thermodynamics and electricity in the first year; thermodynamics and optics in the second year; and electricity, induction and German physicists in the third year.[27] The physics curriculum taught girls about household and kitchen appliances, as well as physics in relation to health and optics, rather than about modern physics per se. Physics, in girls' schools, mainly comprised instruction in the technical and even economic aspects of household management, heating and the practical use of electrical appliances.[28]

Chemists likewise attempted to raise the prestige and status of their subject by underlining its significance to German national goals. In particular, they emphasized its importance to German manufacturing and defence. Ilse Beier, a chemistry teacher from Essen, suggested the possibilities of the subject in underlining 'the educational principles of the Third Reich'.[29] Walther Franck, a secondary school teacher from Hamburg, defended chemistry, stating that it would be inopportune to reduce its teaching 'at a time when political and economic leaders in the whole world are struggling with the problem of materials, their production and their processing'.[30] Chemistry teachers appealed to the armed forces and industrial companies such as I. G. Farben, as well as Nazi leaders who could see the benefits of their subject – in terms of economic self-sufficiency and readiness for war – for support. Chemistry education under National Socialism connected the chemical industry to the German people and the German economy. Chemists argued that their subject was significant for the economy and for defence. Furthermore, the history of science in chemistry teaching was aimed at strengthening national awareness and pride. Important German chemists such as Johann Wolfgang Döbereiner, Carl von Linde and Josef Loschmidt were used to show the importance of German contributions to research and scientific knowledge. Chemistry teachers could also use their subject as an opportunity to discuss 'race' by showing pupils the importance of the Germanic 'race' to the science of chemistry.[31]

Furthermore, the discussion of the Treaty of Versailles in this regard underlined a sense of unfairness that Germany was disadvantaged by the loss of territories rich in raw materials. Connections between raw materials and the national economy were drawn in chemistry teaching. Walter Leonhardt, a secondary school teacher from Dresden, explained that

> chemistry has to do with the instruments of power that first make it possible to wage war, with the most important mineral resources, coal and iron ore, from which steel is produced, with the materials for producing gunpowder and explosives, with the fertilizers to ensure the national food supply, etc. In the years since the lost war, chemistry teachers have considered it their duty to make clear to pupils what instruments of power Germany lost by being robbed of the mineral sources in Lorraine, the Saar and Upper Silesia, and most textbooks have not failed to include notes on this. In future, much more space will have to be devoted to such things so that our young learn to assess Germany's endangered situation from this viewpoint.[32]

New educational guidelines from Rust's Ministry for Education and Science in 1938 stated that chemistry instruction in schools should be aimed at teaching children that 'constant and systematic work on developing natural sciences and technology ensures the high economic and cultural status of our people'. Furthermore, it was to demonstrate 'how chemical science and technology make new, valuable raw materials and synthetics available to German industry from substances found in our native country' and 'how they process and refine imported foreign raw materials'. Moreover, it taught children 'that application of chemical knowledge in agriculture and forestry and in the food industry helps to ensure our food supply, and that chemistry is indispensable for questions of national defence'.[33] These guidelines also indicated that only certain compounds and substances needed to be taught. Pupils were required to learn only about economically significant raw materials, and how they were obtained and processed. New chemistry textbooks that taught in accordance with these stipulations were introduced. In practical terms, pupils worked in groups on chemical processes and analyses. Suggested topics included 'Analyses of Artificial Silks and Rayon', 'Experiments on Producing Artificial Fibres', 'Analysis of a Detergent' and 'Simple Analyses of Soil and Water'.

For girls, chemistry teaching dealt mainly with the chemistry of foodstuffs, fibres, household objects and detergents. Girls were taught about the need for domestic frugality. Both girls and boys were taught about chemical gases and air raid protection, although for boys defence chemistry was deemed particularly significant. Pupils were taught to become fit for defence in the event of gas attacks. They were taught about the nature of chemical weapons, protection against chemical gas, the effects of poisons on human beings and first aid to victims of gas poisoning.[34] Pupils also undertook related chemistry experiments, for example on making gunpowder, on how oxygen masks worked and on protection from gas poisoning in air raid shelters.

Another significant topic in chemistry teaching, particularly after the announcement of the Four Year Plan in 1936, was the 'battle' for production and for collecting and recycling waste. The economic importance of metals, fuels, synthetic rubber and synthetic fibres was examined. Pupils were encouraged to collect and recycle waste. They experimented with producing oil from coffee grounds and they conducted experiments using waste metals that they had collected. This kind of teaching dovetailed with Nazi propaganda on the collection and recycling of waste materials. Chemistry under National Socialism was employed to underline the regime's ideological objectives as much as was possible within the perimeters of the subject area. In particular, production, raw materials and defence as aspects of chemistry teaching, along with attempts to employ the subject to enhance national awareness, were the most significant aspects of this phenomenon.

GEOGRAPHY

The key topics in the geography curriculum under National Socialism were: studies of the homeland, which included love of the fatherland, 'blood and soil' and an idealization of bucolic life; political geography, which focused on the Treaty of Versailles, Germans living in border territories and abroad, Germany's 'enemies' and Germany's requirement for 'living space'; race studies, which included differentiations between 'superior' and 'inferior' races and especially an excoriation of the Jews; defence geography, which included security of German borders, defence preparation, descriptions of military topography; and colonial geography, which dealt with the need to reclaim lost German colonies, the history of Germany's colonial achievements and the crimes of other colonial powers.[35] Geography in the Third Reich aimed to generate a political understanding of Germany's position in the world. The term a '*Volk ohne Raum*' or 'people without space' – originally the title of a serialized novel by Hans Grimm – which suggested that the German *Volk* needed more 'living space', was used to justify Nazi policies of expansionism. Studies of the homeland were a central theme throughout all geography education. The new secondary school curriculum in 1938 allotted two hours per week to geography. It emphasized topics such as the political subdivision of Germany, its racial groups, its 'living space' in Europe, Germans in border areas and abroad, German colonies and culminated in 'German People and German Land: The German Reich and its Position in the World'. There was much emphasis on Germans living in border areas and in territories lost to Germany under the terms of the Treaty of Versailles, which aimed at arousing sentiments of nationalism among German schoolchildren. Similarly to physics and chemistry, the regime found a way to introduce the theme of defence into geography teaching. This began as early as 1933 but was accelerated as the war approached. Defence geography included military topography, as well as a discussion of national borders and arenas of war.

Furthermore, geography teaching was employed by National Socialism in order to expound its racial ideology. In particular, geography pedagogues exploited both traditional and new forms of anti-Semitism in their publications. For example, the image of the eternally wandering Jew was a favourite theme. Walter Jantzen was one of the most prominent geography educationalists in the Third Reich. He integrated Nazi ideology into the geography curriculum, particularly racial concerns about Jews, Blacks and Gypsies.[36] He addressed the subjects of 'living space', 'blood and soil' and the decline in Germany's birth rate since the end of the First World War. Konrad Olbricht and Hermann Kärgel highlighted the ideological distinctions between National Socialism and 'Jewish Bolshevism' in their geography textbook.[37] They juxtaposed their values on a number of themes and issues. For example, whilst National Socialism stood for leadership and loyalty, Judaeo-Bolshevism was characterized as the tyranny of a foreign national authority under the guise of democracy. Whilst Nazism advocated a healthy peasantry, a love for the soil and a dislike of urbanization, Judaeo-Bolshevism stood for the crushing of the peasants and the expansion of big cities.

Hence, geography in the Third Reich was employed to create a sense of love for the fatherland among schoolchildren. Hitler's achievements for Germans everywhere were glorified. The curriculum was very much focused upon topics about the German land. Phrases such as 'people without space' and 'blood and soil', which were really propaganda slogans, found their way into the classroom, as did anti-Semitism.

HISTORY

Hitler was clear in his views about history teaching:

> Particularly in the present method of teaching, a change must be made ... The result of our present history instruction is wretched in ninety-nine cases out of a hundred. A few facts, dates, birthdays and names remain behind while a broad clear line is totally lacking. The essentials which should really matter are not taught at all ... The main value lies in recognising the great lines of development ... For we do not learn history in order to know the past, we learn history in order to find an instructor for the future and for the continued existence of our nationality.[38]

The history curriculum was subjected to considerable change under National Socialism. For example, Hans Schemm stated that 'the prehistory of German history must have a more prominent position in our curricula'.[39] Defence history and frontier studies were also added to the history curriculum.[40] The subject area 'local history' was to include not only knowledge about the local area, but also information about the whole *Volk* and fatherland.[41] It was concerned with the destiny of the nation and an understanding of the homeland. The lore of race and its prehistory, as described in the works of Houston Stewart Chamberlain and Hans Günther, were also significant to this subject area. Local history under National Socialism was, in these ways, different to our understanding of what this subject usually comprises.

A meeting of the NSLB in Eger on history teaching reported that the field of history was unable to keep up with the pace of National Socialist change in terms of its ideological and political world view.[42] It bemoaned the lack of a history book that satisfied the National Socialist view in its evaluation and organization of historical events.[43] National Socialist historians re-examined single chapters of world history anew. Even before new textbooks were available, history teachers were urged to teach their subject in the spirit of National Socialism: 'It is the duty of every history teacher to teach with his National Socialist–trained conviction, even if new teaching material is not yet available'.[44] There was a call for the transformation of the old historical interpretation into a National Socialist interpretation. The great National Socialist revolution needed to situate itself within the course of German history.[45] The current struggle was of a historic nature and had to be understood as such: 'The new self-display of National Socialism ... will be seen in sharp contrast to the democratic era'.[46] Alfred Rosenberg stated: 'I am well aware that this is a huge educational task for our movement. Our task is to write world history anew, and this will take many years, even decades'.[47] Although many of the Weimar history books contained the themes of earlier nationalist thought, the Nazi regime nevertheless aimed to replace them. Nazi history textbooks fostered nationalistic themes more extremely than ever before.

History was interpreted as a struggle for existence between nations.[48] History lessons were used as an opportunity to demonstrate to pupils the greatness of Germany. They were intended to awaken and excite children's sense of national pride and concern about the continued existence of the German state and nation. Hitler believed that: 'From all the innumerable great names in German history, the greatest must be picked out and introduced to the youth so persistently that they become pillars of unshakeable national sentiment'.[49] History under National Socialism was further used to highlight the leadership principle, emphasizing Germany's 'great leaders' and their 'world-historical' achievements. For example, great historical leaders, such as Frederick the Great, were used to illustrate heroic leadership, tireless service to the state, military achievements and parallels to Hitler. The great triumphs of National Socialism were given considerable attention in the history textbooks of the Nazi period.[50] History was an integral part of 'national political' education.[51]

A history textbook for secondary school pupils devoted part of its section on German culture to the position of women in the 'national community'.[52] This outlined Nazi views on women's role in society and stressed the need to reawaken women's desire to have children and indeed to have large families. It underlined the role of mothers in educating their children, claiming that there was no task more noble or more beautiful than a mother making the developing soul of her child receptive to all the goodness and beauty of its nation. Various aspects of the theme of 'national renewal' were indeed common in the history textbooks of the era.[53] Historical atlases illustrated Germany's greatness in her most historically important and expansive periods, and especially in the Third Reich. Furthermore, they employed maps, graphs and charts to highlight population policy issues, such as the declining birth rate and the age make-up of the population to demonstrate that Germany was becoming 'a nation without youth'.[54] Hence, history books were implemented to explain the nature of Nazi population policy.

There was a flurry of activity in writing a new history curriculum in Nazi Germany. Publishers, university professors, teachers and school administrators became involved in this process, often in the pursuit of professional advancement. Dieter Klagges was one of the key history curriculum writers of the Nazi era, underlining the significance of German blood in history teaching. He developed the themes of racial purity and anti-Semitism in his writings.[55] Johann von Leers used history stories as a means of portraying anti-Semitic ideas to young children, stressing the profiteering of Jews at the expense of Germans and depicting Jews as 'swindlers' and 'crooks'.[56] History textbook writers of the Nazi era, such as Hans Warneck and Willi Matschke, portrayed the Jews as 'enemies of the Reich'.[57] In his children's history textbook Johannes Mahnkopf wrote about the historical connection of Jews and Freemasons as a negative force.[58] Such texts aimed to increase children's sense of attachment and loyalty to National Socialism in its struggle against 'the Jewish enemy'. Whilst the Nazi regime was not the first to use *völkisch* ideas in history teaching, Wegner has shown that it was 'the first and only regime to fully institutionalise a racist and anti-Semitic history curriculum'.[59] The glorification of militarism and nationalism that were already extant in the history textbooks of the *Kaiserreich* and the Weimar Republic reached their peak in the history textbooks of the Third Reich.

MATHEMATICS

Nazi maths books seized the opportunity to socialize children through pervading the curriculum in a well-established tradition.[60] Maths questions dealt with 'national political problems'. Calculations of sums were based on examples of bullet trajectories, aircraft, cannons and bombs. For example, pupils were given the following statement: 'A bombing plane can be loaded with one explosive bomb of 35 kilograms, three bombs of 100 kilograms, four gas bombs of 150 kilograms, and 200 incendiary bombs of one kilogram'. The questions that the pupils had to answer were: 'What is the load capacity?

What is the percentage of each type of bomb? How many incendiary bombs of 0.5 kilograms could be added if the load capacity were increased by 50 per cent?'[61] Such arithmetic and mathematical problems were not uncommon in the textbooks of the Third Reich.

Numerical problems based on state expenditure on 'hereditarily ill' and 'inferior' people exemplified the way in which Nazi ideology pervaded the school curriculum. In one exercise, pupils were presented with the following information: 'Every day, the state spends RM. 6 on one cripple; RM. 4 1/4 on one mentally ill person; RM. 5 1/2 on one deaf and dumb person; RM. 5 3/5 on one feeble-minded person; RM. 3 1/2 on one alcoholic; RM. 4 4/5 on one pupil in care; RM. 2 1/20 on one pupil at a special school; RM. 9/20 on one pupil at an ordinary school.' It then asked questions such as 'What total cost do one cripple and one feeble-minded person create, if one takes a lifespan of forty-five years for each?' and 'Calculate the expenditure of the state for one pupil in a special school, and one pupil in an ordinary school over eight years, and state the amount of higher cost engendered by the special school pupil'.[62] The implications of such questions were that state funds were being squandered on 'unhealthy' or 'undesirable' people. This was typical of the way in which data regarding state expenditure on 'hereditarily ill' or 'inferior' people was utilized in 'education'.

Exercises using data based upon the birth rate and other issues relating to population policy were also common in school textbooks of the Nazi era. For example, one exercise was based on the marriage loan scheme, introduced by the Nazi regime in 1933 to promote early marriage and the founding of *kinderreich* families. It gave the figures of the number of loans given each year between 1933 and 1937, together with the value of each loan, and required pupils to calculate the yearly state expenditure on these loans.[63] The association of these figures in the minds of schoolchildren doing these exercises was to indicate to them that money spent on maintaining 'hereditarily ill' people or on children attending special schools could be better spent on other things, such as marriage loans for 'healthy' and 'valuable' families. Furthermore, pupils were given figures relating to the number of Jews ('aliens') living in Germany as compared to the total population and asked to work out 'What is the percentage of aliens?' living in Germany.[64]

Another maths textbook familiarized children with large numbers by using figures relating to the First World War. It stated that 13,250,000 men were called up by Germany, 11,250,000 by her allies, and 47,500,000 by Germany's enemies. The children, whilst doing addition and subtraction exercises, were simultaneously made aware of the 'heroic struggle' of Germany in the conflict.[65] These examples all highlight the way in which Nazi educators used textbooks to disseminate Nazi ideology.

GERMAN

The remit of the Nazi school curriculum was extremely broad and this subject in particular lent itself to the promotion of Nazi ideals. German language and literature found a prominent place in the Nazi school curriculum, teaching children the language of National Socialism. The preface of a German grammar book from the Nazi era states:

> Whatever moves the soul of a people, in joy and sorrow, in meditation and battle, in creation and festivity, vibrates in unison with the entire curriculum, and by no means least in the teaching of language. Here, too, it is a matter of coinciding with life itself! Proximity to the present! Relation to the people! For that reason let us also give utterance to the mighty events of the time in our lessons in German! That which fills the heart of the people is spilled by the tongue of youth! The stream of strong blood-folk thought, feeling, and will must be permitted to flow, warm with life, into the form of the word. The result will be a teaching of folk-culture in the mother tongue: we must make this live and be watchful in the growing generation, so that this may, with its own treasure of words belonging to our day and age, express the new treasure of thought, gather it into itself, and let it root ever deeper in the German essence, growing ever more deeply rooted, growing ever more into the German mode of thought, the German mode of living, and the German view of the world.[66]

Studies of German folklore were regarded as a 'central educational point' in the Third Reich.[67] A document on this subject prepared by Friedrich Dehmlaw argued that no other *Volk* had experienced such change from greatness to profound collapse in its history. Dehmlaw claimed that Germany had been 'internally decayed'. The solution was to create clear goals for future development. He described the historical development of Germany in earlier eras, with a neglect of German traditions and culture. Nevertheless, Germany transformed herself again and again and developed a new folklore. 'In order to bring German qualities to the German mind, the *Volk* must be educated'. It had to be educated to love the nation and 'to be the German people'. Dehmlaw decried the influence of the Jews on Germany and called for their exclusion from German culture, as they were 'foreign' to it. He called for schools to subordinate all their activities to 'the national goal of the making of the German *Volk*'. German folklore was an integral part of education. The great value of German culture and language was emphasized. Whilst Dehmlaw's essay was criticized by other educationalists, the basic premise that German folklore was an important aspect of *Volk* education remained valid throughout the Third Reich.[68]

Lessons in German were designed to foster a sense of 'Germanness' and of national pride and unity among pupils. Nationalist and irrational aspects of German literature were extolled. Poems such as Dietrich Eckart's 'Germany Awake!' were used to ignite a sense of nationalism in German schoolchildren:

Germany Awake!
Storm, storm, storm!
Let the bells ring from tower to tower,
Ring till the sparks begin to shower,

Judas appears, to win the Reich's power.
Ring till the bell-ropes redden with blood.
Ring for the burning, the martyred, the dead.
Ring out the storm, and let the whole earth shake,
Revenge to the rescue, and thunder overhead!
Woe unto those who dream today!
Germany, awake![69]

Furthermore, Kamenetsky has pointed out, many classics were adjusted to the requirements of the Nazi regime by means of 'slanted abridgements or reinterpretations', whilst
others that did not fit into the Nazi 'world view' were simply banned.[70] For example,
attempts were made at an 'Aryan' reinterpretation of Goethe. Literature was rewritten,
with rationalist, enlightened or cosmopolitan influences removed. 'Non-Aryan' writers, such as Heine, were rejected. Individualistic aspects of literature were removed or
ignored in favour of the promotion of *völkisch*ness, with its themes of belonging and
identity. Teachers of German language and literature were urged to stress the nation as 'a
community of blood', 'a community of fate and struggle', 'a community of work' and 'a
community of mind'.[71] Traditional German tales and sagas were supplemented with Nazi
myths and war stories. Hero worship of National Socialist heroes such as Horst Wessel
found their way into school textbooks. Furthermore, there was much emphasis on *Blut
und Boden* (blood and soil) literature, as well as the glorification of war. Considerable
attention was given to the war of 1914–18, in particular. The subject matter of Germans
living outside the nation's boundaries was also treated in reading books. Such books
bemoaned the loss of 'ethnic' Germans, who through 'blood' and 'race' belonged to the
German nation, but who were citizens of foreign states – 'Germans across the borders'.
Schoolchildren were taught the need 'to make Germany whole again'.[72]

School textbooks were employed widely to represent Nazi ideals. Primers introduced
very young children to aspects of Nazi ideology such as faith in the *Führer*, love of the fatherland, and service and sacrifice for the German 'national community'. Initially, primers represented a mixture of old and new values. Publishers reprinted pre-1933 texts with
small alterations, such as the addition of Nazi Party slogans or images of swastika flags.
By the mid- to late 1930s, primers represented Nazi ideology more distinctly as censorship increased and a greater number of new texts and illustrations became available.[73]
They dealt, 'in word and picture, with camp life, marching, martial drums, boys growing
up to be soldiers, and girls to take care of soldiers'.[74] An image of Hitler often appeared
on the page inside the front cover, before the start of the book.[75] A page consisting of the
words *Heil Hitler* followed, with children shown raising their arms in the Hitler salute.[76]
Hitler was portrayed as benevolent, friendly and generous. For example, the story 'A
Happy Day' depicts scenes of great excitement and anticipation, as children prepared
for the *Führer's* visit to their village.[77] Nazi symbols were depicted in textbooks for very
young children. For example, there were illustrations of children waving swastika flags.[78]

There was a poem in the form of a short prayer, in which children expressed their hope to become 'strong and pure … German children' of their *Führer*.[79] This theme of making the *Führer* happy was common in school textbooks of the Nazi era.[80] In addition, there were texts and illustrations of Nazi organizations, in particular the SA and the Hitler Youth. One textbook showed two small boys proudly marching alongside their SA fathers.[81] The combined impact of striking illustrations with simple primer language conveyed the National Socialist message boldly. Primers became more concerned with doing this, than with preparing children to read. Letters of the alphabet were introduced in conjunction with an aspect of Nazism, for example, the letter H for 'Heil, Heil'.[82] Political socialization in readers took the form of stories about 'helping the *Führer*' and the 'national community', for example by taking part in the regime's *Winterhilfswerk* (Winter Relief Agency) and *Eintopf* (one-pot dish) campaigns to help needy 'national comrades'. The 'one-pot dish' campaign encouraged families to give up their usual meal on one Sunday each month, for a cheap 'one-pot dish' and to donate the money saved to a state-sponsored charity. In one story, illustrated with a family sitting around their dining table, a child told her parents that she had thought the *Eintopf* meant that there was a large dish outside the town hall, and that all the people went there to eat. Her brother laughed at her, but their father admonished him, saying that at least now the girl had understood what the *Führer* meant. After that, there was a knock at the door and the collector appeared. One of the children was instructed to fetch the money, and to give double that day, as it was the father's birthday. This story explained the significance of the *Eintopf*, using the family context as a basis for political socialization.[83] Another story told of a mother asking her daughters to fetch potatoes from the cellar in baskets to fill up a sack for the Winter Relief Agency, whose motto was 'no one shall go hungry, no one shall freeze'. They brought up three baskets and asked if that was enough. Their mother told them to bring up another basket, as the sack was not yet full, emphasizing that they should be pleased to make sacrifices for the Winter Relief Agency.[84]

Political socialization was evident too in the way in which family life was portrayed and in stories and images of 'the German mother', which mirrored the Nazi idealization of motherhood. For example, the choice of adjectives employed to describe family members accorded exactly with National Socialist ideals – the 'goodness' of the mother, the 'strength' of the father, the action and 'pride' of the son, the passivity of the daughter were depicted in a description of 'a good type of family'.[85] Illustrations of a mother surrounded by four or five loving children were common. These reflected the Nazi aim of the *kinderreich* family. Short texts and poems about the mother and her tireless work for her family accompanied these images. They listed all the tasks and duties that the mother happily undertook, without becoming fatigued or morose.[86] In readers for younger children, there were stories of children preparing a special treat for their mother on her birthday or on Mother's Day, but in reading books for older children, depictions of the mother were found under the subheading 'heroes of everyday life'.[87] This elevation of 'the German mother' to a heroic status closely reflected Nazi ideology.

A play for Mother's Day was included in one school textbook, portraying four councillors engaged in a discussion of ways to relieve the 'mother' of her many burdens and duties.[88] Just as they were considering the possibility of finding someone to take over some of the duties of the mother, a woman appeared at the door. They asked her if she was a wife and mother, to which she replied affirmatively. Then they asked her if she took care of her family, to which she responded that she did so from dawn to dusk. However, when asked about the possibility of having assistance to lighten her burden, she firmly rejected the idea, claiming that mothers loved their domain and were happy to toil from early in the morning until late at night for their families. The councillors, after she had departed, concluded their meeting by deciding that 'mothers do not want to be relieved' of their duties and tasks. This clearly reflected the Nazi view that German mothers should be willing to work hard and make sacrifices for their families.

Examples of blatant political socialization are found in stories depicting 'the enemies of Germany', in particular Jews, Bolsheviks and Slavs. Such negative stereotypes were used to underline the differences between 'national comrades', who belonged to the 'national community', and 'community aliens' and 'enemies', who did not.[89] For example, in secondary school readers, anti-Semitic quotations from Hitler, Himmler or other Nazi leaders were interspersed with folklore and literature that sought to highlight nationalism. The German need for 'living space' explained in history and geography books also found its way into storybooks.[90]

RACIAL STUDIES

'No boy and no girl must leave school without having been led to an ultimate realisation of the necessity and essence of blood purity'.[91] Many textbooks of the Nazi era focused on this theme. One story that related specifically to Nazi racial ideology told of a cuckoo that met a nightingale in the street.[92] The cuckoo wanted to sing as beautifully as the nightingale. He claimed that the only reason he could not do so was because he had not been taught to sing when he was young. The nightingale laughed and said that nightingales did not learn to sing, but were born with the ability to sing. The cuckoo, nevertheless, believed that if only he could find the right teacher, his offspring would be able to sing as beautifully as the nightingale. His wife had a clever idea. She decided to lay her eggs in the nest of another bird, so that their young would grow up together with those of another type of bird than the cuckoo, and would therefore learn how to sing. She laid an egg in the nest of a hedge sparrow. When the mother hedge sparrow returned to her nest, she was surprised to see the strange egg, but she decided to take care of it as if it were her own. When the eggs hatched, a young cuckoo emerged among the young hedge sparrows. He was nourished and cared for in exactly the same way as them, but he did not grow into a hedge sparrow. In fact, the older he grew, the more noticeable his differences became. He did not fly like the others, but flew like his real parents, that is, like a cuckoo. When he tried to sing, he could not do so. The only sound he could make was that of his own species. Hence, despite being reared in the nest of a hedge sparrow, he grew up to be a true cuckoo. This story was used to pose the questions: 'What is more important? The race from which one stems, or the nest in which one grows up?' The issues raised in this fable are particularly salient, reflecting both the debate about inherited versus acquired characteristics and the fundaments of Nazi racial ideology.

Rassenkunde (racial studies) was a new subject that formed an integral part of the curriculum under National Socialism.[93] 'The battle about *Rassenkunde* is not a matter of theoretical debates, but a battlefield on which, without a doubt, the most important battles of our century are fought out.'[94] The strength of the nation was conditional upon 'pure' blood, and Nazi ideology consistently expounded the evils of 'racial miscegenation'. The NSLB stressed that 'at primary schools in particular we have to work on only the Nordic racial core of the German *Volk* again and again and have to contrast this with the racial composition of foreign populations and the Jews'.[95]

Racial studies became an obligatory subject in all classes. The importance of race and heredity for the future of the nation and the aims of the government was impressed upon pupils. Their sense of responsibility towards their nation was awakened. *The ABC of Race* outlined the following as Germany's main problems: too little territory, the Germans living abroad, the menace of the Jews and the falling birth rate. 'A nation without territory in time becomes a nation without people ... If, however, we all fight together under our mighty National Socialist leadership and under the protection of the new racial laws, then the glorious Nordic future of Germany is assured'.[96] In Nazi textbooks, 'Aryan' and Jewish 'racial types' (often in the form of caricatures) were juxtaposed so that German children would positively identify with the former and reject the latter as 'enemies'. This offered a pedagogical foundation and legitimization to the persecution of the Jews.

Nazi pedagogue, Fritz Fink, called for anti-Semitism to pervade the entire curriculum, at all age levels, in order to disseminate it in the classroom. He furnished educators with information about the Jews that they could use in their lessons, even if they had little experience of the subject. He integrated pictorial distinctions between Jews and 'Aryans' for teachers and school administrators.[97] His work encompassed both traditional and radical anti-Semitism, using economic, religious and racial arguments against the Jews.[98]

Anti-Semitic storybooks were specifically dedicated to propounding Nazi ideology to children and they played a significant part in this regard. Indeed, the publishers of anti-Semitic literature aimed to disseminate their messages in the most direct and appealing way, by incorporating artwork using the most up-to-date techniques in colour printing. The most notable of these was the publishing house of *Der Stürmer*, based in Nuremberg. *Der Stürmer* was the anti-Semitic newspaper founded by Julius Streicher, the ardently anti-Semitic *Gauleiter* of Franconia; it was characterized by a crude writing style, caricatures and cartoons. *Der Stürmer* published an anti-Semitic textbook for young children, written by Elvira Bauer in 1936, entitled *Trau keinem Fuchs auf grüner Heid und keinem Jud bei seinem Eid* (*Trust no Fox on the Green Heath and No Jew Upon his Oath*), designed to show children that Jews could not be trusted. It portrayed the

Jews as inferior, untrustworthy and parasitic. *Der Stürmer* put out a further anti-Semitic children's book entitled *Der Giftpilz* (*The Poisonous Mushroom*), written by Ernst Hiemer, in 1938. It portrayed the Jews, through a text containing seventeen short stories, as the antithesis of 'Aryan' humanity. 'The Jew' was dehumanized and conceptualized as 'the poisonous mushroom'. This book included the entire spectrum of anti-Semitic allegations against Jews, encompassing strands of both religious and racial anti-Semitism. The contents included the following themes: 'How to Tell a Jew', 'How Jewish Traders Cheat', 'How Jews Torment Animals', 'Are there Decent Jews?' and finally 'Without Solving the Jewish Question, No Salvation for Mankind'.[99] *Der Stürmer* published another work by the same author two years later, which propounded racial anti-Semitism and decrying the evils of 'racial miscegenation'.[100] In this text, Hiemer portrayed Jews as 'bloodsuckers'. He equated Jews with tapeworms, claiming that: 'Tapeworm and Jew are parasites of the worst kind. We want their elimination. We want to become healthy and strong again. Then only one thing will help: Their extermination'.[101] The aim of texts such as this was to justify the Nazis' mass destruction of the Jews. *Der Stürmer* itself was also used in schools as part of Nazi 'education'. As well as salacious gossip, scandalous stories and its overtly anti-Semitic content, the paper published letters from approving teachers and children.[102]

'The whole of education must be subordinate to the new principle which aims at every young German person becoming a conscious political bearer of German blood.'[103] Indeed, much use was made of genealogy and family trees in school textbooks of the era, in order to establish 'racial purity'.[104] On this theme, a piece entitled 'You and your Ancestors!' asked pupils: 'Do you know what kind of blood runs through your veins? Do you know your father and your mother, and have you yet seen the ancestry of your forefathers?'[105] This text urged children to be proud, not ashamed, of their ancestors, in their old-fashioned clothes. The writer stated that he had traced his own family tree back to 1500 and that he knew, therefore, what kind of blood ran through his veins. He wrote that ancestors had a bearing upon one's own talents and distinguishing features, a conviction firmly held by the Nazi leadership. Beyond forming a family tree, the author made up a genealogical table, so that instead of simply naming his ancestors, he recorded each one's date of birth and death, as well as details of marriages, professions and titles. The writer made this ancestral knowledge sound very important, exciting and colourful. He encouraged pupils to take an interest in their own ancestry, asking them to consider that one day they would be the ancestors of a future family, and that they were part of a family tree that would continue to grow. The implication was that the reader was culpable if he was ignorant about his line of descent. In addition to pupils' books, there were a number of teaching aids that suggested to teachers the ways in which these issues could and should be taught.[106] Through genealogical activities, children were made aware of their membership of the 'blood community' of the German nation.[107]

Apart from involving children in their own ancestry, numerous poems and stories about heredity, blood and kinship were presented in the textbooks of the Third Reich.[108]

These kinds of texts highlighted the sense of continuity between children, their parents, grandparents and great-grandparents back over the generations. They emphasized the flow of blood from the past, into the present and through into the future of a line of ancestry, and of blood flowing through the veins of a family generation after generation.[109]

One textbook demonstrated the transmission of family characteristics through the generations by considering the composer Johann Sebastian Bach.[110] It illustrated Bach's family tree, in order to show that there were no fewer than thirty-four 'musically competent' people in his family, of whom approximately half were 'outstandingly gifted'. This particular example was part of a comprehensive chapter dealing with heredity, race and family.[111] Within this context, blood was the most significant and penetrating symbol, as 'German blood' was the guarantor of the future of the nation. However, there were other symbols too, such as the family home and traditions. Old furniture was regarded as a representation of continuity, so that the 'old chest' or the 'old table' linked together different generations of a family. The values of kinship were expressed through such symbols, which further represented the desirability of a good German family.

In relation to this theme, the rural family, in particular, was accorded a special significance during the Nazi era. Nazi ideology regarded the rural family to be pure and ideal, untainted by the depravities of urban life. It excoriated many aspects of life in the big cities, not least the tendency of young couples to limit the size of their families. Urbanization leading to the death of the nation was a recurrent theme.[112] This came across especially vehemently in textbooks aimed at pupils in rural areas, designed to demonstrate to them their importance and value in maintaining a healthy nation. Such books showed that what was regarded as a family in the big cities was not a true family, but a distorted image of one. A husband and wife, living in the city, without children, but with domestic pets instead, could be described at best as a 'household', but not as a 'family'. The rural family was portrayed as the 'archetype of a true family'.[113] Children were key components of a true family in Nazi ideology, the greatest blessing for a couple and, more significantly, for the nation. Another aspect of rural family life deemed positive by the Nazi regime was the inclusion of the grandparents in the home. In this way, children were more aware of their family history and ancestry.[114]

Nazi teachers took their role in teaching on the subject of 'blood and soil' very seriously: 'We educators are the proclaimer and communicator for the coming generation, therefore it has to be our holy duty to plant blood and soil as something alive into the hearts and souls of German children.'[115] This argument underlined the role and importance of the German peasantry, for 'only a hereditarily healthy people is capable of passing on the acres from generation to generation'.[116] Peasant poems symbolized the working and struggling German peasantry that formed one of the foundations of Nazi ideology.[117] The oak tree symbolized the eternal, stable German nation.

Nazi family ideology was treated in sections entirely devoted to this theme in schoolbooks for older children. Under the subheading 'the essence of the family; its biological position; its legal establishment', key aspects of Nazi ideology and policy were examined.[118] This began with the statement that the family was the smallest but most important unit of the German nation, followed by an explanation that a true family consisted not just of a married couple, but of children too. It was the duty of parents to provide protection and care for their children, and of children to honour and respect their parents. Among the tasks or obligations of the family were the development of a sense of awareness of the 'national community' and the preservation of the nation through the creation of 'healthy' children. Only spouses who were free of physical and mental disabilities or illnesses were to reproduce. Furthermore, the obligation to know about heredity in general and one's own ancestry in particular was explicitly stated. Textbooks of this period explained why and how the National Socialist state promoted 'healthy' families, as well as its laws, such as the Law for the Prevention of Hereditarily Diseased Offspring and the Nuremberg Laws.[119] As the 'germ cell' of the nation, the family was central to the attainment of blood purity and hereditary health.[120]

GIRLS' EDUCATION

As we have seen, education for girls in Nazi Germany was differentiated from boys' education through its emphasis on motherhood and the family. The Nazi pedagogue Alfred Bäumler stated that under National Socialism there was not to be a general education, but a separate male and female education.[121] Hence, girls' education was considered to require a distinctive character, rather than being part of the overall education of both sexes. The essence of the female nature and its significance to the future of the nation was underlined. The role of motherhood and family life was central to girls' education. To this end, textbooks devoted lengthy chapters to the subjects of cleaning and household care, as well as cooking and nutrition. Some of this education on hygiene and home economics was very practical. For example, one textbook gave detailed nutritional advice.[122] It examined the nutritional value of meat, which differed according to the age of the animal and its diet, and explained the health risks of uncooked meats and liver or blood sausages if they were not properly cooked. It advocated the valuable contribution of fish to the diet, in particular cod, herring and shellfish. It explained the food poisoning risks from fish and how to tell if a fish was going off. It gave nutritional guidance on milk, butter, cheese, eggs, pulses, fruit, vegetables and sugar. It explained how beers, wines and spirits were made and highlighted their lack of nutritional value, as well as their effects upon the mind and body. In particular, the effects of alcoholism on the individual, the family and the state were explained – the illness of the alcoholic, his expenditure of his family's income on alcohol and the costs involved for the state in maintaining chronic alcoholics in hospitals, prisons and asylums. Tea, coffee and cocoa were shown to have little or no nutritional value. The dangers of smoking tobacco were explained. This type of nutritional information was provided in order to promote an awareness of health, as part of the Nazis' comprehensive aim of creating a 'fit' race.

Advice on cleaning and household care followed this nutritional guidance.[123] The daily cleaning of the kitchen, living room, bedrooms, floors and stairs was explained in great detail. Weekly cleaning of the rest of the house was considered to be sufficient. Instructions were then given for a thorough annual cleaning of the house, including all the woodwork, skirting boards, windows, window frames and sills. Instructions were given for cleaning floors, bringing back colour to faded carpets, cleaning china and glass and polishing furniture, as well as on which type of cleaning materials to use. The book gave advice on washing-up and kitchen hygiene. It claimed that the sign of a good housewife was a scrupulously clean kitchen. It gave further advice on washing bed linen, dealing with vermin and cleaning shoes, as well as heating and lighting the home. Another textbook that treated the subject of 'the work of the housewife' examined similar topics, but additionally dealt with the subject of clothing for the family and the part played by the housewife in saving and collecting old material.[124] Such texts aimed to ensure that young women would not stumble into marital life unprepared. In particular, education on hygiene and the prevention of disease was considered to be very important. This was practical and even quite progressive. The advice and instruction in textbooks of the era, sometimes obvious, sometimes over-detailed, demonstrates the seriousness of the intentions of the Nazi regime to educate girls in accordance with its ideological imperatives.

PHYSICAL EDUCATION

An emphasis on physical education was not new to Hitler's Germany. Physical education in Germany had its antecedents in the *Ritterakademien* of the seventeenth century, in which the sons of the aristocracy were educated. Gymnastics also had a long history associated with and developing from the work and writings of Friedrich Jahn in the early nineteenth century. By the second half of the nineteenth century, gymnastics festivals and gymnastics societies were an established feature of German life. The Kaiser had stressed the importance of physical education at the Reich School Conference in 1890 and its significance was emphasized again in the Weimar Republic at the School Conference in 1920. During the Weimar era, the Prussian State Boarding Schools and Salem School exemplified the glorification of militarism in their physical training curricula. The Reich Youth Badge and Reich Youth Sports Competitions were introduced in the Weimar Republic. Hence, Hitler's concerns with physical education were not out of line with certain extant trends.

Hitler emphasized the importance of physical education claiming that the state had to adjust its entire educational work primarily 'to the breeding of absolutely healthy bodies'.[125] He further stated that 'sport does not exist only to make the individual strong, agile and bold; it should also toughen him and teach him to bear hardships'.[126] Nazi educationalists devoted considerable attention to this aim.[127] The NSLB was keen to work to achieve Hitler's goals in this area.[128] It argued that the bias towards intellectual education must be counteracted. Furthermore, racial-biological knowledge and an understanding of its requirements were built on the realization of the worth of the body and its entire development. To this end, physical development and achievement were regarded as very important. 'Where there is no will to defend, there is no ability to defend': this was an argument for inspiring willingness and ability to defend at school, primarily through physical education. The concept of the subordination of the individual to the whole was connected to physical education too, as it led to an understanding of collective effort and comradeship. A sense of responsibility and duty to the nation was encouraged through physical education, which created will and character. Hence, Hitler regarded physical education as fundamental to education as a whole.

The accomplishment of the regime's aims to increase physical education entailed greater demands on all teachers, including older ones. The advancement of physical education was a requirement 'in the interest of the toughening and increased fortification' of the nation.[129] School inspectors were required to 'pay the greatest attention to and support this undertaking' through enquiries about participation, as well as tightened surveillance and monitoring of the lessons.[130] Teachers who showed particular commitment to this goal were compensated by means of their schedules, such as being spared the duty of standing in for sick colleagues. Teachers were advised to become members of the SA, unless they were too old or had a physical infirmity. Otherwise, they were trained in sports courses. Teachers who were members of the SA were at a considerable advantage.

In reforms proposed to the secondary school system in 1936, it was argued that more hours for physical education had to be accommodated in the curriculum.[131] Physical education took on a prominent role within schools, with five hours per week devoted to it, in the secondary school curriculum. In order to achieve the desired position for physical education within the National Socialist state, it was suggested that entry to university be based not only upon an examination of intellectual capacity, but also on the gaining of an official medical certificate pertaining to physical eligibility.[132] There were also calls for grades awarded in physical education to be used for evaluating whether or not pupils advanced to the next higher class. In addition, individual physical performances, effort, discipline and leadership qualities could be assessed and these assessments could be taken into account with regard to entry to university. There was also a suggestion that if a pupil were exceptionally accomplished in terms of physical education this should balance out poor marks in academic subjects, which attracted some controversy among teachers. Additionally, it was to be made much harder for pupils to get exemptions from mandatory physical education. They had to be examined by a public health official or the school doctor. Many of these suggestions were implemented in Nazi education policy.

Curriculum development in the area of physical education was an area of considerable attention during the Third Reich. Nazi educators believed that it was the duty of schools in the National Socialist state to educate the German nation to faith, obedience, strength and glory. Physical education had a new and important role in this: 'Physical exercises are for us no longer empty forms ... but the means for the education of youth to National Socialism'.[133] No other form of education was considered 'to give such possibilities for the education of the character of young people, than the various areas of physical education'.[134] In physical education, 'we have the opportunity to guide the youth away from the "I" sports of past times to the "We" sports of the National Socialist state'. This was part of the process of inculcating youth with a sense of community of spirit and a move away from care for the self to concern for the group. In this way, a National Socialist society could be created.

In primary schools for boys and girls (years 1–3), children were to participate in movement stories based on the curriculum, such as Hansel and Gretel, The Wolf and the Seven Goats, Visit to the Easter Bunny, Strolling, Travels of a Family, exercises based on traffic and imitating the clock. They were to do moving exercises based on the theme of the forest, such as running between trees, jumping, hopping, jumping up to branches, stretching to imitate the height of trees, moving around in the woods and imitating animals in the forests. Other themes around which exercises were based included the river, winter, street life and building a house. Then there were simple songs and simple games such as 'Come and Run', 'Run after Numbers', 'Cat and Mouse', 'Fox and Geese'.[135] In year 4, physical education included walking, running, jumping, imitation games and group activities. These sessions included push fights, pull fights, crawling and wrestling for boys. There was also use of equipment and obstacles, as well as ball exercises and first attempts at high jump and long jump. Gymnastic games and singing games were also part of the curriculum.

In years 5–6, there were more walking and running exercises, including endurance runs.[136] There were balancing and skills exercises, as well as exercises to form the body, without equipment. This was supplemented with exercises using equipment, such as pushing and pulling bars, high bars, parallel bars, ladders and gymnastic rings. In years 7–8, walking and running exercises were intensified, with the use of hurdles and, additionally, the acceleration of training runs over 100 metres. Balance and skills exercises continued from the previous years, with the addition of skipping rope activities. There were more exercises for toning the arm and leg muscles. Exercises with equipment took the form of a more intense progression of bench, bar, ladder and gymnastic ring activities. In school years 9–10 and 11–13, a similar format and concept of physical training was given. The exercises were adapted according to the age groups and became progressively more difficult and demanding from year to year. Exercises for the formation of muscles became more important as the children grew older.

There was also a call for schools to establish an effective *Volkssport* (national sport) in order for a strong German people to emerge.[137] By participating in the national sport, pupils placed themselves in the 'national community' and were willing to make sacrifices for the *Volk*. As the timetable was already full of other physical education, national sport activities took place on field days, exercise marches and play afternoons. For years 5–7, these exercises included 'order exercises' (commands for individuals and groups), 'marching exercises' (duration one to three hours), cross-country games, wrestling, swimming and floor exercises. For years 8–10, there were 'order exercises', 'marching exercises' (duration four hours), country exercises which included orientation, assessment and use of terrain, and camouflage. In addition, there were waving and flashing exercises, pitching of clubs, aerial defence and gas defence exercises, swimming, floor exercises, wrestling and fist-fighting. For years 11–13, the activities were of a similar nature, but order and marching exercises were intensified, and country exercises were extended to include reconnaissance patrol training. In addition to this, at all age levels, there were *Volk* exercises (running, jumping, pitching and hitting) aimed at achieving increased performance and accuracy. These *Volk* exercises included stamina training and relay races, long jump, high jump, triple jump, pole vault, ball, javelin, discus, shot-put, gymnastics and swimming.

Structured games and contact sports were important aspects of physical education. They promoted team spirit and co-operation, as well as self-discipline. These were considered to be perfect for character formation.[138] In addition, hiking expeditions on field days were intended to enable children to get to know their homeland.[139] By hiking and experiencing their 'homeland soil', the Nazis believed that pupils would learn to appreciate their folklore and to love their homeland with all its beauty. For younger children, hiking was intended as a pleasurable experience. Getting to know the homeland was associated with marching and singing songs. Whilst the duration and distance of the hikes varied according to age, there was nevertheless the intention to expose boys to a certain amount of strain. It was believed that enduring heat and cold, as well as hunger and thirst, would make older German boys tougher. In years 10–13 camp-duties were added to hiking exercises, in order to 'strengthen the community of the pupils', in a way deemed impossible at school. A tightly organized camp-structure with a strong leader was aimed at making pupils obedient, as well as ready for action and responsibility. In the winter, field days were based around winter sports, including skiing, tobogganing and ice-skating.

The physical education curriculum for girls was different to that for boys.[140] Girls' gymnastics were aimed at educating German girls to become 'healthy, happy German women and German mothers'. All 'un-German' characteristics were to be avoided and eliminated. There was a particular emphasis on games and dance. There was to be contest and competition among girls, in order to encourage both productive efficiency and a sense of responsibility towards competitors. Responsibility towards the *Volk* would be encouraged in this way. Classes were carefully planned so that all parts of the body were exercised. The aim of gymnastics was the development of a high degree of control of the body. In years 5–6, girls participated in 'order exercises', gymnastics, walking, running, skipping, relaxation exercises, swing exercises, muscle-strengthening exercises, dry swimming exercises, activities with balls and skipping ropes. They learned to use gymnastic equipment including the swinging rope, jumping vault, ladder, climbing pole, horizontal bar, swing rings and parallel bars. In years 7–8, they undertook similar 'order exercises' and a more intensive gymnastics training. As the school years progressed, they continued to follow a prescribed gymnastics programme, but with more demanding exercises. Girls took part in *Volk* exercises similar to those of the boys. Their games lessons began as simple singing and dancing games and developed so that girls acquired the ability, discipline and knowledge to play contact sports competently in years 11–13. Games afternoons were designed not only for the games themselves, but also to further pupils' commitment to their school community. Hiking for girls was intended to create a strong love for the homeland and nation. The girls' marches were not as arduous as the boys' marches. The length and duration of hikes in primary school were based on the pupils' age and ability. Older pupils participated in longer hikes. In secondary school, two-day hiking trips were organized, with pupils staying overnight at a youth hostel. Such activities played an important part in creating a sense of the importance of the homeland and in developing camaraderie among participants. They were designed to encourage a sense of belonging to the national community and a concern for 'we' rather than 'I'.

FILM AND RADIO PROPAGANDA IN SCHOOLS

New compulsory film courses were incorporated into the German school curriculum, and teachers under National Socialism enthusiastically supported the use of film as a supplement to the instruction they gave their pupils. The Nazi propaganda machine carefully and deliberately exploited film propaganda, both in schools and in youth groups, to disseminate Nazi ideology. The Reich Centre for Educational Films was established in June 1934 to oversee the production and distribution of educational films for schools.[141] Furthermore, Rust advocated the showing of political propaganda films in all German schools. He stated that:

> The leadership of Germany increasingly believes that schools have to be open to the dissemination of our ideology. To carry out this task we know of no better means than the film. The film is particularly important for schoolchildren. Film education must not only clarify contemporary political problems but also it must provide children with a knowledge of Germany's heroic past and a profound understanding of the future development of the Third Reich.[142]

The films were silent and typically lasted between ten and twenty minutes. Teachers were provided with a teacher's guide, in the form of a printed lecture, which they were to present to their pupils before the film screenings. Much propaganda was contained in these lectures, which accompanied the films. The pupils were tested on the content of the films by means of a written examination. The content was overtly political, extolling the virtues of discipline, camaraderie and self-sacrifice, as well as the key themes of Nazi propaganda. In particular, military educational films that dealt with the subject of war and the army were very significant in treating important themes. In addition, the School

Radio was employed as a further way of disseminating Nazi ideology and propaganda in the classroom. Typical themes included 'Germany, Land of Beauty', 'A People without Territory', 'The German Spirit of Unity and Will to Sacrifice' and 'Unity of Blood in the German People'.[143]

Nazism used the concept of 'integrated instruction' as a tool for the dissemination of its ideology in schools. It sometimes blurred the boundaries between subject areas in order to achieve an organic curriculum. It emphasized the teaching of particular subject disciplines, especially physical education, and the reduction or exclusion of others, especially religious education. Those subject areas it deemed the most important were those through which it could permeate the curriculum with its ideology. These were biology, physics, chemistry, geography, history, mathematics and German. A new compulsory area of racial studies was introduced. Through school textbooks, Nazi educators sought to develop in children a sense of identity with the nation, the Nazi regime and its policies. The emphasis was placed upon the selection of politically valuable material, with the implementation of a system of strict censorship. *Völkisch* education was directed at the promotion of the German nation. Other educational aims were subordinated to this end. Certain aspects of the curriculum were practical and even progressive; others were not limited to Germany but were comparable to those of other countries. Although there were some similarities to earlier periods, the Nazi curriculum was distinctive from the curricula that preceded it and the curricula that followed it, in particular in its specifically racial and anti-Semitic aspects. The next chapter moves away from the general curriculum to examine the very specific subject of the Nazi elite schools.

NOTES

1. Krieck, *Nationalpolitische Erziehung*.
2. Cited in Samuel and Hinton Thomas, *Education and Society*, p. 83.
3. BA R 4901/1 4620/1, 'Betrifft: Neuordnung des höheren Schulwesens', p. 5.
4. C. Kamenetsky, *Children's Literature in Hitler's Germany: The Cultural Policy of National Socialism* (Athens, Ohio, 1984), p. 187.
5. Cited in ibid., p. 188.
6. See, for example, P. Brohmer, *Biologischer Unterricht und völkischer Erziehung* (Frankfurt am Main, 1933).
7. On this, see Ä. Bäumer, *NS-Biologie* (Stuttgart, 1990), pp. 152–4.
8. Ä. Bäumer-Schleinkofer, *Nazi Biology and Schools* (Frankfurt am Main, 1995), p. 238.
9. ibid.
10. BA NS 12/41, 'Erbbiologie in der Praxis des biologischen Unterrichts', p. 1.
11. Ibid., p. 2.
12. Ibid., p. 5.
13. A. Vogel, *Erblehre und Rassenkunde für die Grund- und Hauptschule* (Baden, 1937).
14. G. Wegner, 'Schooling for a New Mythos: Race, Anti-Semitism and the Curriculum Materials of a Nazi Race Educator', *Paedagogica Historica*, Vol. XXVII (1992), p. 197.

15. Ibid., p. 198.
16. Cited in ibid., p. 200.
17. On this, see G. Knoblauch, 'Der Schulgarten als Erziehungsstätte', *Der Biologe*, Vol. 4 (1935), pp. 76–8 and A. Höfner, *Der Schulgarten in der Unterrichtspraxis* (Munich, 1937).
18. On this, see R. Brämer and A. Kremer, *Physikunterricht im Dritten Reich* (Marburg, 1980), pp. 51–76 and J. Willer, 'Physikunterricht unter der Diktatur des Nationalsozialismus', in R. Dithmar (ed.), *Schule und Unterricht im Dritten Reich* (Neuwied, 1989), pp. 187–204.
19. E. Günther (ed.), *Wehrphysik – Ein Handbuch für Lehrer* (Frankfurt am Main, 1936).
20. E. Günther, 'Die Bedeutung des Physikunterrichts für die Erziehung zur Wehrhaftigkeit', *Unterrichtsblätter für Mathematik und Naturwissenschaften*, Vol. 45 (1939), p. 231.
21. W. Göllnitz, 'Die Schießlehre im neuzeitlichen Physikunterricht', *Unterrichtsblätter für Mathematik und Naturwissenschaften*, Vol. 43 (1937), p. 133.
22. M. Pongratz, 'Schießversuche in der Oberstufe der Oberschule', *Unterrichtsblätter für Mathematik und Naturwissenschaften*, Vol. 46 (1940), p. 161.
23. A. Friedrich, 'Wehroptik', *Unterrichtsblätter für Mathematik und Naturwissenschaften*, Vol. 46 (1940), p. 148.
24. *Erziehung und Unterricht in der höheren Schule. Amtliche Ausgabe des Reichs- und Preußischen Ministeriums für Wissenschaft, Erziehung und Volksbildung* (Berlin, 1938), pp. 173–86.
25. J. Stark, 'Zur Neuordnung des physikalischen Unterrichts', *Unterrichtsblätter für Mathematik und Naturwissenschaften*, Vol. 45 (1939), p. 82.
26. O. Brandt, 'Die neuen Lehrbücher', *Unterrichtsblätter für Mathematik und Naturwissenschaften*, Vol. 46 (1940), p. 152.
27. R. Fricke-Finkelnburg, *Nationalsozialismus und Schule* (Opladen, 1989), p. 202.
28. On this, see for example, H. Oden, 'Hauswirtschaftliche Physik an Oberschulen für Mädchen', *Unterrichtsblätter für Mathematik und Naturwissenschaften*, Vol. 45 (1939), pp. 27–30.
29. I. Beier, 'Zur Schulreform. Chemieunterricht und Erziehung im Dritten Reich', *Unterrichtsblätter für Mathematik und Naturwissenschaften*, Vol. 40 (1934), p. 252.
30. W. Franck, 'Zur Schulreform. Chemieunterricht und Erziehung im Dritten Reich', *Unterrichtsblätter für Mathematik und Naturwissenschaften*, Vol. 40 (1934), p. 68.
31. K. Gölz and W. Jansen, 'Der Chemieunterricht im NS-Staat. Ein Beitrag zur Geschichte der Chemiedidaktik', *Gesellschaft Deutscher Chemiker, Fachgruppe Geschichte der Chemie Mitteilung*, Vol. 4 (1990), p. 31.
32. W. Leonhardt, 'Chemieunterricht und Wehrhaftigkeit', *Unterrichtsblätter für Mathematik und Naturwissenschaften*, Vol. 39 (1933), p. 235.
33. *Erziehung und Unterricht*, p. 165.
34. Gölz and Jansen, 'Der Chemieunterricht im NS-Staat. Ein Beitrag zur Geschichte der Chemie-didaktik', p. 28.
35. H. Heske, *"...und morgen die ganze Welt". Erdkundeunterricht im Nationalsozialismus* (Gießen, 1990), p. 206.
36. W. Jantzen, *Die Geographie im Dienste der nationalpolitischen Erziehung* (Breslau, 1936).
37. K. Olbricht and H. Kärgel, *Deutschland als Ganze. Der Erdkunde Unterricht in der Volks- und Mittelschule* (Berlin, 1938).
38. Hitler, *Mein Kampf*, pp. 382–3.
39. BA NS 12/967, *Der Erzieher*, Nr. 1, 1934, p. 8.
40. Hahn, *Education and Society*, p. 82.
41. On what follows, see BA NS 12/824, Dr. Gerhard Endriss, 'Beiträge zur Heimatkunde'.
42. BA NS 12/327, 'Wandel des geschichtlichen Weltbildes', *Völkischer Beobachter*.
43. Ibid.

44. Ibid.

45. BA NS 12/327, *Kölnische Zeitung*.

46. Ibid.

47. Ibid.

48. On this, see G. Blackburn, *Education in the Third Reich: A Study of Race and History in Nazi Textbooks* (Albany, 1985). See also, H. Genschel, 'Geschichtsdidaktik und Geschichtsunterricht im nationalsozialistischen Deutschland', in G. Schneider and K. Bergmann (eds), *Gesellschaft, Staat und Geschichtsunterricht* (Dusseldorf, 1982).

49. Hitler, *Mein Kampf*, p. 387.

50. See, for example, D. Klagen (ed.), *Volk und Führer: Deutsche Geschichte für Schulen* (Frankfurt am Main, 1943).

51. D. Klagges, *Geschichtsunterricht als nationalpolitische Erziehung* (Frankfurt am Main, 1936).

52. W. Hohmann, *Volk und Reich. Der deutschen Geschichtsbuch für Oberschulen und Gymnasien, Klasse 8. Von Bismarck bis zur Gegenwart* (Frankfurt am Main, 1941), pp. 236–8.

53. See, for example, W. Gehl, *Geschichte für höhere Schulen Mittelstufe, Heft 4* (Breslau, 1936), pp. 145–9.

54. B. Kumsteller, *Werden und Wachsen. Ein Geschichtsatlas auf völkischer Grundlage* (Braunschweig, 1938), p. 60.

55. For example, see Klagges, *Geschichte als nationalpolitisiche Erziehung*.

56. J. von Leers, *Für das Reich: Deutsche Geschichte in Geschichtserzählungen* (Leipzig, 1940).

57. H. Warneck and W. Matschke, *Geschichte für Volksschulen* (Leipzig, 1942).

58. J. Mahnkopf, *Von der Uhrzeit zum Grossdeutschen Reich* (Leipzig, 1941).

59. G. Wegner, *Anti-Semitism and Schooling under the Third Reich* (New York and London, 2002), p. 126.

60. See L. Pine, 'The Dissemination of Nazi Ideology and Family Values through School Textbooks', *History of Education* (1996), Vol. 25, No. 1, p. 105.

61. Cited in E. Mann, *School for Barbarians: Education under the Nazis* (London, 1939), p. 62.

62. *Allgemeinbildender Grundlehrgang, 1. Teil* (Breslau and Leipzig, 1941), p. 226.

63. Ibid., p. 227.

64. Mann, *School for Barbarians*, p. 63.

65. Cited in Samuel and Hinton Thomas, *Education and Society*, p. 87.

66. Cited in Mann, *School for Barbarians*, pp. 64–5.

67. On what follows, see BA NS 12/824, 'Deutsche Volkstumkunde als Erziehungsmittelpunkt im neuen Reich'.

68. BA NS 12/824, 'Gutachten über Fr. Dehmlaw: Deutsche Volkstumkunde als Erziehungsmittelpunkt im neuen Reich', 22 June 1934.

69. Cited in Mann, *School for Barbarians*, p. 71.

70. Kamenetsky, *Children's Literature*, p. 149.

71. Pine, *Hitler's 'National Community'*, p. 47.

72. Mann, *School for Barbarians*, pp. 66–7.

73. Kamenetsky, *Children's Literature*, p. 174.

74. Mann, *School for Barbarians*, p. 50.

75. See, for example, *Mein erstes Buch* (Dortmund, 1935).

76. E. Frank, *Fröhlicher Anfang. Ausgabe für Thüringen* (Frankfurt am Main, 1943), front cover, and *Bei uns in Nürnberg. Erstes Lesebuch* (Nuremberg, 1934), p. 3.

77. *Deutsches Lesebuch für Volksschulen II* (Frankfurt am Main, 1936), p. 9.

78. *Fibel für die Volksschulen Württembergs* (Stuttgart, 1937), pp. 1–3.

79. W. Kohler, 'Gebet', in *Deutsches Lesebuch für Volksschulen, 3. und 4. Schuljahr* (Berlin, 1937), p. 275.

80. See *Mühlenfibel. Erstes Lesebuch für schleswig-holsteinisches Kinder* (Braunschweig/Berlin/Hamburg, 1935), p. 65.

81. *Fibel*, p. 80.

82. *Von Drinnen und Draussen. Heimatfibel für die deutsche Jugend* (Frankfurt am Main, 1942), p. 17.

83. *Fibel für Niedersachsen* (Hanover, 1939), pp. 80–81.

84. Ibid., p. 81.

85. *Hand ins Hand fürs Vaterland. Eine deutsche Fibel von Otto Zimmermann* (Braunschweig, 1943), p. 65.

86. See, for example, *Fibel für Niedersachsen*, p. 51. See also 'Muttersorgen', in H. Dreyer *et al.* (eds), *Deutsches Lesebuch für Mittelschulen. Klasse 1* (Frankfurt am Main, 1942), p. 28.

87. See, for example, *Lebensgut. Ein deutsches Lesebuch für höhere Schulen. Dritter Teil* (Frankfurt am Main, 1937), pp. 152–3. See also, K. Müllenhoff, 'Das brave Mütterchen', in *Deutsches Lesebuch für Volksschulen, 2. Band, 3. und 4. Schuljahren* (Kiel, 1937), pp. 249–50.

88. On what follows, see 'Die Mutter muß entlastet werden!' in *Von neuen Deutschlands. Ergänzungshefte zu deutschen Lesebuchern. Heft 1, 3–5. Schuljahr* (Frankfurt am Main, 1935), pp. 38–40.

89. Pine, *Hitler's 'National Community'*, p. 48.

90. Kamenetsky, *Children's Literature*, p. 195.

91. Hitler, *Mein Kampf*, p. 389.

92. On what follows, see M. Stämmler, 'Was ist wichtiger?', in H. Dreyer *et al.* (eds), *Deutsches Lesebuch für Mittelschulen. Klasse 1* (Frankfurt am Main, 1942), pp. 27–8.

93. For example, see H. Günther, *Rassenkunde des deutschen Volkes* (Berlin, 1938) and J. Graff (ed.), *Vererbungslehre, Rassenkunde und Erbgesundheitspflege: Einführung nach methodischen Grundsätzen* (Munich, 1933).

94. BA NS 12/327, *Die Zeit*.

95. BA NS 12/628, Rundschreiben 'Betr.: Jahresarbeit 1938', 16 February 1938, p. 2.

96. Cited in Mann, *School for Barbarians*, p. 77.

97. F. Fink, *Die Judenfrage im Unterricht* (Nuremberg, 1937).

98. See Wegner, *Anti-Semitism and Schooling*, p. 66.

99. E. Hiemer, *Der Giftpilz* (Nuremberg, 1938), pp. 1–2.

100. E. Hiemer, *Der Pudelmopsdackelpinscher und andere Erzählungen* (Nuremberg, 1940).

101. Ibid., p. 83.

102. Mann, *School for Barbarians*, p. 81.

103. BA NS 12/16, 'Rassenpolitische Erziehung'.

104. See, for example, P. Petersen, *Landvolk und Landarbeit. Lehrbuch für ländliche Berufsschulen. Erstes Berufsschuljahr* (Breslau, 1939), pp. 22–3.

105. L. Finckh, 'Du und deine Ahnen!', in H. Dreyer *et al.* (eds), *Deutsches Lesebuch für Mittelschulen. Klasse 1* (Frankfurt am Main, 1942), pp. 25–7.

106. For example, F. Hayn, *Politische Sippenkunde in der Schule* (Leipzig, 1936).

107. P. Hasubek, *Das deutsche Lesebuch in der Zeit des Nationalsozialismus. Ein Beitrag zur Literatur-pädagogik zwischen 1933 und 1945* (Hanover, 1972), p. 54.

108. See, for example, N. Maaken *et al.* (eds), *Ewiges Deutschland. Schroedels Lesebuch für Mittelschulen für den Gau Schleswig-Holstein, 3. Band, Klasse 3–6* (Halle an der Saale, c. 1942), pp. 153–65, on 'ancestors and descendants'.

109. See H. Stellrecht, 'Das Erbe der Vater', and L. Finckh, 'Heilige Ahnenschaft', in H. Kickler *et al.* (eds), *Dich ruft Dein Volk. Deutsches Lesebuch für Mittelschulen, 4. Band, Klasse 5 und 6* (Bielefeld, 1942), pp. 229–30.

110. L. Kahnmeyer and H. Schulze, *Realienbuch enthaltend Geschichte, Erdkunde, Naturgeschichte, Physik, Chemie und Mineralogie* (Bielefeld, 1938), p. 148.

111. Ibid., pp. 139–60.
112. Flessau, *Schule der Diktatur*, pp. 150–51.
113. Petersen, *Landvolk und Landarbeit*, p. 7.
114. Ibid., pp. 7–8.
115. BA NS 12/41, 'Acht Tage Schulungslager des NS-Lehrerbundes'.
116. Ibid.
117. Kamenetsky, *Children's Literature*, p. 192.
118. F. Sotke, *Deutsches Volk und deutscher Staat. Staatsbürgerkunde für junge Deutsche* (Leipzig, 1936), pp. 83–6.
119. J. Fischer, *Volks- und Staatskunde, 1. Teil* (Selbstverlag, 1938), pp. 76–9.
120. A. Waetzig, *Volk, Nation, Staat. Ein Beitrag zur staatspoliticshen Schulung unserer jungen Volksgenossen* (Stuttgart, 1937), pp. 5–7.
121. A. Bäumler, *Männerbund und Wissenschaft* (Berlin, 1934).
122. On what follows, see *Kamps Neues Realienbuch für Schule und Haus* (Bochum in Westfalen, 1937), pp. 151–6.
123. On what follows, see ibid., pp. 158–67.
124. Kahnmeyer and Schulze, *Realienbuch enthaltend Geschichte, Erdkunde, Naturgeschichte, Physik, Chemie und Mineralogie*, pp. 46–55.
125. Hitler, *Mein Kampf*, p. 371.
126. Ibid., p. 373.
127. See for example, H. Eckhardt, *Die Körperanlage des Kindes und ihre Entwicklung. Ziel und Weg einer biologische Körpererziehung* (Stuttgart, 1935), which advises on the physical development of children from birth until the age of 18.
128. On what follows, see BA NS 12/814, 'Denkschrift für die Fachschaft für körperliche Erziehung'.
129. BA NS 12/1400, 'An alle Volks- und Hilfeschulen'.
130. Ibid.
131. BA R 4901/1 4620/1, 'Betrifft: Neuordnung des höheren Schulwesens', p. 5.
132. BA NS 12/814, 'Denkschrift für die Fachschaft für körperliche Erziehung'.
133. BA NS 12/813, 'Lehrplan für die Körperliche Erziehung in den Thüringer Schulen (Jungen und Mädchen)', 1934.
134. Ibid.
135. BA NS 12/813, 'Lehrplan für die Körperliche Erziehung in den Thüringer Schulen (Jungen und Mädchen): Die Leibesübungen in der Grundschule. Jungen und Mädchen 1.– 4. Schuljahr'.
136. On what follows, see BA NS 12/813, 'Lehrplan für die Körperliche Erziehung in den Thüringer Schulen (Jungen und Mädchen): Lehrplan für Knaben-Schulen 5.–13. Schuljahr'.
137. On this, see BA NS 12/813, 'Lehrplan für die Körperliche Erziehung in den Thüringer Schulen (Jungen und Mädchen. Volkssport)'.
138. On this, see BA NS 12/813, 'Lehrplan für die Körperliche Erziehung in den Thüringer Schulen (Jungen und Mädchen). Spiele'.
139. On what follows, see BA NS 12/813, 'Lehrplan für die Körperliche Erziehung in den Thüringer Schulen (Jungen und Mädchen). Wandern und Lagerdienst'.
140. On what follows, see BA NS 12/813, 'Lehrplan für die Körperliche Erziehung in den Thüringer Schulen (Jungen und Mädchen). Lehrplan für Mädchen-Schulen. 5.–13. Schuljahr'.
141. D. Welch, 'Educational Film Propaganda and the Nazi Youth', in D. Welch (ed.), *Nazi Propaganda: The Power and the Limitations* (London, 1983), pp. 66–7.
142. *Völkischer Beobachter*, 23 June 1934.
143. Mann, *School for Barbarians*, p. 99.

4 THE NAZI ELITE SCHOOLS

Nazi elite educational institutions performed a special function within Nazi education and socialization processes as a whole. In the 1960s and 1970s German scholars carried out some excellent pioneering research into Nazi elite educational institutions. However, developments in the historiography of the Nazi era have necessitated a reconsideration of these establishments in the light of current knowledge.[1] It is important to underline the significance of these institutions in the Third Reich, particularly as they have received very little scholarly attention in the English-language historiography.[2] In order to achieve its aims of creating a greater German empire, the Hitler regime was committed to a policy of elite education that would provide the Third Reich with future leaders. In order to try to comprehend how the Nazi system consolidated its power and advanced its imperial ambitions, it is useful to look at the institutions in which the new ideal National Socialist man and leader was created. As Scholtz has pointed out, the regime described these schools as *Ausleseschulen* (selection schools), rather than elite schools.[3] This referred to the 'selection' of a certain type of pupil who had the capacity to become part of the future elite leadership of the nation. The concept of elitism was fundamental to the way in which the Nazi regime sought to organize and refashion German society, with the SS at the pinnacle of the Nazi elite. Far from creating a 'classless society', not only did the Nazis fail to eliminate class distinctions, but also they imposed a different type of hierarchical structure upon German society, based on race and fitness, in which some sectors were valuable and others were expendable.[4] Hence, whilst Nazi policy appears ambivalent, on the one hand claiming to advocate 'classlessness', and on the other hand fostering elitism, its true concern was to try to create a new kind of elite identity. This was based upon race rather than class or social status. The Nazi leadership, with Hitler at the helm, represented the elite of the German 'national community'. The purpose and function of elite education in Nazi Germany was to train a leadership cadre for the next generation. The Nazi elite schools claimed to be meritocracies, but in reality they only selected pupils from within a racially defined framework.

As Baumeister has shown, the Nazi elite institutions were formed to recruit the future Nazi elite and to prepare them for their leadership tasks.[5] The Nazi regime established three main types of educational institutions to train the future elite of German society: the *Nationalpolitische Erziehungsanstalten* (National Political Educational Institutions or

Napolas), the *Adolf Hitler Schulen* (Adolf Hitler Schools or AHS) and the *Ordensburgen* (Order Castles). These institutions represented a microcosm of the Nazi *Weltanschauung* by fostering the leadership principle, promoting competitiveness and emphasizing life as a struggle and survival of the 'fittest'. They encouraged physical prowess. They excoriated the 'enemies of the Reich', in particular the Jews, Communists and Socialists. They emphasized racial purity, glorified war and fostered militarism. They underlined the necessity for *Lebensraum* and had a role in the achievement of a 'greater German empire'. Hitler took a strong personal interest in the elite institutions, particularly during the war, when their functions were linked to expansion and the conquest of *Lebensraum*. He was determined that 'our future elite must be given a tough upbringing'.[6]

Institutional and personal rivalries played a significant role in the development of Nazi elite educational institutions. In particular, competition and antagonism between Bernhard Rust, the Minister of Education, Robert Ley, the leader of the German Labour Front and Baldur von Schirach, the leader of the Hitler Youth, as well as their overlapping areas of competence in relation to the Nazi elite educational establishments, served to underline the tensions between Party and State. This created a lack of coordination in educational policy-making as in many other areas of Nazi policy-making. As functionalist historians have shown, this wrangling created problems in terms of inefficiency and lack of coordination; however, it also demonstrated the status and significance attached to the elite institutions by the Nazi leadership.

Elite consciousness was central to securing the eternal life of the German *Volk*, as exemplified by the Nazi elite formation, the SS. These aims were also found in the Nazi elite educational institutions, which were designed to shape the destiny of the best and most valuable of the nation's stock. Did Nazi elite schools represent anything novel or unique to National Socialism? In one sense, they did not, because elite educational establishments already existed both in Germany and elsewhere. Elite schools were not an invention of the Nazis. On the contrary, special establishments for elite education had existed in many forms long before the Nazi era, such as boarding schools for young members of the German aristocracy set up in the seventeenth and eighteenth centuries and the military schools set up for officer cadets in nineteenth-century Prussia.[7] There were some similarities between the cadet schools and the Nazi elite schools in educational aims, such as the inculcation of strength, courage, discipline and awareness of duty. However, there were also marked differences between the cadet schools and the Nazi elite schools, in terms of both organization and educational aims. The cadet schools took in only the sons of officers as pupils; the Nazi elite schools took in pupils from all walks of life, providing that they were 'racially valuable'. The cadet schools prepared their pupils only for careers as officers; the Nazi elite schools prepared their pupils for a variety of careers. Most significantly, in the cadet schools there was no political training; in the Nazi elite schools political training was an integral part of life, as pupils were reared in National Socialist ideology.

MODELS OF ELITE EDUCATION IN THE USSR AND BRITAIN

A contemporaneous example of a similar type of educational institution was provided by the educational colonies established by Anton Makarenko in the USSR in the 1920s. The Nazi elite schools and Makarenko's colonies shared the objective of creating bearers of their respective totalitarian ideologies. Both types of institution aimed at forming the ideal members of their societies, through discipline and collective consciousness, the use of symbols, uniforms, military drills, marches and physical education. However, there was also a very significant distinction between the Soviet and Nazi institutions. Makarenko was involved in re-educating *besprizorniki* – outlawed, homeless and delinquent youths – with the aim of turning them into model Soviet citizens. His objective was to direct these youths to meaningful and purposeful tasks of re-education and to create 'the new Soviet man'.[8] Makarenko was engaged in a type of social engineering programme. By contrast, the Nazi elite schools accepted only their 'ideal' entrants as pupils.[9] Hence, what differentiated the Nazi elite institutions was a specific understanding of 'elitism' in terms of social Darwinist principles. The most significant prerequisite of Nazi elitism was 'racial blood purity'. In this sense, the Nazi elite schools were unprecedented and unparalleled. The Nazis utilized their own version of elite schools for their own ends, for a particular function that was distinctive from previous or contemporaneous examples.[10]

It is important to recognize that Nazi elite education consciously took on the examples of English public schools in its aims, and yet, simultaneously, it shunned them ideologically. In order to consider this, a brief overview of the English public school tradition is helpful. Public schools had a long history in England, dating back to the fourteenth century when William of Wykeham (1324–1404) founded Winchester College. From the start, such institutions aimed 'to socialise future members of an elite'.[11] By the nineteenth century, many prominent public schools had been established, at which pupils boarded and a classical curriculum featured strongly. English public schools underwent a transformation during the course of the nineteenth century in response to the changing structure of society, and education at a public school became the defining mark of a 'gentleman'. The sons of the aristocracy, gentry and the professional and mercantile classes were educated at the public schools and this trend gradually replaced the status of the gentleman being based purely on ancestry.

The English public schools sought to create a political and administrative elite. Whilst the historical and structural features of the schools were not changed, they did begin to function in new ways. They have been described as 'incipient total institutions'.[12] Whilst the traditions of both boarding and education in the classics were maintained, moral and religious expectations were inculcated in a new way, with sets of rules for behaviour and conduct.[13] Boys were often isolated in these institutions – the advent of the railway meant that it was possible for schools to be located at some distance from their homes – which served the purpose of elite education in 'total institutions'. Self-indulgence and self-interest were to be eliminated. Organized games were introduced to instil obedience to a leader, restraint and self-control. As well as their classical education, the games these pupils played (notably rugby, tennis and cricket) integrated the new elite and distinguished them from the rest of society. These were the hallmarks of their public school education.

The authoritarian structure of the schools as total institutions was established by the accretion of powers to the headmaster. The headmaster directed the activities of the boys in minute detail through the prefect system, which worked directly under his control. The prefect system itself fitted with the responsibility of public schools to educate an elite. Boys were trained to wield power from an early age. The 'fagging' system – in which junior boys were menials for prefects – was another element of power relationships. In addition, public schools took over much of the responsibility for education and socialization that belonged to the family. In many senses, the closed community of the public schools eclipsed the role of the family. Hence, the English public school became an impregnable total institution and an enduring and 'powerful device for insulating and socialising an elite'.[14]

In the Nazi elite schools, the ethos of English public schools was imitated in certain respects. There was a distinct attempt by Nazi educationalists to emulate British public school traditions as they perceived them. However, the Napolas did not imitate the class distinctions that were the hallmark of the British public school system. Instead, they sought to take in the best of German youth, regardless of their social status. Nazi educationalists compared their Napolas with British public schools in terms of their ethos and aims:

> The boy is removed from the spoiling influence of the parental home at an early age, and at first has difficulty in establishing his own position among his fellows. But as a rule, the need to survive wakens the necessary forces in him, which toughen him and provide him with security and a firmness of will ... Public schools are explicit instruments for shaping the individual pupil into a uniform national type, with an equally uniform system of values. Our most recent educational endeavours in the Napolas ... run along the same principles. Like the public schools in England, they are meant to train an elite, a reservoir for leadership.[15]

The emphasis on competition and compulsory participation in sports was particularly strong. Furthermore, 'Through the strengthening of historical consciousness, German consciousness ... an awareness of the national community, perspectives are being created which ultimately culminate in an organic view of the whole. As in public schools, the authoritarian principle is indispensable'.[16] The aim was to create a new leadership elite drawn from across the social spectrum in Germany to rule the greater German empire.[17] In a speech to armaments workers in Berlin on 10 December 1940, Hitler extolled the greatness of the Nazi elite schools in comparison with the English public schools, which he scorned as perpetuating the English moneyed aristocracy.[18] He stated that 'we take the gifted children of the masses, sons of workers, of peasants' into the Napolas and AHS.

> Thus we have created great opportunities to rebuild the state from below. This is our aim. It is a marvellous thing to be able to fight for an ideal like this ... We imagine a state in which in the future every position will be occupied by the ablest sons of our people, irrespective of their origin, a state in which birth means nothing and achievement and ability everything.

In comparison, he described Britain as 'a state governed by a thin crust, the upper class, who send their sons automatically to specific educational institutions like Eton College'.[19] Hitler described two different worlds, in which he clearly praised the Napolas and AHS and denigrated the British public schools: 'in the one case the children of the people, in the other only the sons of a financial aristocracy'.[20]

NAPOLAS

The Napolas were designed to educate future top-ranking government and army personnel. They were state-run boarding schools under the aegis of the Ministry of Education. They were not affiliated to either the Party or the Hitler Youth. The first three Napolas were established in April 1933 in Plön, Köslin and Potsdam, in former cadet school premises. In 1934, five further Napolas were set up in Berlin-Spandau, Naumberg an der Saale, Ilfeld, Stuhm and Oranienstein. In 1935, another five Napolas were established. They were housed in either renovated or newly constructed buildings that corresponded to Nazi ideals, with exacting standards of hygiene in the living, sleeping and washing areas.[21] Communal rooms were designed to strengthen the sense of spirit and value of the young men. Sports facilities and equipment were comprehensive, including a gymnastics hall, a swimming pool, a boathouse and stables. As boarding schools, the Napolas offered the possibility of extensive control of the education and socialization processes of their pupils.

August Heißmeyer, the SS Napola inspector, declared that the Napolas represented 'something different from the mere transformation of any type of school within the framework of the old secondary school system'. He described the aims of the Napolas as follows:

> All true education is education for real life in its full extent; it is political education. The purpose of political education, however, is the education of a posterity carrying its own community of life into the future. It is formative education, education designed to mould a type, and such education is achieved in our nation today through community and team education. The National Political Educational Institutions have the aim of removing the education of youth from the plane of

intellectual education to that of true education, that is to say, of total education in a tightly-knit community, of education which embraces, as far as possible, all human powers and which, as political education, is always education which moulds the individual and forms the team.[22]

Admission to the Napolas was very strict. Entrants had to pass a double selection process, consisting of a pre-inspection and an entrance examination.[23] In order to be admitted, a prospective pupil had to be of 'Aryan' descent, a member of the Hitler Youth, physically fit, healthy and sponsored by his *Gauleiter*. In a series of endurance tests, over the course of one week, Napola selectors checked prospective pupils for courage, stamina and physical ability. In October 1937, Bernhard Rust, the Minister of Education, stated: 'It is of the utmost importance that the Napolas receive those German boys who by their attitude and ability meet the special requirements of these institutes'.[24] Once admitted, pupils had a six-month probationary period, during which time they could be expelled from the institution if they failed to fulfil the expectations of them. The Napolas were 'total institutions', designed to give a complete National Socialist education to their pupils, who would then be able to provide exemplary service to the *Volk* and state. In addition to the usual school syllabus, there was education in National Socialist principles, for example, through daily discussions about the editorials in the *Völkischer Beobachter*, as well as a great emphasis upon physical activities, including boxing, war games, shooting, rowing, sailing, riding, gliding and motorcycling. Physical education was considered to be crucial to character formation.[25] Pupils had to undertake 'toughening up exercises' such as grappling with Alsatian dogs. Hans Müncheberg, a former pupil of the Napola school at Potsdam recounts: 'If anyone showed weakness he was considered a wet, a weakling, a coward, a disgrace to the whole platoon or the whole company'.[26] In the Napola at Plön, recalls Napola student Theo Sommer, 'physical stamina was driven to the limit'.[27]

The Napola pupils spent six to eight weeks on a farm and a further six to eight weeks working in a factory or coalmine as part of their training. This was designed to give the pupils an inside view and experience of the workers and their lives. Placement in agriculture and industry was not a new phenomenon, but a tradition that could be traced back to the earlier youth programmes. However, the highly political aspect of the programme designed to prepare the pupils for service to National Socialism was novel. Scholtz has described the training in the Napolas as a mammoth programme. A Napola pupil was referred to as a *Jungmann* (young man). School classes were called 'platoons'. Pupils engaged in manoeuvres and field exercises, military marches and war games, as well as learning orientation skills. The pupils were to have 'soldierly' characteristics and leave the Napolas with a capacity to lead and an in-depth knowledge of National Socialism.

In his autobiography, Peter Neumann, a junior SS officer, who received a Napola education at Plön, describes it as 'gloomy, icy and horrid'.[28] He outlines the racial instruction there and tells of his gliding experiences: 'I am a little giddy from this first solo flight and my ears are buzzing slightly. But what will one not do to gain the admiration of one's friends?'[29] There is some suggestion here of the need to behave in a particular manner and to appear courageous. Other former pupils recollect the prestige associated with belonging to the elite school and the opportunities it afforded. Hans-Georg Bartholomäi, a former pupil of the Napola at Naumburg, recalls: 'There was a wide range of travel and "manoeuvres", as we used to call them. We could go skiing and gliding. We went to the Alps, we went to the lakes. That was pretty unusual for any boy in those days ... People made a fuss of us. And of course we picked up on that.'[30] Yet the Napolas removed young boys from their families and friends into a strict, unfamiliar, military environment, to which they had to adapt swiftly, showing no signs of personal weakness or homesickness. Simultaneously, the tough demands placed upon the boys made them feel special and chosen.

Rust called for 'total education' in the Napolas. Pupils were educated with a consciousness of racial selection of the German *Volk*. Their education was not aimed at the development of individual or critical thought, but at service to the *Volksgemeinschaft*. Indeed, this was noted by a foreign observer of the Napola at Bensberg, a Dutch educationalist, Dr Goedewaagen, who reported that: 'In the Napolas the foundation is laid out for the education of personality free of any individualistic attachment'.[31] Goedewaagen was impressed with the ethos and *modus operandi* of the Napolas and recommended their replication in the Netherlands.[32]

Another significant feature of Napola education in the period before 1939 was the organization of exchange visits abroad. Exchange programmes were arranged in German Southwest Africa, America and Britain.[33] They were designed to confirm to Napola pupils their own superiority and to consolidate Nazi doctrines.[34] Napola pupils were instilled with the main tenets of Nazi ideology – anti-Bolshevism, anti-Semitism and nationalism. The *Führer* stood at the centre of the *Weltanschauung*. The pupils were taught that life was a struggle and that a militaristic spirit was necessary in order for the German *Herrenvolk* to survive and create a new ruling order. As the political soldier of the *Führer*, the *Jungmann* had to become an unconditional and ardent advocate of the Nazi *Weltanschauung*.[35] The regime also attached significance to the training of teachers in the Napolas. Special training courses were set up for this purpose and records kept of the performance and outlook of Napola teachers.[36]

The conception and aims of the Napolas changed during the course of the war. Physical training was extended more specifically to weapons training.[37] The Napolas became part of the process of building, consolidating and securing a 'greater German empire'. They became 'forts of the Führer for the protection and strengthening of the Reich'.[38] They came increasingly under the direction of the SS, which exerted its influence upon them by claiming the monopoly on political education.[39] Even before the war, as Kogon has shown, the SS intended to create a new generation of leaders through the Napolas.[40] Between 1936 and 1939, under a new SS Napola inspector, August Heißmeyer, the Napolas had already become increasingly influenced by the disciplinary and racial ideas of the SS. During the war, Heinrich Himmler, the head of the SS, clearly wanted to subordinate the Napolas to the SS entirely and to use them to further his expansionist aims.[41] With the military successes of the Third Reich, a role developed for the Napolas in securing its racial and ideological goals. Rust explained their function and task as education of the imperial idea. They were linked to the concept and goal of *Lebensraum*. Between 1941 and 1944, new Napolas were established across the occupied territories to educate those young people that were considered to be 'racially valuable'.[42] Himmler discussed specific plans with Hitler to create Napolas in Holland and Norway.[43] By 1944, there were thirty-seven Napolas. Hitler supported the expansion of the Napolas during the war and the Nazi regime aimed to establish a total of 100.[44] Whilst the Napolas were scarcely able to carry out the new task assigned to them, it is significant to note how different this mission was from their original conception and *raison d'être*.

Hence, the Napolas combined some of the traditions of the earlier cadet schools and the English public schools in their brand of elite education, but blended them with a National Socialist ethos that was distinctive from both models. The Napolas were based upon the overriding idea of 'political soldierliness' and the fight for National Socialism. They combined elite consciousness and leadership education for all professions, with political training in the Nazi *Weltanschauung*, racial awareness and an emphasis on physical education as a means to character formation. The Napola has been described as truly 'a National Socialist institution *sui generis*'.[45]

Not surprisingly, elite education for girls was not deemed as significant as for boys; nevertheless, three Napolas for girls were established in the Third Reich. The first Napola for girls was set up at Hubertendorf-Türnitz in Austria following the Anschluß in 1938. In 1941 and 1942 respectively, two further Napolas for girls were founded at Achern in the German state of Baden and at Castle Kolmar in Luxembourg.[46] The existence of these three Napolas for girls appeared as an anomaly in a state in which ideological values placed girls in the role of mothers and guardians of the hearth and home. Yet, ideological tensions existed between the majority of the Nazi leadership, who maintained that girls should remain in the domestic sphere, and a small group of women in the Nazi power structure, who viewed elite schooling for girls as a means of access to the professions for capable girls. There was a lengthy struggle over the *raison d'être* and aims of Napolas for girls. Hitler was clear in his view that women's role as mothers was the most important.

> If today a female jurist accomplishes ever so much and next door there lives a mother with five, six, seven children, who are all healthy and well brought up, then I would like to say: From the standpoint of the eternal value of our people, the woman who has given birth to children and raised them and who has given back our people life for the future has accomplished more![47]

Alfred Rosenberg also firmly believed that leadership roles in the state belonged to men.[48] Why then did the Napolas for girls come into being?

Wegner argues that the elite schools for girls 'grew out of changing economic realities that challenged Nazi assumptions about gender and the workplace'.[49] By the late 1930s, a shortage of technically skilled and professionally qualified workers led to a need for the Nazi leadership to compromise its ideological beliefs and to allow elite educational institutions for girls to be established. Hence, practical concerns overcame ideological tenets about the suitability of women working in the professions. Yet those calling for the opening of Napolas for girls, among BDM leaders and from the Ministry of Education, envisaged them as institutions in which girls could be educated 'in body and soul to become wives and mothers'.[50] Whilst Heißmeyer stated that girls would eventually take on leadership roles in Nazi organizations, he equally stressed the expectation that they would give birth to many children.[51] Hence, the girls' Napolas had an ambivalent position from the outset.

The selection process, like that in the Napolas for boys, was based upon 'blood' and 'race', rather than class or parental income. Girls also had to be actively involved in the BDM. As in the boys' Napolas, classes were called 'platoons' and the curriculum included drills, marching and education in key aspects of Nazi ideology. The curriculum at the Austrian Napola consisted of a combination of academic subjects with domestic science. It had space for between 200 and 250 girls, but only 123 girls enrolled there, half of whom were Austrian.[52] The contradiction remained apparent between schooling them for motherhood and schooling them for the professions. The same type of tensions existed at the German girls' Napola at Achern in 1941. Indeed, due to financial constraints, this institution shed its elite status after only one term, becoming a *Heimschule* (home-making school) instead. At Castle Kolmar too, the curriculum was a blend of home economics to prepare pupils for motherhood and academic subjects that would allow pupils to enter university, along with physical education and performing arts. In 1942, Castle Kolmar enrolled 192 female pupils from all parts of the Reich. This Napola lasted for two years.

The Napolas for girls were a short-lived experiment, ambivalent from the start in terms of their existence and their goals. The nature of the Nazi state and the ideology that underpinned it did not lend itself to girls' elite education. Although the girls' Napolas came into existence for pragmatic reasons, ideological concerns about girls' roles in Nazi society never really left them to the task of training girls for professional or leadership roles. The girls' Napolas did not receive a comparable level of funding and status to the boys' Napolas.

ADOLF HITLER SCHOOLS

The Adolf Hitler Schools (AHS) were established in 1937, as conscious and direct rivals to the Napolas, which had been formed during the first year of Nazi rule. They were set up, with Hitler's approval, under the aegis of Robert Ley and Baldur von Schirach, in order to train future political leaders. Hitler ordered that they should take his name and he continued to show an interest in their development throughout their existence. The AHS were purely Party schools and remained outside the realm of the Ministry of Education and therefore outside Rust's jurisdiction.[53] Ley's office, the German Labour Front (DAF), was in charge of the initial organization and administration of the AHS. Schirach appointed an Inspector of the AHS, within his National Youth Leadership, who was directly responsible to him.[54] Rust had initially agreed to the foundation of the new AHS on the condition that his Ministry would participate in the selection of pupils and teachers. However, Ley and Schirach deliberately bypassed Rust, presenting the foundation document to Hitler without any mention of this agreement. Hence, Hitler signed the foundation document which granted neither Rust nor his Ministry any control in the AHS. Rust's subsequent protestations were ignored.

Significantly too, with their status as purely Party schools, the AHS were unprecedented as educational institutions in Germany. Indeed, in his speech given at the laying of the foundation stone of a new AHS on 14 January 1938, Schirach clearly stated: 'We have not reformed something extant, but begun something new'.[55] The AHS deliberately and consciously distanced themselves from the Napolas, exalting their own status and significance as 'Party schools'.[56] They were designed to educate the youth who would take over and secure National Socialist power in the future by working in the offices of the Party. The principal purpose of the AHS was to develop a 'leadership corps' that was devoted to the Party with unconditional loyalty and obedience.

On 10 December 1940, in a speech to armaments workers in Berlin, Hitler spoke about the purpose and aims of the AHS:

> We are bringing talented youngsters, the children of the broad mass of our population. Workers' sons, farmers' sons, whose parents could never afford to put their children through higher education ... Later on, they will join the Party, they will attend an Ordensburg, they will occupy the highest positions. We have a goal which may seem fantastic. We envisage a state in which each post will be held by the ablest son of our people, regardless of where he comes from. A state in which birth means nothing, but performance and ability mean everything.[57]

In total, there were twelve AHS. Each *Gau* (Party region) selected prospective AHS pupils from all 12-year-old boys who demonstrated distinctive *Führereigenschaften* (leadership qualities or characteristics). Prospective pupils had to be selected from the *Deutsches Jungvolk* (the Hitler Youth group for boys aged 10–14). Applications made by parents were automatically rejected.[58] The AHS prided themselves on offering opportunities for social advancement, as social class was not a barrier to entry. The Party allocated funding to the Adolf Hitler Schools, and, in principle, the parents of AHS pupils were not obliged to pay for their education, although, in practice, many did contribute towards its cost. In reality, the majority of pupils came from middle-class backgrounds. Almost half of the pupils (49.7 per cent) who joined the AHS in the first two years stated that their fathers were civil servants, teachers, office workers or officers, whilst a considerably smaller percentage (19.5 per cent) stated that their fathers were craftsmen, agricultural labourers or industrial workers.[59] The percentage of Party officials' sons in the AHS was also significant. The national average was 2.3 per cent, but in the *Gau* of Munich-Upper Bavaria, the early stronghold of the NSDAP, 11.7 per cent were the sons of Party officials.[60]

The AHS admitted pupils that had been pre-selected in the Hitler Youth, but with the additional 'sifting' process of a two-week selection camp, which took place at the beginning of each year. This was preceded by a 'racial examination'. Boys who did not pass this examination were not allowed to take part in the camp. The proportion of prospective candidates who failed to get through this stage was quite high. For example, of forty-eight candidates in Baden in 1940, fourteen failed the first medical examination.[61] The *Gau* youth camps allowed the Party to assess and observe the physical and mental capacities of the AHS candidates. The candidates were split up into groups of six to eight boys. Each group was monitored and observed by a Hitler Youth group leader. The leader spent the whole time with the boys for the duration of the camp in order to observe not only their performance in their tasks, but also their behaviour during their leisure time.[62] At the end of the two-week camp, the candidates were assessed according to character and competence ratings.[63] Strength of character and toughness were tested by a range of activities including war games, gymnastics, marches and tests of courage.

Hereditary health and racial purity were the fundamental criteria for admission. 'Proof of absolute health, without physical disabilities or deformities', as well as 'hereditary health of family' and 'proof of Aryan descent' were the essential conditions for admission to the AHS.[64] To this end, prospective pupils had to include in their application a photograph, hereditary health certificate and genealogical table.[65] Their parents were responsible for writing the genealogical table, with help from the Party. In addition, prospective pupils had to be able to demonstrate physical toughness, a strong character and an instinct to dominate others. Bravery was another significant characteristic that was required by the assessment panels, as indicated by instructions for selectors, which stated: 'We can only use boys who have courage'.[66] A number of exercises and activities, particularly boxing and wrestling, were used as tests of courage. The daily schedule of the selection camps included a full day of mainly physical activities, starting at 7 am with an hour of early sport before breakfast and ending at 8 pm.[67] The selection camps placed much greater emphasis upon physical capacity than mental ability. After 1938, when the AHS boys came under increasing criticism for their lack of intellectual capability, the admission process was amended to include academic criteria. New selection guidelines introduced in 1938 attached greater significance to the level of intelligence of prospective pupils. Furthermore, a new requirement stipulated that only teachers who were qualified to teach at the *Gymnasien* were allowed to teach at the AHS after 1938. By 1941, more than half of the pupils selected for the AHS had passed the *Gymnasium* entrance examination. From 1942 onwards, the search for intelligent boys continued and intensified and by the end of the war, physical and intellectual entry requirements had become more or less equal. However, the initial stigma of intellectual inferiority remained with the AHS throughout their existence.

The Party demanded a new type of educational institution to train the future leading class. The architectural style of the school buildings, as well as the timetable, was to express this desire, with new methods of education for the leadership class. The AHS had three main goals in the education of its pupils: the pupils were to be politically moulded in the National Socialist *Weltanschauung*; they were to be physically fit; and they were to be trained to become future Party functionaries. The superiority of the 'Aryan' race was emphasized in textbooks provided specially for the AHS.[68] History, literature and biology were all taught within the context of the Nazi *Weltanschauung* in order to imbue pupils with its tenets. The incompatibility of the National Socialist world view and Christianity was emphasized in AHS education. Themes in literature included heroic death, the struggle for the fatherland and the significance of the German landscape. In this way, the *Blut und Boden* myth was propagated. The glorification of war was another popular theme. Between 1941 and 1944, new textbooks were issued on the subject of Germany's need for the conquest of *Lebensraum*. As well as National Socialist ideology, the AHS placed great importance upon physical education, particularly combat sports such as boxing, wrestling and fencing, as well as pre-military training. Physical education took up a high proportion of timetabled hours: for example, in the AHS weekly timetable in 1941, it took up fifteen out of thirty-seven hours.[69] Slavic languages were taught with the aim that AHS pupils would be able to give orders to subordinated people in the Nazi-occupied eastern territories during the war. Foreign languages, mathematics and the natural sciences were taught at a basic level, but not in depth. A former AHS boy, Harald Grundmann, recalls his education with regret: 'I am ashamed how little we knew about German poets and men of letters – from Thomas Mann to Gottfried Benn; how scanty our knowledge of mathematics was ... our qualifications were pretty miserable'.[70] The AHS considered it to be 'timewasting' to teach these subjects in detail to pupils who were destined to become political functionaries and Party 'large-capacity administrators' (i.e. those with wide-ranging functions). It was more important for them to be imbued with the Nazi *Weltanschauung*. The pupils were to be turned out confident in Nazi ideology and its legitimacy. The method of teaching employed was designed to ensure this. Furthermore, the AHS had no grading system or school reports. Instead, there were written assessments of the pupils, which focused in particular on the development of the students into 'leader' personalities.

The AHS pupils spent time undertaking practical work in different Party offices, in order to round out their skills and give them an insight into jobs they might undertake in the future. In addition, there was handicraft instruction. Practical work was designed to broaden competence and knowledge, as well as to enhance economic understanding. 'Working with material' was intended to broaden the outlook of the boys and to give them respect for people who worked in handicrafts.[71] The aim was not to create 'ready-made locksmiths or carpenters', but 'men who can be useful in the workforce, in the army and in the battle for life', who have acquired a feeling for handicrafts and technical aspects of their environment.[72] As with the Napolas, the education of boys in the AHS played a significant role in the Nazis' long-term plans for a New Order in Europe, creating an administrative corps of enthusiastic and trained Party leaders, with an unconditional belief in the Nazi *Weltanschauung*.

ORDENSBURGEN

The *Ordensburgen* (Order Castles) were intended to be the finishing schools for the Nazi elite. Scholtz has described them as a 'characteristic product' of the Nazi era.[73] The decision to begin the construction of the Order Castles originated with a discussion between Hitler and Ley, in July 1933, on a visit to a workers' school in Berlin.[74] Ley 'intuitively' began to plan four 'Education Castles' based on Hitler's ideas to establish institutions to train Party officials. The building of the first Order Castle began in February 1934. Alwin Seifert, the construction supervisor, stated that the Order Castles were to display 'superhuman magnitude' and to inspire 'knightly actions'.[75] However, the completion of the four Order Castles was never achieved and Ley's plans were not fully realized.

The *Ordensburgen* attracted much attention from German and foreign observers, both during the Third Reich and in the early historiography of the Nazi era. However, there has been no recent analysis of the role of the *Ordensburgen* in the Nazi state. The *Ordensburgen* were to be set up in four locations across Germany: Crössinsee in Pomerania; Vogelsang in the Eifel Mountains near the Belgian border; Sonthofen near Lake Constance in Bavaria; and Marienburg in East Prussia, near the Polish border. Having completed their AHS secondary education, a six-month period of compulsory Labour Service, two years in the army and entered their chosen profession, selected future political leaders were to be trained on a four-year programme, one year at each Order Castle. At Crössinsee, students underwent pre-military training, took part in parachute jumping and learned about German history and race. They were educated about the dangers of 'racial pollution' and trained to view themselves as racially superior, as 'the aristocracy of the earth'.[76] At Vogelsang, they were instilled with bravery and heroism.[77] At Sonthofen, they were to study Hitler's *Mein Kampf* and the works of other Nazi ideologues, such as Alfred Rosenberg. Extended skiing and mountaineering expeditions here were designed to test their physical capacity and endurance. By the end of 1939, Peter Neumann, a junior SS officer, writes that: 'The training is getting more and more tough, cruelly tough'. He describes the rise in the number of accidental deaths at Sonthofen: 'The weak must go to the wall here. Only those who survive will have the right to form part of the National Socialist elite'.[78] Finally, at Marienburg, the students were to learn about Nazi foreign policy, *Ostpolitik* (policy towards the East) and the need for 'living space'. Here the students would complete their political education. The four-year programme was designed to equip students for their role as leaders of the

Third Reich.[79] During the course of their *Ordensburg* training, the students were obliged to spend three months of each year working in Party organizations in order to accrue practical experience.[80]

The *Ordensburgen* were not spartan, but, on the contrary, provided comfortable accommodation to their students. The buildings were lavish in design and immense in scale. The students had their meals served to them in the large dining halls. They were allowed visits from their wives at certain times. Funds were made available to them for theatre trips and other visits, even abroad. They enjoyed special privileges and distinctions, whilst being educated for their 'elite function'.[81] Ley promised the *Ordensburg* students that 'we open doors to the highest positions in the Party and in the State'.[82] In return, he expected total obedience and trust.

A paean to the Order Castle Vogelsang in *The Order* magazine evokes the sentiments inspired by the *Ordensburgen*:

> Ruins surrounded by tales of sentimental knighthood romance,
> The wanderer shall not search, your tower greets him from far away.
> Your walls are represented through Nordic strength,
> Like a stone finger of vow you stretch above the Eifel and Urft
> Your staggered building issues from the bitterness of the landscape,
> No petty ornaments ruin the praise of clear lines.
> You are appointed to announce heroic loyalty and strength:
> Deep into the hearts of youth may the Führer's law descend.[83]

A number of interesting metaphors have been applied to the *Ordensburgen*. The one most consciously and deliberately employed by the Nazis was that evoked by their name – Order Castles. This had obvious associations with medieval knights, and there was symbolic significance attached to the mission of this new generation of 'knights' as creators and leaders of the Nazi empire. A contemporary foreign reporter commented on this: 'The young men are told that they form a Nordic Crusading Order like that of the Knights Templar of old'.[84] A great sense of the historical past and its connection with a grandiose current mission was conveyed. The careful selection of their location and the grandeur of the *Ordensburgen* buildings underlined this. Their interiors were grand and lavish. Vogelsang, designed by the architect Clemens Klotz, boasted both a dining hall and a lecture hall for 1,000 people. On a platform at the front of the lecture hall stood a massive statue of an idealized Aryan male – 'powerful, muscular, saluting with a raised right arm'.[85] The communal rooms at Sonthofen included a vast dining room for 1,500 people, with marble walls and floors, a 'hall of the community' for 2,500 people, lecture halls for 1,500 people, as well as a ceremonial council room.[86] The *Ordensburgen* were also associated with the Valhalla, the palace of Norse mythology, in which the souls of slain heroes lasted for eternity. A foreign commentator described the *Ordensburgen* pupils as prospective leaders of 'the Hitlerite Valhalla'.[87] In this way, the students of the

Ordensburgen were conceived of as 'heroes' and the grandiose plans of the Nazi leadership for the longevity of the Third Reich as an empire to last a thousand years were evoked.

Another foreign commentator conceived of the *Ordensburgen* in different terms, however. He saw them as pagan, anti-Christian institutions, in which 'monks of a new kind' were trained. Reporting on his visit to Vogelsang in November 1937, a correspondent for *The Manchester Guardian* wrote that 'the keepers of the consciences of these monks direct them to the worship of blood, of the soil'.[88] He added too that he left Vogelsang 'profoundly disturbed, astounded at the emptiness of the teaching given there'.[89] He described the pupils as 'impeccably aligned' as they marched and sang.[90] Peter Neumann recounts his experiences at Vogelsang in his autobiography: 'Combat training is terrifying'.[91] He describes animal combat sessions and, in particular, fighting between specially trained Alsatian dogs and the *Ordensburg* students: 'This is the kind of exercise which contributes to the "character forming" process at Vogelsang'.[92]

Another student at Vogelsang gave his view of the institution:

> We have gathered from all regions of the German *Volk*, to spend a year together here. We are at an age, at which the learning period is generally assumed to be over, in which most have started to work independently. A majority of us has already founded a household ... Now that we have left profession and family and gathered here, it shows the awareness that there is a duty beyond our individual lives – the duty towards the people.[93]

What were the expectations of these 'leader candidates'? The foremost expectation was obedience and the knowledge that they had to learn to listen and obey in order to be able to lead. Obedience training required a 'constant hardness' of the individual on himself and a battle against the inclination to let himself go.[94] The students knew that this was not easy, but hoped to emerge from the year strengthened through this training. The next expectation was ideological training. They required a deep and enhanced knowledge of National Socialist ideology and of the *Volk* to prepare them for their future role as leaders. Their living together in comradeship 'in a small people's community' would prepare them for future lives and tasks in the real *Volksgemeinschaft*. Hence, the comradeship at Vogelsang was 'not just a pleasant way of living together', but also 'the highest duty' of daily lives.[95] The students realized that their year at Vogelsang would not be easy, but its 'beauty' lay in that very difficulty, as they felt their mental and physical powers tighten and they learned how to overcome all obstacles to their goal.[96]

The students of the *Ordensburgen* were called Junkers. This was a term deliberately adopted by the founders of the *Ordensburgen*, as the term Junker referred to the Prussian aristocracy. The *Ordensburgen* 'Junkers' were groomed to be 'the aristocracy of the earth'. Scholtz has argued that the *Ordensburgen* were proof of Hitler's will to create a 'New Order' in society.[97] They were conceived of as part of the SS state, whose aim was to rule over a great German empire. Together with the *SS-Junkerschulen* (Junker Schools or SS elite schools), the *Ordensburgen* were to be 'the real colleges of the future National Socialist aristocracy'.[98] In Hermann Rauschning's conversations with Hitler, the relationship between Hitler's will to create a new man and the *Ordensburgen* is established.[99] Robert Ley, who was in charge of the organization of the *Ordensburgen,* stated that the curriculum represented 'four years of the hardest possible physical and mental exertions'. He was very clear about the main aims of elite education at the *Ordensburgen*: 'Firstly, we want to test the initiative, courage and daring of a man and to promote these qualities where they exist. Secondly, we want to know whether these men are fired by an overweening ambition to become leaders of men, to dominate, to become masterful … Thirdly, anybody desiring to govern over others must be able to rule himself'.[100] There were obvious echoes here of Friedrich Nietzsche's concepts of the *Übermensch* (superman) and the 'will to power'.

However, in reality, the academic standard of education in the *Ordensburgen* was not particularly high. There was no fixed educational schedule. Indeed, there was a popular perception and some official criticism of the *Ordensburgen* that the educational standards were low and that their pupils were not necessarily clever. One headteacher reported that the knowledge of his *Ordensburgen* pupils was limited and that it took them a lot of time to process the material they were being taught.[101] Indeed, Scholtz has shown that education became a secondary function of the Order Castles, which increasingly became used as 'drinking halls' for Party comrades, in which they could relax, feel 'at home' and 'remember the old times'. At one point, Ley even envisaged a role for the *Ordensburgen* as 'Strength through Joy' hotels with 2,000 beds to enable German workers to use them for weekly holidays.[102] This was a gross deviation from their original purpose. Scholtz argues that only occasionally were the buildings used for their original design as 'Education Castles'.[103] Furthermore, the outbreak of the war prevented the possibility of the *Ordensburgen* training being completed, as their students and prospective students were called into the armed services. After the invasion of Poland, the *Ordensburgen* were used to 'educate members of the Party about tasks in the *Ostgebieten*' (eastern regions). In addition, the *Ordensburgen* were used to accommodate pupils from the AHS, as the latter were running out of space.

The role of the *Ordensburgen* extended beyond the initial and main function of training future Party leaders. They were also to be 'the spiritual and ideological centres' of the NSDAP.[104] The *Ordensburgen* were used for training courses for existing political leaders, including *Gauleiter* (regional leaders) and *Kreisleiter* (district leaders), who were evaluated and assessed.[105] The training courses, with a maximum number of 200 attendees, were split into working groups of twelve to eighteen political leaders. The rationale for this was mainly personnel planning for the future leadership of the party, based on the example of selection processes that already took place for the AHS and the *Ordensburgen* pupils. The aim was to check 'if each political leader is appropriate in terms of his performance and his whole attitude, if shortcomings can be eradicated by further training courses, if he has to be posted somewhere else, or sacked due to ineptitude'.[106] This would help the Party to make good choices in the efficient and effective selection of leaders, from among whom the best could be cultivated if they showed the correct aptitude and performance:

> A high degree of racial value and faultless characteristics, matched with determination, will power and readiness for action are requirements which have to be met by each political leader. Furthermore, a disposition for above-average performance and good appearance which compliments and rounds off the personality is absolutely essential, so that the political leader, through the combination of his inner and outer attitude, can lead the *Volk* and have its absolute acceptance.[107]

By pursuing these goals, the Party would not have to worry about future leadership.

Furthermore, the *Ordensburgen* were used during the wartime period for short residential courses for various other groups. For example, a training course was held at Sonthofen between 12 August and 4 September 1940 for 'ethnic Germans' from the former South Tyrol.[108] Once they were resettled and trained, they would be used for Party work, as *Blockleiter* (block leaders) and *Zellenleiter* (ward leaders). The course of instruction included daily lectures on themes including: 'Greater Germany'; 'The Party as the Führer's Tool'; 'The Organizational Composition of the Party'; 'Jewry'; 'The Biological Principles of National Socialism and the Struggle for the Conservation of the German *Volk*'; 'National Socialist Economic Policy' and 'National Socialist Social Policy', as well as lectures on the duties of the key organizations of the Party including the DAF, the NSF, the HJ, the NSV, the KdF, the SS and the SA.[109] In this way, the participants learned intensively about all aspects of National Socialism and the workings of the NSDAP. The course also included film screenings, working groups and an excursion.

An exploration of the lecture themes, which were designed to cover all aspects of the Party and its policies, gives a good indication of the ideological training given at Sonthofen. In each case, a Party member with an expert knowledge of the particular theme was appointed to give the lecture. A lecture given by Danninger on 'The Duties of the Great German Farming Community' explained Walther Darré's agricultural ideology and National Socialist agricultural policies. It emphasized the connection of 'German blood' to 'German soil' and the need for German farmers to settle and cultivate the land. Danninger described the farming community as 'the ultimate bearer of the German people'.[110] This lecture was supplemented by one from Hörgenrode on the theme of 'The Agricultural Production Battle', which further stressed the significance of 'blood and soil', as well as the need for autarky. It concluded with the principle that 'the Reich should be like a great farm, which should produce everything it needs for itself'.[111]

Lectures on Party organizations, such as the SA, the SS, the HJ, the NSV, the KdF and the DAF, examined the duties of each organization. Kulisch, who spoke on the subject of the DAF, emphasized the 'common duties' of German workers and concluded that: 'the strength of a nation lies in its readiness to make any sacrifice … The enjoyment of leisure time would not be of any value, if it were not preceded by the achievement of duties. Adolf Hitler has taught us over and over again that work is the blessing of the German *Volk*'.[112] Helmreich's talk on a similar theme described 'work duty' as 'an essential expression of the German people'.[113] Not surprisingly, lectures on racial ideology formed an important part of the training. In particular, Wölpl's lecture on the 'biological foundations of National Socialism' examined the essence of German blood purity, the evils of 'racial miscegenation', the 'danger of hereditary disease', and the need for the German nation to reproduce and to have large families.[114] Hartlieb's lecture on 'Jewry' described the perils of Jewish 'world power' as well as the National Socialists' 'ideological war' against Judaism.[115]

A course was put on at Crössinsee for South Tyrolese settlers in November 1940.[116] This course included speeches and lectures on a number of themes, particularly relating to folklore and border issues.[117] Party members addressed participants on a variety of subjects, for example 'The Tasks and Aims of the SA'.[118] The programme of the training courses held at the *Ordensburgen* reveals much about their purpose and structure. A course held at Sonthofen in August 1941 was based around the theme of national folklore and tradition.[119] Each day began with a wake-up call at 7 am, with flag-raising and breakfast at 8.15 am. The morning session consisted of singing and then either rehearsal of a play or a lecture. Lectures were on topics such as 'Folklore Work as a Political Task' or 'Practical Folklore Work'. After lunch, there was a film, play rehearsal or preparation for the social evening. After dinner, there were 'folklore evenings', puppet shows or a folk play. Hence, the aim was to promote a sense of national affinity.

The *Ordensburgen* were also used to hold special courses for 'resettlers' wives'.[120] For example, a course at Crössinsee held from 14 January to 4 February 1943 schooled 196 women. It covered all aspects of National Socialist life through a series of thirty-seven lectures. Themes included political subjects, such as 'The Structure and Composition of the NSDAP' and 'The Foundations of the National Socialist World View', as well as practical topics such as 'Healthy Food' and 'Hygiene Care'. The report of the training course written up by its leader concluded that 'the resettlement women were open and positively joyous towards the tasks of our time after the three weeks of the training course'.[121]

OTHER ELITE INSTITUTIONS

There were two other attempts at the creation of elite institutions in Nazi Germany: the *Hochschule der NSDAP* and the *SS-Junkerschulen*. Alfred Rosenberg's *Hochschule der NSDAP* (High School of the Party) at Chiemsee in Bavaria was intended as the ultimate stage in the selection of elite leaders. However, despite gaining Hitler's approval for the project, the circumstances of the war stymied Rosenberg's plans.[122] Himmler established *SS-Junkerschulen* in Bad Tölz (1934) and Braunschweig (1935) for men designated for high office by the SS. The *SS-Junkerschulen* were the academies within which Himmler 'strove to create a "professional" SS officer corps by means of the establishment of a standardised military training system and the creation of the "political soldier"'.[123]

During the war, three other *SS-Junkerschulen* were established at Posen-Treskau (1943–4), Klagenfurt (1943) and Prague (1944). However, in the war the aims of the *SS-Junkerschulen* changed from their original purpose.[124] Between 1934 and 1945, the *SS-Junkerschulen* existed as political institutions to serve National Socialism, in particular, the SS elite armed vanguard the *SS-Verfügungstruppe* and during the war, the *Waffen-SS*. Himmler considered it to be very important that a standardized, professional educational process was developed for his elite troops. The SS elite sought to project itself as a highly disciplined and well-trained racial *Führerkorps*. As Hatheway has argued: 'it was essential that the leadership corps of the armed SS consist of "professionally" trained SS officers who would have the physical, mental and "moral" courage necessary to carry out whatever needed to be accomplished in order to further the goals of the National Socialist Revolution'.[125] Himmler's new, elite man was the political soldier of the armed SS who would be trained in the *SS-Junkerschulen*, the new SS institutions established for that very purpose. Racial selection was the pre-eminent elite characteristic for the SS. The cadets were encouraged to see themselves as future leaders and the academies were constructed 'to create an air of privilege befitting a new elite', with the symbolism of German historic grandeur.[126] They combined modern technology with the traditions of 'Teutonic' aristocracy. The curriculum included in-depth instruction in National Socialist ideology.[127] As well as Nazi ideology, military training and sports – in particular riding because of its associations with aristocratic elites – were the key elements in the *SS-Junkerschulen* education. It was at the *SS-Junkerschulen* that Himmler built his elite leadership corps aimed at ruling the 'New Order' Nazi empire. The bulk of the cadets were not of noble birth, but they constituted what the SS regarded as 'an aristocracy of blood'.[128]

The Nazi elite schools had a specific political task allotted to them – to train a new generation of leaders. They were significant institutions in the Third Reich and Hitler took a personal interest in them. They were a microcosm of the Nazi *Weltanschauung* as a whole. They fostered the *Führerprinzip* (leadership principle) and promoted physical fitness and prowess. They purported to be meritocracies and to advocate classlessness, but, in reality, the concept of racial superiority underpinned them. The most significant prerequisite of Nazi elitism was 'racial blood purity'. The ideology taught in the elite institutions promoted National Socialism and excoriated the enemies of the regime. The Nazi elite educational institutions, particularly the Napolas, had a specific role assigned to them in the war – a function in the achievement of a 'greater German empire'. As boarding schools, these institutions offered the possibility of a 'total education' to their pupils, giving the opportunity to the regime to extensively control the socialization process. The pupils were removed from the influence of their parents, and the institutions replaced the family as their focus of socialization. However, the Nazi elite schools placed too much emphasis upon physical training and ideological education, to the detriment of academic subjects. As Evans has pointed out: 'Eclectic and often contradictory in their approach, they lacked any coherent educational concept that could serve as the basis for training a new functional elite to rule a modern technological nation like Germany in the future.'[129] In the end, as Koch has stated, none of them 'produced an elite that outlived their creators'.[130] Furthermore, once the regime collapsed so too did the value system of all these young pupils. This came as a great shock to those educated to be the future Nazi elite, who had been inculcated with Nazi ideology. Hans Buchholz, a former pupil at the Napola in Naumburg, sums this up aptly: 'Everything that had worth and value for me was suddenly no longer worth anything. The men I had looked up to were branded as criminals. The ideas by which I had lived, and for which I had been prepared to die, had become the products of criminal minds.'[131]

NOTES

1. Important early works on the Nazi elite schools included the following: D. Orlow, 'Die Adolf-Hitler-Schulen', *Vierteljahrshefte für Zeitgeschichte*, Vol. 13 (1965), pp. 272–84; H. Scholtz, 'Die "NS-Ordensburgen"', *Vierteljahrshefte für Zeitgeschichte*, Vol. 15 (1967), pp. 269–98; H. Ueberhorst (ed.), *Elite für die Diktatur. Die Nationalpolitischen Erziehungsanstalten 1933–1945. Ein Dokumentarbericht* (Düsseldorf, 1969); and H. Scholtz, *NS-Ausleseschulen. Internatsschulen als Herrschaftsmittel des Führerstaates* (Göttingen, 1973).

2. There have been a number of significant German studies including: H. Arntz, *Ordensburg Vogelsang 1934–1945. Erziehung zur politischen Führung im Dritten Reich* (Euskirchen, 1986); S. Baumeister, *NS-Führungskader. Rekrutierung und Ausbildung bis zum Beginn des Zweiten Weltkriegs 1933–1939* (Konstanz, 1997); J. Leeb (ed.), *'Wir waren Hitlers Eliteschüler': Ehemalige Zöglinge der NS-Ausleseschulen brechen ihr Schweigen* (Hamburg, 1998); B. Feller and W. Feller, *Die Adolf-Hitler-Schulen. Pädagogische Provinz versus Ideologische Zuchtanstalt* (Weinheim and Munich, 2001).

3. Scholtz, *NS-Ausleseschulen*, pp. 9–10.

4. Pine, *Hitler's 'National Community'*, p. 227.

5. Baumeister, *NS-Führungskader*, p. 2.

6. *Hitler's Table Talk*, p. 394.

7. On this, see K. Demeter, *The German Officer-Corps in Society and State 1650–1945* (London, 1965), pp. 66–70. See also, G. Craig, *The Politics of the Prussian Army 1640–1945* (Oxford, 1955), p. 79 and C. Barnett, 'The Education of Military Elites', *Journal of Contemporary History*, Vol. 2, No. 3 (1967), pp. 15–35. The cadet schools were officially closed down on Allied orders in 1920 in the aftermath of the peace terms of the Treaty of Versailles.

8. On this, see J. Bowen, *Soviet Education: Anton Makarenko and the Years of Experiment* (Madison, 1962). On Makarenko, see also W. Goodman, *Anton Simeonovitch Makarenko: Russian Teacher* (London, 1949).

9. On distinctions between Nazi and Soviet ideals, see R. Overy, *The Dictators: Hitler's Germany and Stalin's Russia* (London, 2004), pp. 261–4.

10. On other elite educational systems, see R. Wilkinson (ed.), *Governing Elites: Studies in Training and Selection* (Oxford, 1969), which examines the different criteria by which elites are selected and the ways in which they are trained.

11. I. Weinberg, *The English Public Schools: The Sociology of Elite Education* (New York, 1967), p. 26. On this, see also, G. Brauner, *The Education of a Gentleman. Theories of Gentlemanly Education in England 1660–1775* (New Haven, 1959) and N. Orme, *From Childhood to Chivalry: The Education of the English Kings and Aristocracy 1066–1530* (London, 1984).

12. Weinberg, *The English Public Schools*, p. 38.

13. On what follows, see ibid., pp. 42–6.

14. Ibid., p. 52. On the ethos and development of English public schools, see also B. Simon and I. Bradley (eds), *The Victorian Public School: Studies in the Development of an Educational Institution* (Dublin, 1975); J. Honey, *Tom Brown's Universe: The Development of the Victorian Public School* (London, 1977): G. McCulloch, *Philosophers and Kings: Education for Leadership in Modern England* (Cambridge, 1991).

15. H. Heuer, 'Englische und deutsche Jugenderziehung', *Zeitschrift für neusprachlichen Unterricht*, Vol. 37 (Berlin, 1937), pp. 215 ff.

16. Ibid.

17. H. Koch, *The Hitler Youth: Origins and Development 1922–1945* (London, 1975), p. 182.

18. Ueberhorst (ed.), *Elite für die Diktatur*, p. 93.

19. Cited in Koch, *The Hitler Youth*, p. 191.

20. Ibid.

21. Ueberhorst (ed.), *Elite für die Diktatur*, p. 64.

22. Cited in Samuel and Hinton Thomas, *Education and Society*, p. 52.

23. Koch, *The Hitler Youth*, p. 185. On the selection process, see also Ueberhorst (ed.), *Elite für die Diktatur*, pp. 77–9.

24. Cited in Koch, *The Hitler Youth*, p. 183.

25. Ueberhorst (ed.), *Elite für die Diktatur*, p. 12.

26. Cited in Knopp, *Hitler's Children*, p. 116.

27. Cited in ibid., p. 146.

28. P. Neumann, *Other Men's Graves* (London, 1958), p. 48.

29. Ibid., p. 52.

30. Cited in Knopp, *Hitler's Children*, p. 132.

31. BA NS 15/205, Dr Goedewaagen, 'Die Nationalpolitischen Erziehungsanstalten in Deutschland', p. 8.

32. Ibid., p. 13.

33. Koch, *The Hitler Youth*, p. 188.

34. Ueberhorst (ed.), *Elite für die Diktatur*, p. 12.

35. C. Schneider, C. Stillke and B. Leineweber, *Das Erbe der Napola: Versuch einer Generationengeschichte des Nationalsozialismus* (Hamburg, 1996), p. 34.

36. BA NS 15/107, 'Schulungslehrgang der Referendare der nationalpolitischen Erziehungsanstalten vom 19 Oktober bis 19 Dezember 1937 in Berlin'.

37. Ueberhorst (ed.), *Elite für die Diktatur*, p. 93.

38. Ibid.

39. Schneider, Stillke and Leineweber, *Das Erbe der Napola*, p. 33.

40. E. Kogon, *Der SS Staat* (Stockholm, 1947), p. 20.

41. Ueberhorst (ed.), *Elite für die Diktatur*, p. 28.

42. Koch, *The Hitler Youth*, pp. 192–3.

43. Ibid.

44. J. Noakes (ed.), *Nazism: A Documentary Reader, 1919–1945*, Vol. 4 (Exeter, 1998), p. 415.

45. Schneider, Stillke and Leineweber, *Das Erbe der Napola*, p. 48.

46. G. Wegner, 'Mothers of the Race: The Elite Schools for German Girls under the Nazi Dictatorship', *Journal of Curriculum and Supervision*, Vol. 19, No. 2 (2004), p. 171. On the Nazi elite schools for girls, see also, U. Aumüller-Roske, 'Weibliche Elite für die Diktatur? Zur Rolle der nationalpolitischen Erziehungsanstalten für Mädchen im Dritten Reich', in U. Aumüller-Roske (ed.), *Frauenleben-Frauenbilder-Frauengeschichte* (Pfaffenweiler, 1988), pp. 17–44 and U. Aumüller-Roske, 'Die Nationalpolitischen Erziehungsanstalten für Mädchen im Grossdeutschen Reich: Kleine Karriere für Frauen?', in L. Gravenhorst and C. Tatschmurat (eds), *Töchter-Fragen: NS-Frauen Geschichte* (Freiburg, 1990), pp. 211–36.

47. Cited in *Völkischer Beobachter*, 13 September 1936.

48. A. Rosenberg, *Der Mythos des 20. Jahrhunderts: Eine Wertung der seelisch-geistigen Gestaltenkämpfe unserer Zeit* (Munich, 1934).

49. Wegner, 'Mothers of the Race', p. 178.

50. Cited in ibid., p. 179.

51. Ibid., p. 181.

52. Ibid., p. 182.

53. Orlow, 'Die Adolf-Hitler-Schulen', p. 273.

54. Koch, *The Hitler Youth*, p. 196.

55. BA NS 22/889, 'Abschrift der Rede des Reichsjugendführers anlässlich der Grundsteinlegung der neuen Adolf-Hitler-Schulen. Veröffentlicht im R. J. P. vom 14.1.38.', p. 2.

56. Scholtz, *NS-Ausleseschulen*, p. 11.

57. Cited in Knopp, *Hitler's Children*, p. 124.

58. BA NS 22/889, 'Arbeitsanweisung zur Auslese und Musterung der Adolf Hitler-Schüler', 12 October 1938, p. 2.

59. Orlow, 'Die Adolf-Hitler-Schulen', p. 277.

60. Ibid.

61. Ibid., p. 276.

62. BA NS 22/889, 'Anweisung für den Ausleselehrgang 1938 für die Adolf-Hitler-Schulen', 9 February 1938, p. 2.

63. BA NS 22/889, 'Richtlinien für die Auswahl, Ausmusterung und Einberufung der Adolf-Hitler-Schüler', 15 October 1938, pp. 4–5.

64. ibid., p. 1.

65. Ibid., p. 2.

66. BA NS 22/889, 'Anweisung für den Ausleselehrgang 1938 für die Adolf-Hitler-Schulen', 9 February 1938, p. 2.

67. BA NS 22/889, 'Anweisung für den Ausleselehrgang 1938 für die Adolf-Hitler-Schulen', 9 February 1938, Anlage 1, 'Vorschlag eines Tagesplanes'.

68. Koch, *The Hitler Youth*, p. 197.

69. Orlow, 'Die Adolf-Hitler-Schulen', p. 282.

70. Cited in Knopp, *Hitler's Children*, p. 116.

71. BA NS 22/997, Franz Albert Schall, 'Grundgedanken zum Aufbau des Werksunterrichts an den Adolf Hitler Schulen', 9 August 1938.

72. Ibid.

73. Scholtz, 'Die "NS-Ordensburgen"', p. 269.

74. Ibid., p. 272.

75. Cited in ibid., p. 274.

76. E. Lengyel, 'Incubators for Heroes', *The Daily Herald*, 13 July 1938, p. 8.

77. On Vogelsang, see Arntz, *Ordensburg Vogelsang*.

78. Neumann, *Other Men's Graves*, p. 71.

79. Lengyel, 'Incubators for Heroes', p. 8.
80. R. Evans, *The Third Reich in Power* (London, 2006), p. 287.
81. Scholtz, 'Die "NS-Ordensburgen"', p. 289.
82. Ibid., p. 290.
83. BA NS 22/998, Neumayr, 'Ordensburg Vogelsang', in *Der Orden: Blätter der Ordensburg Vogelsang*, Jahrgang 1, Folge 1, p. 1.
84. W. Teeling, 'Training for Life', *The Listener*, 10 November 1937, p. 1,003.
85. '"Führers" of the Future: The Chosen Few', *The Manchester Guardian*, 17 November 1937, p. 12.
86. E. Hearst, 'Ordensburgen: Finishing Schools for Nazi Leaders', *Wiener Library Bulletin*, Vol. XIX, No. 3 (1965), p. 38.
87. Lengyel, 'Incubators for Heroes', p. 8.
88. '"Führers" of the Future', p. 11.
89. Ibid., p. 12.
90. On education at Vogelsang, see Arntz, *Ordensburg Vogelsang*, pp. 102–35.
91. Neumann, *Other Men's Graves*, p. 59.
92. Ibid.
93. BA NS 22/998, P. Waiblinger, 'Ein Jahr Ordensburg: Ausblick', in *Der Orden: Blätter der Ordensburg Vogelsang*, Jahrgang 1, Folge 1, p. 4.
94. Ibid., p. 5.
95. Ibid., p. 6.
96. Ibid.
97. Scholtz, 'Die "NS-Ordensburgen"', p. 270.
98. Kogon, *Der SS Staat*, pp. 21–2.
99. Rauschning, *Hitler Speaks*, pp. 241–2.
100. R. Ley, *Schmiede des Schwertes* (Munich, 1942), p. 134.
101. Scholtz, 'Die "NS-Ordensburgen"', p. 284.
102. Ibid., p. 278.
103. Ibid., p. 274.
104. BA NS 12/1196, Robert Ley, 'Die Burgen der Partei und die Erziehung des Führernachwuchses', p. 2.
105. BA NS 22/27, 'Über personelle Auswertung der Schulung zur Personalpolitik', 18 Jan. 1941.
106. Ibid., p. 3.
107. Ibid., pp. 3–4.
108. BA NS 22/284, 'Betrifft: Schulung von Volksgenossen aus dem ehemaligen Südtirol', 26 July 1940. For full course content and rota, see also BA NS 22/280, 'Dienstplan'.
109. BA NS 22/281, 'Schulungslehrgang der Südtiroler Politischen Leiter auf der Ordensburg Sonthofen vom 12. 8. bis 4. 9. 1940', pp. 1–5.
110. BA R 49/2219, Ordensburg Sonthofen: Schulungsthemen, 'Aufgaben des grossdeutschen Bauerntums', 2 September 1940, p. 1.
111. BA R 49/2219, Ordensburg Sonthofen: Schulungsthemen, 'Die Landwirtschaftliche Erzeugungsschlacht', 2 September 1940, p. 3.
112. BA R 49/2219, Ordensburg Sonthofen: Schulungsthemen, 'Betriebsgemeinchaftliche Aufgabe der Arbeitsfront', 29 August 1940, p. 3.
113. BA R 49/2219, Ordensburg Sonthofen: Schulungsthemen, 'Arbeitsdienst', 28 August 1940, p. 1.
114. BA R 49/2219, Ordensburg Sonthofen: Schulungsthemen, 'Die biologische Grundlage des Nationalsozialismus und der Kampf für die Erhaltung der Rasse', 21 August 1940, pp. 1–3
115. BA R 49/2219, Ordensburg Sonthofen: Schulungsthemen, 'Das Judentum', 21 August 1940, pp. 2–3.

116. BA NS 22/282, 'II. Lehrgang für Südtiroler vom 4. November bis 24. November 1940 auf der Ordensburg Krössinsee', 4 November 1940.

117. BA NS 22/282, 'Auszug aus dem Vortrag des Pg. Dr. Luig, über das Thema: "Volkstums- und Grenzlandsfragen"'.

118. BA NS 22/282, 'Auszug aus dem Vortrag des Pg. Bennecke, SA-Obergruppenführer, über "Aufgabe und Ziele der SA"'.

119. BA NS 22/950, 'III. Lehrgang Volkstum/Brauchtum auf der Ordensburg Sonthofen. Allgäu vom 6.-16.-8.-41.'

120. BA NS 22/938, 'Reichslehrgang für Umsiedler Frauen auf der Ordensburg Die Falkenburg am Krössinsee vom 14/1 bis 4/2/1943'.

121. BA NS 22/938, 'Bericht über den 1. Reichslehrgang für Umsiedlerfrauen auf der NS-Ordensburg "Die Falkenburg am Krössinsee" vom 14.1 bis 4.2.1943', p. 6.

122. On Rosenberg, see E. Piper, *Alfred Rosenberg: Hitlers Chefideologe* (Munich, 2005).

123. J. Hatheway, *In Perfect Formation: SS Ideology and the Junkerschule-Tölz* (Atglen, 1999), p. 7. See also R. Schulze-Kossens, *Militärischer Führernachwuchs der Waffen SS: Die Junkerschulen* (Osnabruck, 1982).

124. On this, see Hatheway, *In Perfect Formation*, pp. 109–24.

125. Ibid., p. 10.

126. Ibid., p. 83.

127. ibid., pp. 92–103.

128. Ibid., p. 132.

129. Evans, *The Third Reich in Power*, pp. 288–9. See also p. 502.

130. Koch, *The Hitler Youth*, p. 203.

131. Cited in Knopp, *Hitler's Children*, p. 171.

5 THE HITLER YOUTH

In his speech at the Nuremberg Party Rally in September 1935, Hitler stressed his requirements for the new image of German youth. He stated that: 'In our eyes, the German youth of the future must be slim and slender, swift as the greyhound, tough as leather, and hard as Krupp steel'.[1] Hitler firmly believed that the education and socialization of German youth should not be limited to the schools, but extended to incorporate the activities of the youth groups. The Nazi youth groups were accorded a very significant task in Nazi educational aims and in Nazi society as a whole. This chapter examines the role and ethos of the *Hitlerjugend* (HJ) or Hitler Youth as an organization for the regimentation and socialization of German boys. It analyses the aims of the HJ and their implementation. First, however, in order to place the Hitler Youth movement into its historical context, a brief examination of the German youth movement is necessary.

GERMAN YOUTH GROUPS BEFORE NATIONAL SOCIALISM AND THE ORIGINS OF THE HJ

The *Wandervogel* (birds of passage) came into existence at the end of the nineteenth century. In these groups, young people endeavoured to create for themselves an alternative to the formal education and discipline in schools. They roamed the German countryside, dressed in traditional costumes and sang folk songs. They cherished the landscape, exploring forests, hills, villages and castles. Most of the groups were against authority and discipline. In 1913, representatives of the Free German Youth met on the Hoher Meißner mountain near Cassel to proclaim the aims of the German youth: 'to mould its own life, in accordance with its own nature, on its own responsibility and in inner integrity'.[2] German youth leader Gustav Wyneken stated that:

> youth, hitherto merely an appendage of the older generation, excluded from the life of the community and given only the passive role of learning and with opportunities only for a dilettante form of social life, is beginning to become conscious of itself . . . It is striving for a way of life which corresponds to the nature of youth, but which at the same time will enable it to take itself and its activity seriously.[3]

Wyneken regarded youth not only as a time of transition, but also as a time which had 'its own unique value' and 'its own beauty'.[4] The *Wandervogel* movement reacted against suppression and lack of freedom. It proposed the right of youth to independence. As Hahn states, it was 'both nostalgic and utopian, celebrating simple country life and folklore while working for the development of the individual within free communities'.[5] It made a statement that youth should have its own sphere and, in this period, it stood against *völkisch* and nationalist sentiments. Not surprisingly, both the state and the Churches regarded the youth groups with distrust and dislike. The state, in particular, attempted to undermine these youth movements by expanding its own programme of youth welfare.

The approach and outbreak of the First World War stymied the attempts of the youth movement at independence, anti-*völkisch*ness and 'youth for youth's sake'. The war brought to the fore feelings of nationalism and chauvinism. After the war, German youth groups moved towards a more reactionary and conservative position. By the late 1920s, the *Bündische Jugend* came to emphasize more organized and formalized activities than the carefree wanderings of the earlier *Wandervogel* movement. Leadership and uniform came to play an increasing role. The *Bündische Jugend* rejected the Weimar system and everything it represented, including modernity and urbanization. It became increasingly concerned with nostalgia for a 'national community', as well as more exclusively middle-class, Protestant and increasingly nationalist in its orientation. New groups sprang up for Catholic youth, Jewish youth and working-class youth. Youth groups representing all political parties and the Churches existed before the advent of the Nazi *Machtergreifung*. During the Weimar Republic, some five to six million young Germans belonged to this assortment of youth groups.[6]

Youth had come to attract more public awareness and a more prominent role during the Weimar years through social change and the proliferation of youth movements that shaped the image and cult of youth in the 1920s. The Weimar era gave youth a new prominence, yet the economic and social situation from the late 1920s presented German youth with problems too. Faced with an array of difficulties and tensions, many young Germans felt alienated from the Republic. Radical youngsters turned increasingly to the youth groups of the parties on the two political extremes, the NSDAP and the KPD, both of which appealed to them. The NSDAP was able to capitalize on the crisis of youth, as well as the tensions that existed between the older and the younger generations, and made many recruits among young Germans.

The earliest National Socialist youth group was organized by Adolf Lenk. Lenk had wanted to become a member of NSDAP in 1920, but was denied entry as he was not yet 18 years old. He had asked Anton Drexler, the first leader of the NSDAP, if he could found a youth group. First Drexler, and then Hitler in 1921, encouraged him in this aim. Lenk started his movement with seventeen boys gathered in the Bürgerbräukeller in Munich on 5 May 1921, where Hitler came to address them. Lenk stated: 'Starting with the seventeen, more people joined, then further local groups grew out of the Munich group, it developed quickly'.[7] The Youth League of the NSDAP was publicly announced and its statutes were proclaimed in March 1922.[8] Most significant among its points were Clause 3, which stated that the purpose of the movement was 'to awaken and nurture those values within our youth which have their roots in Germanic blood' and Clause 5, which stated that 'foreigners and Jews cannot be members'.[9]

The next year, at the Party conference, the youth group was given its own flag. In May 1923, at the youth group's first conference, Lenk addressed the boys as follows: 'As boys we appeal to the blustery, thunderous youth, who does not doubt and is not afraid, but hopes and believes, who wins, as it dares. We need a youth which believes in the mission of National Socialism ... the German youth must be trained intellectually, morally and physically, only in this triad will we achieve our goal'.[10] Lenk's youth group engaged in clashes with the Communist youth and courted the displeasure of the authorities. It had a very short lifespan, surviving only until the fiasco of the Munich Beer Hall Putsch in November 1923 when Hitler's attempt to seize power failed, after which Lenk was arrested and imprisoned.[11] After his release, Lenk tried to continue his work and was arrested again for his activities in a banned organization. Despite this, he claimed: 'We, the old fighters, only knew one goal: "Germany". For this we sacrificed life, blood, freedom, existence and wealth ... we were proud to have served our country'.[12]

A National Socialist youth group was resurrected in 1925, by Kurt Gruber, a law student from Saxony. He introduced a uniform and established an administrative apparatus for his organization, the Greater German Youth Movement. At first, it attracted mainly working-class youth. Gruber's organization gradually evolved into the official youth group of the NSDAP and in 1926, it took on the name Hitler Youth. But Lenk was careful to ensure that his formative youth group was not forgotten in the history of the Party and that Gruber did not take all the credit for the creation of the National Socialist youth movement.

> When the roots of today's magnificent tree were laid in the year 1921, the thought ruled me to serve this movement in its young years, as this movement, for which back then blood was flowing from our heads on a daily basis, was nothing else for us than Germany itself. Only pure dedication and continuous preparedness was for us, who were only a few back then, the most sacred task.[13]

Lenk stated that Hitler subsequently appointed Gruber to become leader of the National Socialist youth 'on my request'.[14]

Following a protracted power struggle between Gruber and Baldur von Schirach, who had in the meantime become prominent in the National Socialist German Students' Association, Hitler appointed Schirach as head of all youth activities for the NSDAP in 1931. On 17 June 1933, Schirach was made Youth Leader of the German Reich, within the Ministry of the Interior. By 1 December 1936, Schirach had succeeded in persuading Hitler to let him have his own headquarters in Berlin, at which time he was no longer responsible to Wilhelm Frick, the Minister of the Interior, but directly to Hitler. He retained his position as Youth Leader of the German Reich until August 1940, when Artur Axmann replaced him.[15]

From a very early date, even before the regime came to power, the *Jungvolk* (for boys aged 10–14) was determined to be an organization not of words, but of action: 'How can we win those who we care about and whom we need? Again, not through words, but through actions! ... Only achievement and action can prove authenticity and truth.'[16] According to the *Jungvolk* bulletin, the organization and each new boy within it had to go through three steps. The first and foremost stage was to create and become part of a community. The second step was the consolidation of the community. The third stage was attack and outward struggle.[17] Team spirit and commitment to the community was to be fostered through common experiences, in particular, hiking trips. Consolidation was to be achieved through the boys adopting 'an unrelenting acerbity' towards themselves. Through this, they would develop 'a clear conscience' with regard to their 'inner judgement' and 'true and insuperable strength' would grow within them. This, in turn, would drive them to attack and success. At the heart of all this was 'the experience of the German *Volkstum*'.[18] This was demonstrated in a variety of ways, not just in daily politics and political struggle. The organization emphasized the spirit of German life, in terms of dance, games, songs, music and clothing, as well as language, land and national heroes. This is why a wide range of activities was suggested to *Jungvolk* leaders for its members to undertake, including theatre, puppet shows, circus, dancing and singing, music recitals, handicrafts, drawing, woodcutting and photography.[19] And so, the movement emphasized the creation of a 'new community', 'not with words, but with actions', at the heart of which lay the *Volkstum*. Its task was to create 'a new Nordic youth'. Furthermore, it called for 'a link to the countryside, which has seen the birth of the soul of our *Volk* ... we have to be rooted with the oak and the fir tree!'[20] This love of the countryside was significant to National Socialist youth and something it picked up on and followed from the traditions of the *Wandervögel*. These excerpts from the early bulletins of the *Deutsches Jungvolk* are useful sources as they are indicative of the direction in which the movement was intended to develop as it grew. Indeed, the new exemplary man it sought to create would become 'the primary type' of the Third Reich.

At the end of 1932, the Hitler Youth had a comparatively small membership of 107,956.[21] At this time, in the months before the Nazi *Machtergreifung*, HJ members actively took part in propaganda campaigns, distributing leaflets, putting up posters and engaging in street fights with their counterparts in the Communist youth group. Schirach's main objective in 1933 was to build a state youth organization and to try to consolidate all Germany's youth into the Hitler Youth. At first, the Hitler Youth appeared attractive and exciting. It presented young boys and teenagers with the opportunity to take part in a new movement, to escape from parental control and boredom at home. It offered them a sense of purpose, belonging and unity. The Hitler Youth also provided a new opportunity for participation in youth activities to some youngsters, particularly in rural areas, who had not previously had access to youth movements. By the end of 1933, the Hitler Youth had more than two million members. In order to join, young boys had to present a statement of application for admission, which included details of the name and occupation of their parents, their religion, as well as a confirmation that they were of 'German origin', which they had to sign.[22] The young boys who joined the HJ at this time were motivated by a sense of excitement, peer camaraderie and the youthful enthusiasm of its leaders. In addition, many enrolled in order to become involved in the national cause and to gain more independence from their parents.

THE HJ AFTER JANUARY 1933

Once the NSDAP gained power, with its radical ideas for state and society, its youth group acquired a new status and new tasks. The HJ became involved in a host of activities in building the National Socialist state, including health care of the youth, recreation, labour service and the *Winterhilfswerk* (Winter Relief Agency), as well as career counselling and apprenticeship procurement.[23] In particular, its health remit meant that its doctors had to ensure the health of all HJ members and leaders. All HJ (and BDM) members had to undergo a health check before they were admitted into the movement. Furthermore, HJ doctors were to educate the youth in 'hereditary biological and racial thinking'. HJ doctors and leaders were to encourage German youth to understand the importance of choosing a 'racially valuable' partner and furthering the nobility of the German *Volk* through their offspring in the future.

Hitler addressed the first National Socialist Youth Day in Potsdam:

> The German must once again learn how to feel like one *Volk* … our *Volk* fell from its proud height as it forgot that, and you, my German boys and girls should learn it again in the National Socialist movement, to feel as brothers and sisters in one nation. You shall, beyond all professions and social classes, beyond everything which threatens to splinter you, search and find the German community; you shall preserve and hold on to it and no one shall rob it from you … At the moment there might be quite a lot of Germans who deny the value of ideals. But National Socialism educates you, young people, to become believing idealists; as only ideals can forge together the German *Volk* to unity![24]

He sparked great enthusiasm for the National Socialist movement among those gathered. Axmann underlined this theme of national unity and the elimination of class barriers in the Nazi youth movement in a radio lecture on 3 May 1933: 'We do not ask about coincidences of birth and origin, but we ask about character and achievement. We do not ask: "Where do you come from?" but we ask "What is your will and where are you going?"[25] Youth was encouraged to play its part in the future of the national movement.

Whilst part of the explanation for the rapid growth of the movement was its attraction to youth after the Nazi 'seizure of power', a large part of the reason was the process of *Gleichschaltung* (coordination) of youth by the Nazi regime. The Communist Youth Association of Germany (KJVD), the Social Democratic Socialist Working Youth (SAJ) and the German Socialist Youth Association (SAP) were all dissolved. In December 1933, Bishop Ludwig Müller agreed to sign over the members of the Evangelical youth movement into the Hitler Youth. The autonomy of the Catholic youth groups was temporarily protected (until 1936) by the July 1933 Concordat between Hitler and the Vatican. In 1936, the Gestapo banned any remaining youth groups outside the Hitler Youth, and the Catholic youth groups were dissolved. By the end of 1936, the Hitler Youth had 5.4 million members.

On 1 December 1936, the Law on the Hitler Youth stated that: 'The future of the German nation depends upon its youth and German youth must therefore be prepared for its future duties.' It decreed that:

1. The whole of German youth within the borders of the Reich is organized in the Hitler Youth.
2. All German young people, apart from being educated at home and at school, will be educated in the Hitler Youth physically, intellectually, and morally in the spirit of National Socialism to serve the nation and the community.
3. The task of educating German youth in the Hitler Youth is being entrusted to the Reich Leader of German Youth in the NSDAP. He therefore becomes the 'Youth Leader of the German Reich'. His office shall rank as Supreme Governmental Agency with its headquarters in Berlin and he will be directly responsible to the Führer and Chancellor of the Reich.
4. All regulations necessary to execute and supplement this decree will be issued by the Führer and Reich Chancellor.[26]

The Hitler Youth Law was significant because it officially and legally gave the Hitler Youth an equal status to the home and the school in educating German children. However, in spite of its first provision, membership of the Hitler Youth organization was not yet compulsory. Nevertheless, there was much social pressure to join after 1936. Schirach proclaimed 1936 to be 'the year of the German *Jungvolk*' and orchestrated a huge propaganda campaign, as well as pressure on schoolteachers, in order to initiate as many 10-year-olds as possible into the movement in that year. On 19 April 1936, the eve of Hitler's birthday, Schirach proudly presented Hitler with the 'gift' of this cohort of young boys, who took their oath of loyalty to Hitler at Marienburg Castle in West Prussia. In his radio broadcast, Schirach claimed that 90 per cent of all 10-year-olds were members of the Nazi youth movement. However, even despite this immense pressure and compulsion to join, it is noteworthy that a substantial number of young people managed to remain outside the Hitler Youth movement.[27]

The organizational briefs and guidelines for the *Jungvolk* and its leaders were circulated by the National Leadership of the HJ department. The *Jungvolk* was organized into three different types of organisational unit. The *Jungenschaft* comprised 8–16 boys; the *Jungzug* was made up of two to four *Jungenschaften* and comprised 32–64 boys; and the *Fähnlein* was made up of two to four *Jungzüge* and comprised 128–250 boys.[28] The uniforms for both the *Jungvolk* members and the *Jungvolk* leaders were carefully designed. The members' uniform consisted of an open brown shirt, a black neck scarf with a leather knot, brown knee breeches, a belt, with brown leather buttons. Two leather buttons affixed to each other were to be worn as cufflinks. The *Jungvolk* emblem was to be worn on the left chest pocket below the button. The emblem could only be worn once the boy had passed his probation period and had been admitted officially into the *Jungenschaft* with a handshake. There was also a *Jungvolk* cap, with stripes in colours according to region. Leaders' uniforms were marked out by their leadership badges. The *Jungenschaft* leader wore a green disk on the left arm, the *Jungzug* leader wore a blue disk and the *Fähnlein* leader a white disk.[29] This appealed to young people who wanted to wear the uniform and the badges and therefore tried to excel within the movement.

Leaders were given careful guidelines for training and educational work in the *Jungvolk*. They were called upon to educate their boys in 'love of the country' and through group work to eliminate the gap between 'the proletarians and the bourgeois'.[30] This intention was part of the National Socialists' wider aim to destroy class barriers in German society. In the youth group, this was to be achieved through a weekly meeting called the *Heimabend*, in which boys came together to read, sing, listen to stories and do handicrafts. In good weather, this was supplemented with outdoor activities in the form of games and exercises to strengthen the body. In addition, a key activity was the excursion. This was particularly favoured by the Nazi leadership as there the boy was 'totally cut off from home' and could really show 'whether he is a man and knows how to help himself' and 'whether he is a good comrade'. There he learned how to put up tents in different ways and how to secure and heat a camp – 'in short, everything that a good German boy can, will and must know'.[31] German boys acquired knowledge of their homeland and of nature on these excursions. They also learned the group rule that the common good took precedence over self-interest. Beyond these excursions, which took place once a month for a day and a half, were the longer camps that took place in the school holidays. Each month, the *Jungvolk* published a booklet for its members, which included excursion reports, experiences, poems, stories, photographs and drawings. At parents' evenings, exhibitions of *Jungvolk* work were shown, as well as group songs, music recitals, games and exercises. These evenings were designed to show parents what the boys were doing at the youth group and to encourage their support of it. In addition, it was hoped that parents whose boys were not already members might be encouraged to enrol them once they had been to the parents' evenings. Hence they had to be appealing, with no 'feeling of boredom' for the audience.[32]

On 25 March 1939, a further Youth Ordinance decreed that: 'All young people are obliged from the age of 10 to their 19th birthday to serve in the Hitler Youth'. Boys aged 10–14 were to join the *Deutsches Jungvolk* (DJ), whilst boys from 14 to 18 were to join the Hitler Youth. German girls were to join the corresponding Nazi girls' organizations, the *Jungmädel* (JM) for girls aged 10–14 and the *Bund Deutscher Mädel* (BDM) for girls aged 14–18, which are examined in the next chapter. It was the responsibility of the parent or legal guardian to register the children or young people in the Hitler Youth and they could be fined or imprisoned for deliberate failure to do so. Furthermore, the decree stated that: 'anyone who maliciously prevents or attempts to prevent any young person from serving in the Hitler Youth will be punished by fine or imprisonment'.[33] Hitler Youth members were obliged to swear an oath of loyalty to Hitler.

After the Hitler Youth had established itself as the 'state youth', three other influences on children's education and socialization came to stand in opposition to its power: the Church, the school and the parental home.[34] Tensions increased between HJ members and traditional figures of authority, in particular clergymen, teachers and parents. HJ members considered the movement as their 'world ... and not school, nor church nor home could offer competing alternatives'.[35] In HJ newspapers and journals, as well as its training manuals for HJ leaders, the presentation of arguments against the Churches was a significant and recurring theme. HJ leaders encouraged their members to flout the authority of conventional figures and even to scorn them. The Hitler Youth made some attempts to get parents on its side, for example introducing HJ parents' evenings and broadcasting radio programmes on parenthood to secure the loyalty of parents. However, HJ members were encouraged to spy on their families and friends for anti-Nazi activities, which increased tensions between the HJ and the parental home. Furthermore, tension increased between the NSLB and the HJ leadership. The main source of concern for the NSLB was the lack of respect for the teaching profession displayed by HJ members.[36] There was a growing number of complaints by teachers that pupils ridiculed them and undermined their authority.[37] Yet, from the perspective of a young HJ boy, this position was not necessarily so clear-cut. Jurgen Herbst writes in his memoir: 'Did we leaders of boys leave our parents and teachers, or did our parents and teachers leave us? We could not have said.'[38] Nevertheless, in the KLV camps during the war, the regime came closest to achieving its aim of total education – for here the influence of parents was eliminated, the influence of schoolteachers was reduced and the influence of the HJ became the decisive factor.[39]

By the time membership became compulsory, the Hitler Youth had lost some of its original appeal. The initial enthusiasm for the movement waned as military drills took precedence over hikes, camps and sporting activities, and the dissemination of Nazi propaganda became more pronounced. The HJ was becoming an instrument of authoritarianism and indoctrination. The initial enticement of the slogan 'youth leads youth' wore off. There was also a growing number of duties, including collecting money for the Winter Relief Agency and picking berries and herbs. Land Service involved Hitler Youth members in helping with harvesting, milking cows and chopping wood. This was aimed at emphasizing the 'blood and soil' doctrine and at providing experience of life in the countryside to young people from the cities. It fitted in with the Nazi view of the cities as asphalt jungles, which engendered an unwholesome lifestyle. A Hitler Youth circular dated 8 January 1940 stated: 'Land service is a political task of National Socialism. Its purpose is to bring back boys and girls from the cities to the land, to create new recruits for the agricultural occupations and thus secure their continuous existence. The best of them should be given an opportunity to settle. The Hitler Youth is the sole executor of the land service.'[40] From February 1940, Hitler Youth members had to report for duty on two Sundays each month. Some young people came to see the Hitler Youth as a restriction on the freedom of their leisure time, as it took up more and more of their waking hours outside school. State control had replaced parental control. Parents too expressed concern about the amount of time their children were spending on Hitler Youth activities.

Indeed, HJ members recall how busy their HJ schedules were. Erich Loest remembers: 'Twice a week we had HJ service and as soon as I became a leader, there were extra leadership duties on Mondays; and on Sundays we had shooting, or we went bicycling somewhere, or we had a parade. So for four or five days a week I was busy with the Hitler Youth. We had no time to think about what we were actually doing. The next thing was always coming up. It was non-stop action.'[41] However, it is also worth remembering that in many senses, boys living through the Nazi era were still just boys as in other places and times. Herbst makes this point clearly in his memoir:

> As we boys lived our lives, day by day and week by week, they moved along in all the ordinariness of daily existence as ordinary lives unfold everywhere. Dramatic and traumatic events did not occur every day. When they did, they broke into and interrupted the ordinariness of everyday life, but then they were absorbed in the rhythm of our daily doings and became themselves ordinary parts of it.[42]

How were HJ members socialized? As Klönne has suggested, the HJ boy was characterized as outwardly active, capable of physical achievement, fit for work, used to organizational discipline and bound to the norms of the organization.[43] Certainly there was a significant distinction between the socialization of girls and boys. There were specific gendered expectations of boys as boys. Training in the HJ involved a variety of aspects including physical fitness, discipline, adherence to the organization and its dress codes. Physical fitness was one of the most important attributes of the HJ. Its members had a 'duty' to be physically fit. In order to be accepted into the organization, the new recruits of the *Jungvolk* had to pass a physical assessment, which included running and long jump, as well as 'tests of courage'. The boys had to demonstrate their strength and bravery. Once they joined, they took part in physical exercises and military drills. They did roll calls and marched in columns. They participated in numerous sporting events and competitions. The 'HJ National Sports Contest' was the culmination of these events. It showed off the strength and fortitude of the German youth. At the 1937 Party Congress Hitler addressed his youth as follows: 'In place of young people who were previously brought up to enjoy themselves, a generation is now coming of age, brought up to privation, self-sacrifice and above all to the development of a healthy, resilient physique'.[44]

The desire to belong to the Nazi youth movement and to wear the uniform was a significant factor in the appeal of the HJ. The younger boys recall their haste to join and desire to reach the age of 10 so that they could do so. For example, Hans Jürgen Habenicht describes his agonizing wait to be admitted into the *Jungvolk*: 'I really longed for the day and was proud when it finally arrived. My elder brother was already in the Hitler Youth. I too wanted to belong one day to that organization, which was bound up with ideas like comradeship, Fatherland and honour. In uniform, you felt you were taken more seriously. Now I was one of the big boys'.[45]

The Hitler Youth uniform consisted of brown shorts with a brown shirt, a black kerchief, a leather belt, leather shoulder straps, white socks, brown shoes and a brown cap. The boys took pride and pleasure in wearing the HJ uniform, which signified their belonging. Jobst-Christian von Cornberg recalls that 'to wear the uniform was an honour'.[46] The membership of the movement and its uniform appealed to the boys' self-esteem and their desire to be recognized as important to the national cause. Werner Hanitzsch remembers: 'The uniform was first and foremost a symbol of belonging. And for us that was actually the most important thing. We were a community. We were a blood brotherhood and the uniform was the external symbol of this'.[47]

Ideology was presented in a thoroughgoing manner in the HJ *Heimabend*. The HJ leaders were primed with training manuals about what to include and how to run these sessions. They told the boys legends of German heroes and read battlefield literature to them. They were taught about the need to preserve 'the purity of German blood', the menace to Germany presented by the Jews and the importance of gaining 'living space in the East'. The Third Reich would rightfully subjugate its 'inferior', 'sub-human' eastern neighbours and be heroic in battle. Rudolf Hiemke remembers that 'the pattern of the *Heimabend* was strictly laid down, all creativity was suppressed. There was no debate, everything was dictated and organized on military lines. We had absolutely no opportunity to express ourselves freely and dared not offer any criticism.'[48] Herbst recalls the *Heimabend*:

> We listened to our leaders telling us over and over again of the history of the Nazi party, of the exploits of its heroes ... we viewed rows of pictures showing the heads and bodies of men and women who were supposedly representatives of various racial groups. We soon learned that the blond, tall, slender, and straight figures were the Nordic, Aryan types that we all were supposed to be. The dark, small, thick, and bent bodies, on the other hand, belonged to undesirable ... and less worthy races. We should look down on them as inferior beings.[49]

Hence, the Nazi racial stereotypes were clearly and firmly established during the HJ *Heimabend* sessions.

The camping trips excited more enthusiasm among HJ members. They took part in leisure activities that previously had been available only to the children of affluent families. They escaped the monotony of their homes during the long summer holiday to hike through the countryside and camp. The communal spirit formed a great part of the popularity of the HJ camps. Peter Löhrer recalls: 'In the evening we all sat around the fire. And then we sang together. It was dark. The stars shone above us. It was a thrilling feeling.'[50]

The Hitler Youth socialized German youth in militarization and the ultimate aim of acquiring new *Lebensraum* (living space) in the east. Its members played war games, studying maps and spotting enemies. They learned how to master their terrain, as well as orientation skills in darkness. They camped in tents, sang *völkisch* songs, marched and engaged in rifle practice. Boys aged 10 to 18 were taught how to shoot as part of their pre-military training, which also consisted of sports, including boxing, strenuous hikes, marches and drills. Pre-military training of the HJ was carried out by the Reich Youth Leadership in conjunction with the high command of the *Wehrmacht*.[51] These activities prepared them for active combat in the field once the war began. Herbst recalls a memorable night in 1944 on his annual skiing camp when he and his *Jungvolk* comrades had to climb the 3,040-foot-high Achtermann peak on a stormy night. He describes his immense joy on reaching the summit: 'We felt proud and elated. We had proved ourselves, had shown that we knew how to follow orders and that we were ready to move and persevere as soldiers'.[52] In addition to their physical training, Hitler Youth members were inculcated with a militaristic spirit during their *Heimabend* sessions. Topics included great soldiers of Germany's past and the war itself. These sessions were supplemented with films and pamphlets that treated the subject. In addition, soldiers visited the Hitler Youth groups and told them about their experiences at the front. Military preparation camps trained youth in map reading, reconnaissance activities, shooting, guard duty and camouflage.

Herbst describes his time as a *Jungvolk* leader as 'most exhilarating'. He recalls: 'The *Jungvolk* ... gave me responsibility at a young age and taught me what it meant to become a leader of men. It was the comradeship of us boys and the awareness of the duties the war imposed upon us that sustained my enthusiasm and made life meaningful.'[53] Yet, when he recounts his military training at the Labour Service camp at Rodewald in early 1945, the enthusiasm and exhilaration are no longer in evidence:

> The weeks at Rodewald were cold, wet and miserable. We sixteen-year-old recruits were drilled in the basics of infantry combat. From mid-January to mid-March we were sent out day and night through swampy meadowlands that made us sink knee-deep into mud. Every ditch, hidden under snow-crusted ice, had us plunge into freezing water. We were taught how to storm make-believe enemy trenches with

drawn bayonets and how to fire bazookas at haystacks. We were doused with tear gas and sent through billowing clouds, sometimes crawling and sometimes running at full speed, with our gas masks on our faces until our lungs gave out and we collapsed in the icy mud. Our barracks were cold, and we suffered from diarrhoea and fevers.[54]

And still this was easy compared to what awaited the HJ boys at the front.

Another significant aspect of training in the HJ was through the medium of film. From 20 April 1934, the HJ organized the *Jugendfilmstunde* (Youth Film Hour) for its members. At first, these took place once a month, but by 1936 they were organized every week.[55] With the help of the Ministry of Propaganda, the HJ was able to make these screenings an integral part of its members' activities. Most of the feature films that were designated 'valuable for youth' were commissioned by the Ministry of Propaganda. These films were either overtly political or underpinned National Socialist objectives in a less direct manner. They included: *Heimkehr* (*Homecoming*, 1941), *Der grosse König* (*The Great King*, 1942) about Frederick the Great, and *Die Entlassung* (*The Dismissal*, 1942). In 1942–3, the HJ screened more than 45,290 Reich Film Hours, with an attendance of 11,215,000.[56] These screenings supplemented the film education that was given in schools. During the war, films with themes such as self-sacrifice, camaraderie and heroic death were regarded as particularly valuable. These films included *Stukas* (*Dive Bombers*, 1941), *Himmelhunde* (*Sky Hounds*, 1942) and *Junge Adler* (*Young Eagles*, 1944).

In addition, the HJ taught its members film making, as part of its educational work. The argument for films created by the young for the young was that HJ members shared their comrades' experiences and therefore knew what kind of themes to portray and what would be of interest to them. The films made by the HJ between 1939 and 1942 tended to be on the subject of youth, war and sacrifice. They included *Einsatz der Jugend* (*Youth's Mission*, 1939), *Der Marsch zum Führer* (*The March to the Führer*, 1940), *Unsere Kinder – Unsere Zukunft* (*Our Children – Our Future*, 1940) and *Soldaten von Morgen* (*Soldiers of Tomorrow*, 1941).[57]

The HJ also commissioned eight documentary films entitled *Junges Europa* (*Young Europe*) between 1942 and 1945. These showed the work carried out by the HJ during the war, from collecting the harvest to working in armaments factories. Their main purpose was to highlight to the civilian population the role of the HJ in the war. They showed their discipline, organization, obedience, camaraderie and self-sacrifice. They depicted the many activities of the HJ and the ideological commitment to National Socialism of its members. Hence, film was widely used for propaganda purposes by and within the HJ. The advocates of Nazi film propaganda in the HJ claimed that: 'Thanks to the National Socialist film educational work, youth is directed towards the heroic and is therefore psychologically prepared and entirely capable of withstanding all pressures'.[58] Nazi film propaganda played a significant part in the activities of the HJ and formed part of the reason for which German youth was willing to sacrifice itself until the very end of the Nazi regime.

The HJ laid down strict regulations for its leaders.[59] Boys appointed as HJ leaders had to be aware that this was not a 'privilege' but an 'obligation'. The honour and status of the HJ had to be at the centre of a leader's thoughts and actions and he had to advance this through his own impeccable behaviour both 'in service and in leisure time'. In service, he had to be appropriately attired in a clean and orderly uniform. Those promoted to leadership in the HJ had to be loyal and devoted to the organization and 'must never leave for frivolous or futile reasons'. In the HJ, the will of the individual had to take second place to that of the movement as a whole. Orders were to be given 'with personal responsibility' on the part of the person giving the order and were never to 'lack tactfulness and comradeship spirit'. Orders were to be 'short, clear, necessary and easy to understand'. Leaders themselves as subordinates to others at a higher level were to follow orders and directives given to them in an accurate and obedient way, thus setting the best example for their own subordinates. Leaders had to maintain a calm and professional manner and to keep their nerve, 'even in critical moments'. They were to maintain discipline among and care for their subordinates. They were to ensure that their boys wore the appropriate clothing for any weather and that they ate and drank enough during hikes and marches. In addition, every leader was obliged to follow the service regulations and guidelines of the HJ organization.

However, despite its attempts at thoroughgoing socialization and leaders' obligations, Kater has shown that the Hitler Youth 'was not always an expression of monolithic cohesiveness'.[60] Inadequate training and leadership structure gave way to much incompetence, abuse and corruption on the part of the youth leaders. Schirach and Axmann tried to limit incompetence and abuse by establishing leadership courses and sessions for Hitler Youth leaders, such as the Academy for Youth Leadership in Brunswick, set up in 1939. In 1942, an Office for Leadership Training and Instruction was established to deal with all aspects of leadership within the HJ organization.[61] Nevertheless, leadership problems remained and indeed were exacerbated when older leaders were conscripted for military service. By 1940, 25 per cent of all Hitler Youth leaders were at the front, and by 1944 boys in their mid-teens were being commanded by boys of the same age.

Did all German youths participate and willingly so? Certainly, some boys were very enthusiastic about the movement and the leadership positions and experiences it offered to them. They were trained for command and ardently supported the regime and its aims. Erich Loest recalls: 'They enticed us for their own ends, but we were glad to go along with it. Many like me did absolutely nothing to resist, we saw no reason to resist, and in turn, when we became leaders, we enticed the others'.[62] Many others went along with HJ membership without being particularly committed to its ideology, but because it was necessary to belong for apprenticeships and other work opportunities, as many craft guilds and businesses would only take on young boys and girls if they belonged to the Party youth groups. Many had unexpressed reservations or misgivings, despite their outward conformity. There was also a relatively small group of dissenting youth. As Kater points out, even after membership became compulsory, 'too many teenagers came and went or did not enrol at all'.[63] Some disliked the monotony of the drills and routine; others were individualistic enough to reject the norms of the organization as a whole. Many cliques and bands of youth sprang up across the Reich.[64]

GERMAN YOUTH OUTSIDE THE HJ

Dissenting youth included those who belonged to the Hitler Youth, but did not turn up regularly to its meetings, those who had left the Hitler Youth, bored or disillusioned with its requirements, or those who had never enrolled in the Nazi youth movement in the first place. In Munich, the *Blasen* (Bubbles) were made up of anti-authoritarian workers and apprentices. They resisted the limits placed upon their personal freedom by the Hitler Youth. They remained aloof from the official youth group and engaged in theft, sabotage and other transgressions of the law. Similar cliques existed in other cities. In Hamburg, working-class gangs such as the Jumbo Band wore distinctive clothing and attacked the Hitler Youth. Other dissident youth groups sprang up that had ideological affinities to the outlawed Communists and Socialists, such as the *Meuten* (Packs) in Leipzig, which had approximately 1,500 members.[65] They were blue-collar workers and apprentices who met at local cinemas and bars. They went on hikes, listened to Radio Moscow, dressed in unconventional clothes and wore red handkerchiefs. Moreover, they engaged in open confrontations with the Hitler Youth.

The Edelweiss Pirates sprang up spontaneously in many German cities.[66] These young people were typically aged between 14 and 18. In Cologne, the Navajos, in Dusseldorf, the Kittelbach Pirates and in other cities in the Rhineland and Ruhr, other groups of Edelweiss Pirates all attracted the animosity of the Hitler Youth because of their non-conformity. They represented a challenge to the authority of the Hitler Youth and sought conflicts with its members and patrols. In contrast to the state youth groups, the Edelweiss Pirates mixed groups of girls and boys and their sexuality was open. The Hitler Youth and the Nazi government frowned upon this. The Edelweiss Pirates congregated in gangs at local parks, bars, squares or street corners. At weekends, they hiked and camped in the countryside, where they chatted, sang traditional youth songs or adapted the words to reflect their own experiences. During holidays, they undertook longer journeys to assert their independence from both their parents and the regime.[67] The existence of these dissenting youth groups and bands within the totalitarian system of the Third Reich – with all its pressures to conform – is significant.

Another type of non-conformist youth, from a middle- and upper-middle-class background, belonged to the Swing Youth. The Swing Youth listened to jazz and swing music in private or at carefully selected nightclubs and cafés. They dressed distinctively and ostentatiously, wore their hair long and imitated American or British attitudes and styles. The Swing Youth originated in Hamburg, but groups established themselves in other cities including Frankfurt and Berlin. They attracted the attention of the authorities, both for their open sexuality and for their rejection of National Socialist cultural norms.

The Hitler Youth *Streifendienst* (Patrol Service) had been established in July 1934 to police German youth. Its original function had been to combat crime, delinquency and undisciplined behaviour within the Hitler Youth. Its service regulations stipulated that 'the *Streifendienst* has to keep watch that the manner of all members of the National Socialist youth groups is in keeping with the dignity and honour of the NSDAP'.[68] The *Streifendienst* reported any criticism of the regime to the Gestapo. By 1937, however, the remit of the *Streifendienst* had been extended to dealing with former Hitler Youth members that had left the organization and members of the numerous cliques and bands of youth outside the Hitler Youth.

The Hitler Youth and the Gestapo regarded all these groups as a challenge to their authority, and the regime clamped down upon them more and more as the war years progressed. On 9 March 1940, Himmler issued a police ordinance for the 'protection of youth'. This was aimed at repressing cliques and gangs. It prohibited young people from meeting in bars or on the streets after dark. Many young people who failed to comply with this restriction were arrested and placed in youth custody camps, such as Moringen. On 25 October 1944, Himmler issued an ordinance for the 'combating of youth cliques':

> In the last few years, and recently in increased numbers, gatherings of youths (cliques) have formed in all parts of the Reich ... Cliques are groupings of juveniles outside the Hitler Youth, who lead a separate way of life, whose principles are irreconcilable with the National Socialist worldview. Collectively, they reject or are indifferent to their duties towards the national community, or towards the Hitler Youth, and in particular evince a lack of will to conform with the dictates of wartime.[69]

In November 1944, the leaders of the Edelweiss Pirates were publicly executed in Cologne.

The White Rose movement was a resistance group that appeared in Munich during 1942 and 1943, centred round Hans and Sophie Scholl.[70] Together with fellow students Alexander Schmorell, Christoph Probst, Willi Graf, and Professor of Philosophy at Munich University, Kurt Huber, Hans and Sophie Scholl wrote and circulated a series of leaflets that openly told of the murder of Jews in Poland and called for popular mobilization against Hitler. Between the summer of 1942 and February 1943, the White Rose distributed a series of six pamphlets at night in a number of German cities, including Cologne, Essen, Stuttgart, Frankfurt and Nuremberg, as well as Munich. The first leaflet urged Germans to resist the regime. The second leaflet told of 300,000 Jews already killed in Poland. The third asked Germans to sabotage the war industry. Moll has argued that 'their will to topple the system and their ingenuity drove them to ever more reckless campaigns'.[71] On 18 February 1943, Hans and Sophie Scholl distributed their leaflets around Munich University for the last time. Having thrown between 1,500 and 1,800 leaflets down the staircase of the main entrance at Munich University, they were caught by the caretaker and arrested. Willi Graf was arrested later the same day. The remaining three members of the White Rose were arrested within the next ten days. A Special Court was set up under Roland Freisler on 22 February 1943, which sentenced Hans Scholl, Sophie Scholl and Christoph Probst to death, and they were executed the same day. Schmorell and Huber were executed on 13 July 1943 and Graf on 12 October 1943. Sophie Scholl had said to a fellow prisoner on the day of her execution: 'What does our death matter if thousands will be stirred and awakened by what we have done? The students are bound to revolt'. But they did not. On the contrary, the National Socialist German Students' Association organized a demonstration of 3,000 students to show their loyalty to the regime.

Less well known than the White Rose movement, the members of the Hübener group were among the youngest Germans to resist the Nazi regime, acting independently, without the guidance of adults.[72] This group of four teenagers from Hamburg – Helmuth Hübener, Karl-Heinz Schnibbe, Rudolf Wobbe and Gerhard Düwer – took a moral stance against the Nazi dictatorship. In contrast to the majority of German Mormons who accepted the Nazi regime, Helmuth Hübener, a 16-year-old Mormon, distributed anti-Nazi leaflets with the aid of his three co-conspirators. They continued to do this for approximately six months before they were reported to the Gestapo. Arrested in February 1942, Hübener was given the death penalty for committing treason, whilst his three comrades received prison sentences of between four and ten years for their part in the conspiracy. Hübener was executed in October 1942.

THE HJ DURING THE WAR

During the war, HJ duties became increasingly time-consuming and dangerous. At first, Hitler Youth members served in auxiliary positions on the home front. They made door-to-door collections of paper, cloth and scrap metal for the war effort and foraged for medicinal herbs and mushrooms. Later, they worked as couriers and messengers. Herbst recalls his time as a courier and how it raised his self-esteem: 'Here I was, a sixteen-year-old boy, having an official pass for any railroad train I chose to enter, carrying important messages – it all seemed very exciting and flattering to me'.[73] HJ members distributed ration cards and propaganda leaflets. They also worked as air raid wardens and firefighters. As the war progressed, their obligations increased, not just on the home front. Hitler Youth members were sent to the newly conquered Polish territories to re-educate the *Volksdeutsche* (ethnic Germans) who lived on the land there. At first, this was a voluntary service. Tens of thousands of young Germans went to the borderlands where they both taught proper German to the *Volksdeutsche* and worked in the farms and fields. They helped in the process of 'settling' young people who were 'worthy of Germanization' and prepared them for agricultural work. By 1942, it became compulsory for Hitler Youth members to serve for a six-week period in this duty.

As the HJ became increasingly involved in war duties, tensions sometimes arose with their parents. Herbst remembers his experiences: 'I had war duties to carry out, I told my mother, such as standing fire watch during air raids and helping with clean-up work thereafter. Such tasks made it seem somehow inappropriate that I ask her for permission or promise to be back home at a certain time in the evening ... I also grew increasingly on edge listening to my mother's daily questions of whether I had done my school work. I became less and less willing to accept her directions for how I should spend my time out of school'.[74] These types of intergenerational tensions were commonplace and, as we have seen, they were often deliberately fostered by the HJ movement.

The HJ became involved in anti-aircraft work and its members were drafted into fighting units as the tide of the war turned against Germany. Most Hitler Youth members joined the *Wehrmacht* feeling optimistic that Germany would achieve a speedy victory and with a determination to defeat their 'inferior' enemies. They were convinced of their own superiority. Once serious setbacks and defeats occurred, however, these feelings changed to disillusionment.[75] Young soldiers were also frustrated by the duplication of their Hitler Youth drills and training when they entered the *Wehrmacht*. Physical injuries, fatalities and inadequate food provision, as well as psychological scarring, all had a damaging impact on morale. Some HJ members came to have doubts about the war and about the honourableness of their country's cause.[76] They soon came to realize that this 'was not the war of the textbooks, the war of glory and heroic death, but the war of blood and gore, of terror and shame, and of bodies torn and mutilated'.[77] The young soldiers began to question the Nazi stereotype of the cowardly, 'sub-human', 'swamp Russian', once they encountered their Soviet counterparts. Difficulties faced by young soldiers even before Stalingrad led some of them to doubt their own function and to question the regime. Deserters experienced the SS's 'emergency justice' in the form of summary executions and hangings.

Between 1943 and 1945, some 200,000 teenagers served as canoneers to destroy enemy planes.[78] The anti-aircraft artillery training, which showed the boys how to handle searchlights and anti-aircraft guns, lasted just four weeks. After that, the flak helpers (as young as 15) experienced active combat, at first in their own localities, but then in destinations far from their homes. Obliged to work during the night, as well as during the day, they were deprived of sleep, as well as terrified. Casualties were heavy. Despite this, the boys continued to fight, driven on by a sense of duty to the *Führer* and fatherland. Bloodshed was a symbol of valour and heroism. This experience was also difficult for them in terms of their identity and status. These young people saw themselves as outgrowing the Hitler Youth and parental control, yet they were not accepted as 'soldiers'.[79]

On 19 October 1944, the *Volkssturm* was established to draft all men aged between 16 and 60 that were capable of bearing arms to defend the homeland. In many cases, entire HJ groups enlisted together. They were given tasks such as digging trenches, guarding, and defending towns and villages. Dietrich Strothmann recalls: 'I was just a very ordinary kid, obedient, docile, compliant ... ready for duty at all times, available and, ultimately, willing to die'.[80] Despite the insistence that these young boys and old men were imperative to the war effort, they were given inadequate equipment and weaponry. In the last months of the war, the Hitler Youth formed anti-tank brigades against the Soviet advance and units to secure strategic bridges. They greatly feared revenge by their enemies and this made them more determined to keep fighting. The spirit of boys as young as 15 in these circumstances was driven by a determination to destroy as many Soviet tanks as possible. Gerd Häffner remembers:

> They went for the tanks with a fearlessness that is simply indescribable. And they really were just children. I was seventeen, but they were fifteen or younger. Without a thought for themselves, they walked into certain death. And at many points they actually forced the Russians to pull back. But then the children in their HJ uniforms were left lying in the street.[81]

Hitler's youth was required to take its part in the struggle – in the face of death – until the very end of the war. Herbst recalls mid-March 1945, when he was 'being groomed to enter the fight in the war's last, decisive hour … No matter how sombre the outlook was … we were going to live up to our oath and fight for Germany'.[82] In April, he describes how his platoon came under attack from enemy fire for the first time: 'Artillery shells hurled towards us with unnerving shrieks … Dirt, stones, tree branches, and shrapnel hurled through the air. I tasted sulphur between my teeth … My stomach turned, my knees trembled. This then, was … the baptism of fire, I thought.'[83] In April 1945, HJ members engaged in street battles with Soviet soldiers in Berlin.[84] Beevor describes how HJ detachments desperately held on to the Pichelsdorf and Charlotten bridges over the Havel.[85] The HJ boys were cheated of their youth, their humanity and, in many cases, their lives.

'Never before in German history had the young been so courted – and never so abused'.[86] In the HJ, young Germans were seduced by the Nazi regime and ultimately betrayed by it. Young Germans gave up their independence to the greater cause of the 'national community'. In certain ways, the HJ was similar to youth groups that had preceded it, in terms of encouraging a love for the German countryside and for German folklore. Like its predecessors, the HJ engaged German youth in peer camaraderie and popular activities like camping and hiking. This accounted for much of its attraction, particularly in its early years. The most significant difference was that it imbued its members with Nazi propaganda and increased their duties. The other important distinction was that once enrolment into the HJ became compulsory, youth group membership was not a matter of desire or choice, as it had been in the past, but one of obligation. The sense of belonging and of duty to the organization and its demands were central to the nature of the HJ. Clearly in the HJ, as in other Nazi formations, the individual was subordinated to the group. Conformity to the organizational norm was designed to create true believers in the National Socialist system. HJ members were bound to the community of the organization, and, above and beyond that, to the 'national community'. Indeed, the continued commitment, involvement and service of the HJ contributed to the prolonging of the war. Paul Kehlenbeck recalls the war years: 'Anyone fighting for Germany was also fighting for Adolf Hitler, of course. It was almost the same thing. Only towards the end of the war did these attitudes begin to change and lose their hold, but Hitler retained his authority right to the end.'[87] Ultimately, Nazi 'total education' was intended to create such strong devotees to the regime that they would be willing to sacrifice their lives for it – and many did. After the capitulation on 8 May 1945, Peter Boenisch recalls: 'We were really in a state of total physical and psychological exhaustion. Then, when the growing realization came to us that it had all been pointless and in vain, that one's friends had died for nothing, that one's brother had died for nothing, we were utterly embittered'.[88] In the end, the youth of the Third Reich were the victims, as well as the perpetrators, of its bestial criminality.

NOTES

1. Cited in J. Noakes and G. Pridham (eds), *Nazism 1919–1945: A Documentary Reader*, Vol. 2, (Exeter, 1984), pp. 416–17.
2. Cited in Samuel and Hinton Thomas, *Education and Society*, p. 18.
3. Cited in ibid., pp. 29–30.
4. G. Wyneken, *Der Gedankenkreis der freien Schulgemeinde* (Leipzig, 1913), p. 10.
5. Hahn, *Education and Society*, p. 39.
6. On this, see P. Stachura, *The German Youth Movement 1900–1945: An Interpretative and Documentary History* (London, 1981) and W. Laqueur, *Young Germany: A History of the German Youth Movement* (London, 1981).
7. BA NS 26/336, 'Der Wimpel des Jungsturms Hitler!', Rundfunkvortrag des ehem. Führers A. Lenk am 8. November 1933, p. 2.
8. BA NS 26/331, 'Satzungen des Jugendbundes der NSDAP', March 1922. See also Koch, *The Hitler Youth*, p. 47.
9. BA NS 26/333, 'Satzungen des Jugendbundes der NSDAP', March 1922, in 'Das Werden der nationalsozialistischen Jugend'.
10. BA NS 26/336, 'Der Wimpel des Jungsturms Hitler!', pp. 3–4.
11. BA NS 26/332, 'Anerkennung des Jungsturms als Vorläufer der Hitler-Jugend'.
12. BA NS 26/336, 'Der Wimpel des Jungsturms Hitler!', p. 8.
13. BA NS 26/336, 'Das Werden der nationalsozialistischen Jugend', II. Teil, 14 May 1934, p. 1.
14. BA NS 26/336, 'Das Werden der nationalsozialistischen Jugend', Teil 1, 10 April 1934, pp. 3–4.
15. On Schirach, see M. Wortmann, *Baldur von Schirach: Hitlers Jugendführer* (Cologne, 1982).
16. BA NS 26/353, 'Bundesblätter des Deutschen Jungvolkes, Bund der Tatjugend', Folge I, no date, p. 1.
17. Ibid.
18. Ibid., p. 2.
19. BA NS 26/353, 'Bundesblätter des Deutschen Jungvolkes, Bund der Tatjugend', Folge II, Weihnachten, 1930, p. 3.
20. Ibid., p. 6.

21. Koch, *The Hitler Youth*, p. 101.

22. BA NS 26/331, 'Hitlerjugend Aufnahme Erklärung'.

23. BA NS 26/336, 'Die Aufbauarbeit der Hitlerjugend im Staat', pp. 1–3.

24. BA NS 26/336, 'Hitlerrede auf dem 1. Nationalsozialistischen Reichsjugendtag in Potsdam', no date, pp. 1–2.

25. BA NS 26/336, 'Deutsche Arbeiterjungen unter Hitlers Fahnen', Artur Axmann, 3 May 1933, p. 9.

26. Cited in Noakes and Pridham (eds), *Nazism 1919–1945*, p. 419.

27. Hahn, *Education and Society*, pp. 78–9.

28. BA NS 26/353, 'Richtlinien für den Jungvolkführer', 24 March 1932, p. 1.

29. Ibid., pp. 1–2.

30. Ibid., p. 4.

31. Ibid.

32. Ibid., pp. 5–6.

33. Cited in Noakes and Pridham (eds), *Nazism 1919–1945*, p. 420.

34. A. Klönne, *Jugend im Dritten Reich: Die Hitler-Jugend und ihre Gegner. Dokumente und Analysen* (Cologne, 1984), p. 50.

35. J. Herbst, *Requiem for a German Past: A Boyhood among the Nazis* (Madison, 1999), p. 95.

36. BA NS 12/1438, 'Verhältnis HJ. – NSLB'.

37. Stachura, *The German Youth Movement*, p. 148.

38. Herbst, *Requiem for a German Past*, p. xv.

39. Klönne, *Jugend im Dritten Reich*, p. 55.

40. Cited in Koch, *The Hitler Youth*, p. 231.

41. Cited in Knopp, *Hitler's Children*, p. 11.

42. Herbst, *Requiem for a German Past*, p. xiv. See also M. von der Grün, *Wie war das eigentlich?: Kindheit und Jugend im Dritten Reich* (Darmstadt, 1979).

43. Klönne, *Jugend im Dritten Reich*, p. 82.

44. Cited in Knopp, *Hitler's Children*, p. 16.

45. Cited in ibid., p. 12.

46. Cited in ibid., p. 12.

47. Cited in ibid., p. 30.

48. Cited in ibid., p. 18.

49. Herbst, *Requiem for a German Past*, pp. 44–5.

50. Cited in Knopp, *Hitler's Children*, p. 19.

51. BA NS 26/336, 'Vormilitärische Wehrertüchtigung der Hitler-Jugend', 17 December 1941.

52. Herbst, *Requiem for a German Past*, p. 98.

53. Ibid., p. 81.

54. Ibid., p. 174.

55. D. Welch, 'Educational Film Propaganda and the Nazi Youth', p. 73.

56. Ibid., p. 77.

57. Ibid., p. 80.

58. C. Belling and A. Schütze, *Der Film in der Hitlerjugend* (Berlin, 1937), p. 36.

59. On what follows, see BA NS 26/353, 'Führerordnung'.

60. M. Kater, *Hitler Youth* (Cambridge, Mass. and London, 2004), p. 15.

61. Stachura, *The German Youth Movement*, p. 130.

62. Cited in Knopp, *Hitler's Children*, p. 2.

63. Kater, *Hitler Youth*, p. 25.

64. See E. Boesten, *Jugendwiderstand im Faschismus* (Cologne, 1983) and D. Peukert, *Die Edelweißpiraten. Protestbewegung jugendlicher Arbeiter im Dritten Reich. Eine Dokumentation* (Cologne, 1980).

65. Kater, *Hitler Youth*, p. 137.
66. On this, see Peukert, *Die Edelweißpiraten* and M. von Hellfeld, *Edelweißpiraten in Köln* (Cologne, 1983).
67. D. Peukert, *Inside Nazi Germany: Conformity, Opposition and Racism in Everyday Life* (London, 1987), pp. 156–7.
68. BA NS 26/338, 'Vorläufige Dienstvorschrift für den HJ-Streifendienst', 15 May 1936, p. 8.
69. Cited in M. Burleigh and W. Wippermann, *The Racial State: Germany 1933–1945* (Cambridge, 1991), p. 238.
70. On the White Rose, see H. Siefken (ed.), *The White Rose: Student Resistance to National Socialism 1942–1943* (Nottingham, 1991) and I. Jens (ed.), *At the Heart of the White Rose: Letters and Diaries of Hans and Sophie Scholl* (New York, 1987).
71. C. Moll, 'Acts of Resistance: The White Rose in the Light of New Archival Evidence', in M. Geyer and J. Boyer (eds), *Resistance against the Third Reich 1933–1990* (Chicago, 1994), p. 200.
72. On this, see B. Holmes and A. Keele (eds), *When Truth was Treason: German Youth against Hitler* (Urbana and Chicago, 1995).
73. Herbst, *Requiem for a German Past*, p. 164.
74. Ibid., pp. 88–9.
75. Kater, *Hitler Youth*, p. 178.
76. See, for example, Herbst, *Requiem for a German Past*, pp. 116–17.
77. Ibid., p. 128.
78. Kater, *Hitler Youth*, p. 199.
79. Ibid., pp. 206–7.
80. Cited in Knopp, *Hitler's Children*, p. 240.
81. Cited in ibid., p. 276.
82. Herbst, *Requiem for a German Past*, p. 177.
83. Ibid., p. 181.
84. On this, see R. Bessel, *Nazism and War* (London, 2004), p. 148; A. Beevor, *Berlin: The Downfall 1945* (London, 2002), pp. 281 and 316; N. Stargardt, *Witnesses of War: Children's Lives under the Nazis* (London, 2005), pp. 313–14 and 316.
85. Beevor, *Berlin*, pp. 340 and 356.
86. Knopp, *Hitler's Children*, p. ix.
87. Cited in ibid., p. 174.
88. Cited in ibid., p. 276.

6 THE LEAGUE OF GERMAN GIRLS

This chapter examines the role and function of the League of German Girls (BDM) as the Nazi organization for the regimentation and socialization of girls. It analyses the aims of the BDM and their implementation. Since 1980, when Klaus published his pioneering book on the BDM, there has been a proliferation of books and articles on the subject.[1] In addition, the memoirs of girls who grew up in the Third Reich and were affiliated to the BDM enhance our knowledge and understanding of the movement by providing accounts of their personal experiences.[2] Within the secondary literature on the BDM, a number of issues remain disputed and others inadequately addressed. Reese's contribution to the historiography of the BDM highlights some of these controversies, such as whether or not motherhood was the overriding objective for German girls and what 'type' of girl the regime aimed to create within the BDM.[3] Furthermore, Reese indicates that the question of the extent to which the BDM had a modernizing effect on German girls has not been adequately treated. She notes that 'in the early 1930s girls were often drilled to march in formation and trained in field exercises and sometimes marksmanship with air rifles'.[4] This was not the traditional gender expectation for girls. The purpose of this chapter is to analyse the role of the BDM in the training and socialization of girls. An analysis of BDM training manuals and guidelines, as well as its magazine, *Das Deutsche Mädel*, and other literature, gives a clear indication of the norms, values, expectations and political ethos of the organization and the way in which it imbued German girls with the National Socialist *Weltanschauung*. Before embarking upon an examination of the BDM, it is useful to contextualize this subject with an overview of the girls' youth movement before the Nazi 'seizure of power'.

YOUTH GROUPS FOR GIRLS BEFORE THE NAZI ERA AND THE ORIGINS OF THE BDM

The development of youth movements and girls' leagues in Germany had its cultural, socio-economic and ideological foundations in Germany's particular, modern history, with its 'late' industrialization and rapid pace of modernization, its demographic change and urbanization. The *Wandervogel* movement incorporated girls as well as boys from 1905 onwards. Young men and women explored the German forests, hills and villages and hiked through the countryside. It is important to note, however, that the defining image of the youth culture was male. Whilst sports clubs and youth groups admitted girls as members, there were 'no independent forms of leisure for girls'.[5] Nor yet was there the type of distinctive girls' leisure subculture that defined the youth groups and subcultures for boys. Girls joined mixed groups of girls and boys. They gradually began to establish their own single-sexed girls' groups. The groups and organizations for girls came to be characterized by a number of significant aspects, as girls came to establish a culture of their own.

Between 1918 and 1928 girls were expelled from the male youth movement and they established their own autonomous leagues and groups. In particular, as a result of the First World War, girls came to call for a realm of their own, distinctive from that of boys. Girls constructed separate, new identities for themselves for the first time during this period. A gender polarization occurred between *Wandervogel* boys and *Wandervogel* girls. Girls opened up social, geographical and political 'space' for themselves, which they had never claimed before and which had never before belonged to them. These girls sought role models in legendary and historical figures, such as Brunhilde and Queen Luise. De Ras has typified this 'new breed of girls and young women from the youth movement' as 'the New Gretchens'.[6] These girls expressed loathing and disgust for 'modern' girls. They disliked metropolitan girls, Jewish girls, 'French' girls, 'Gypsy' girls, 'unhealthy' girls, and lesbians, as these 'types' went against their conservative conceptions of what a 'German' girl should be. The idyllic, rural past formed the core of their world view.

The girls differentiated their identity with concepts such as 'female culture' and 'sacred island' within their girls' leagues and communities. The 'sacred island' was a phase representing a search for 'the link between "nature" and "femininity", of romancing the German female body, soul and mind, a desire for wholeness'.[7] It was outwardly expressed by the wearing of a loose, white dress – the 'island dress'. A number of girls' leagues retreated into country homes whilst others were secret societies, hidden in the countryside. Settlements of young women and girls, such as those at Schwarzerden and Loheland, became islands of female culture and activity, entirely independent from and impenetrable to male influence. In terms of constructions of the body within the girls' leagues, the 'body culture' that was idealized was neither a 'motherly' body, nor a 'Lolita figure'. Rather, the body type that was advocated was 'androgynous' and as de Ras writes, 'a closed off and closing off young female body'.[8] Lust and sexuality were frowned upon.

The period between 1928 and 1934 was characterized by the growth of extreme nationalist youth groups and leagues, such as the *Jungnationaler Bund* (Young-National League), the *Freischar Junger Nation* (Free Band of the Young Nation) and the *Großdeutscher Bund* (Greater German League), which attracted girls as members. Girls' groups continued to be semi-autonomous within these organizations. Whilst the girls groups were not homogeneous, they did have a number of common aspects: 'the idealisation of *Kultur*; the worship of wholeness and aversion to fragmentation; the love for and glorification of German history, tradition, folklore, language; the emphasis on the importance of soil, nature, landscape, the rural and a dislike of modernity ... and the wish to remain physically, psychologically, and racially pure and natural'.[9] Their vitality and patriotism came increasingly to be bound up with anti-Semitism and 'racial' exclusivity. As the Nazi *Machtergreifung* approached, these 'new radical nationalist girls', who were eager to become part of the state, were ripe to become 'absorbed' into the National Socialist movement.[10]

In the meantime, the National Socialists' own girls' league, the BDM, emerged in 1930 after a number of previous attempts to set up a youth group for girls within the Nazi movement had failed. Adolf Lenk had set up the first group in the early 1920s. This was followed by a number of sororities or sisterhoods within the HJ in 1927. However, these groups had little popular appeal. Groups for girls began to be created within the context of local National Socialist women's associations. They tended to put the emphasis upon girls' duties, such as mending and cooking. Before 1930, there was a large number of small Nazi and *völkisch* groups for girls, such as the *Deutscher Mädel Ring*, set up in Bavaria in 1927, that competed with each other for membership. In 1930, the BDM came to prominence. As part of the HJ, it had a stronger bureaucratic structure and it was marked out by its uniform. On 7 July 1932, Gregor Strasser and Baldur von Schirach dissolved all the other girls' groups that were part of the Nazi women's associations and ordered their membership to be transferred directly into the BDM. Hence, the BDM became the only National Socialist association for girls. However, prior to the Nazi *Machtergreifung*, the BDM was just one of many youth groups for girls in Germany. By the end of 1932, it had a membership estimated at between 10,000 and 15,000 girls.[11]

BDM MEMBERSHIP

After Hitler came to power on 30 January 1933, the BDM rose to a much more significant position. This was partly the result of the process of *Gleichschaltung* or 'streamlining', by which other girls' youth groups were dissolved, and partly due to the desire of girls who had never been in a youth organization before to take part in the National Socialist movement. Both of these factors led to a substantial increase in the membership of the BDM after 1933. In many cases, schools and teachers were encouraged to put pressure on girls to join. Between 1933 and 1936, the BDM experienced a vast expansion in its membership, encompassing almost half of all German girls aged between 10 and 18. The BDM considered the old youth movement to be uncreative and lacking in true value. It came to regard the *Wandervogel* girl as an 'anti-type'.

Many girls were attracted to the BDM because it gave them the chance to do 'what hitherto only boys were allowed to do', for example, to have more independence from their parents, go on trips and take part in group activities.[12] Others joined because they wanted to feel important, and not to be excluded from the world of adults.[13] Entry into the BDM allowed girls to escape from their tedious home lives, where they were usually under the constant scrutiny of their parents. The BDM gave girls the chance to be independent from their parents and to play a role within an organized, hierarchical social institution. They had the opportunity to become leaders within the organization. Reese argues that this led to 'an enhanced sense of female self-esteem'.[14]

Girls from middle-class families, in particular, often eagerly seized upon the opportunities offered to them by the BDM, because of their childhood experiences. In the aftermath of the Wall Street Crash, shattered prestige and finances were strongly felt by all members of middle-class households. In addition, the children of such families were subjected to very strong parental discipline, and girls felt especially intimidated by their fathers.[15] Consequently, they felt insecure, useless, unconfident and insignificant. The BDM gave girls an opportunity to break out of this pattern and style of their lives at that time. Indeed, some girls joined the BDM as a sign of their rebellion against the authority of their parents. The BDM gave young girls a sense of peer camaraderie, involvement in their national cause and independence from their parents. Melita Maschmann has described how she wished to escape from her 'childish, narrow life' and 'to follow a different road from the conservative one prescribed ... by family tradition'.[16] Many of her contemporaries joined the BDM for similar reasons. In this respect, there is some indication that the BDM had a modernizing and liberating effect upon German girls. However, in the place of maternal and paternal influence came societal authority and state force.[17]

An important reason for the popularity of the BDM was the sense that girls were participating equally within the German youth movement. The BDM had its own role, and the Nazi regime exploited a sense of competition and rivalry between the sexes. As a girls' organization, the BDM offered a range of roles and career paths for girls. A mass organization that grew quickly in size, the BDM needed leaders and many girls were appointed as leaders. Leaders had to exhibit the correct type of personality and characteristics. Through their active commitment, leaders had the opportunity of rising up through the hierarchy of the organization to higher leadership positions. Whilst many leaders on the lower levels were volunteers, those at the top end of the leadership scale were paid a salary for their work. Such career possibilities led to increased enthusiasm for the organization.

Reese argues that girls were influenced and shaped by their 'living practice in the National Socialist organization'.[18] The BDM allowed them to take part in activities that were beyond the horizons of their social milieu and to have access to a variety of new experiences. This accounted for much of its initial popularity. However, the appeal of the BDM differed across areas, as well as social and cultural milieus.[19] There was sometimes significant parental resistance to the membership of their daughters into the BDM, on grounds of political or social outlook. Furthermore, in 1936, once membership became compulsory, apathy and disinterest came to replace the earlier enthusiasm among girls to join the BDM. As the years passed, it became increasingly difficult to evade service in the BDM, particularly after the second HJ decree of 1939.

THE NORMS AND REQUIREMENTS OF THE BDM

The National Socialist regime claimed that youth autonomy and the principle of self-leadership of youth were central to the BDM.[20] However, there is much evidence to show that the BDM did not foster true independence among either its members or its leaders. Trude Mohr, the first BDM *Reichsreferentin*, appointed in June 1934, had the following expectations for behaviour in the organization: 'Don't talk, don't debate, live a National Socialist life in discipline, composure and comradeship!'[21] As was the case in all Nazi formations, the ethos of the BDM entailed a loss of individuality for its members. They were bound to a community of peers, and, above and beyond that, to the community of the nation. The BDM, therefore, was not an aggregate of the individual personalities of its members, but rather a community into which individuality was dissolved. As Maschmann's memoir describes: 'Everything that was "I" had been absorbed into the whole!'[22] This community ethos, which was a central part of the character formation of the group's members, was closely tied to National Socialist ideology. There may have been a degree to which the individuals involved believed that they were acting on their own initiatives on behalf of the nation, but this feeling was manufactured. They were, instead, being manipulated and were very much a part of the socialization process. The objectives of the BDM were in no way directed at fostering the individual development or independence of its members. Maschmann has described how: 'No one made us think for ourselves or develop the ability to make moral decisions on our own responsibility. Our motto was: The *Führer* orders, we follow!' Hence, the BDM attempted to create devoted 'believers' in the system.[23] A foreign observer noted about both BDM and HJ members that 'their attitude of mind is absolutely uncritical … They are nothing but vessels for State propaganda'.[24] The network of social control became ever tighter and the grip of the National Socialist movement on its youth members increasingly comprehensive.

The first prerequisites of a BDM member were that she had to be of German origin and of sound heredity. The model German girl had to be prepared to work hard to serve the 'national community', to recognize National Socialist norms and values, and to accept them unquestioningly. She was to be physically fit, healthy, clean, dressed in an orderly manner and domestically capable. Characteristics of cleanliness, rectitude, faith and honour were to be formed by means of discipline.[25] Above all, the BDM girl was to be aware of her future duty as a woman, to become a mother. She had to be well-versed in German culture and music. As a future mother, she was to develop a knowledge of traditional German songs, tales and dances, so that she could be a 'culture bearer' to the next generation.[26] It was important, therefore, that girls took advantage of their 'natural' closeness to their homeland and understood the 'laws of nature'.

Girls in the BDM were educated and socialized quite differently from their male counterparts in the HJ, especially, of course, in terms of ideals and aims.[27] There was, however, one main similarity in the way in which they were trained, and this was that both boys and girls had to be prepared to fulfil their obligations – albeit different obligations – towards their nation and fatherland. In the first place, both had 'the duty to be healthy' and 'to remain pure'.[28] Both were trained to be capable of physical achievement, fit for work and compliant to organizational discipline. Industriousness, hygiene and obedience were expectations in both male and female youth groups. These values appealed to the lower middle classes in particular. Nazi youth group members were, in effect, unthinkingly and unquestioningly bound to the norms of their respective organizations, developing initiatives only within the framework of these norms, not independently. As Maria Eisenecker recalls, 'our own opinions were not asked for'.[29] Apart from that, comparisons of the ideal boy and girl, and of their duties, showed marked differences.

Even the kind of language in which role models were described gives a strong indication of the dissimilarities between the expectations of girls and boys.[30] Girls were to react to circumstances with their emotions, whereas boys were to react with their minds; girls were to store their experiences internally, whilst boys were to use theirs actively and creatively; girls were to be docile and to give of themselves, whilst boys were to affect others, gain victories and conquer; girls were to be passively content, whereas boys were to be active builders or destroyers of cultures; girls were to care for the family and household, whilst boys were to lay the foundations for the state; girls were to view life as a gift, whereas boys were to consider it as a struggle; for girls 'motherliness' – not femininity – was the ultimate aim, whilst for boys it was very clearly 'manliness', in a militarized sense. In certain respects, this kind of language portrayed a very passive role for girls as compared to that for boys, which does not seem surprising considering the ideological tenets upon which the Nazi state was founded. However, this only gives a partial picture, for girls were not to be totally passive. Indeed, the anti-image of the ideal BDM girl was that of the feminine 'young lady', an idea that was taken from the *Wandervogel*.[31] Frivolity and luxury were frowned upon by BDM leaders, who wanted to create strong and hardy young women. Indeed, the BDM even went as far as promoting the books of certain authors, such as Marie Hamsun and Erika Müller-Hennig, who wrote about young people that led 'brave and courageous lives', whilst discouraging the reading of 'sentimental' writers, to the extent of recommending to parents which books to buy for their children.[32] It also made recommendations of 'books that you should read' to its members. These largely comprised German *völkisch* literature, the works of 'blood and soil' novelists, such as Josefa Berens-Totenohl, and those that gave a sense of the German past.[33] Similarly, special recommendations of books were made for the BDM camps. For the summer camp in June 1937, for example, Hitler's *Mein Kampf* and Alfred Rosenberg's *The Myth of the Twentieth Century* headed the list of recommended reading.

TRAINING AND ACTIVITIES IN THE BDM

How were girls in the BDM trained and educated? Jutta Rüdiger, the BDM *Reichs-referentin* from 1927 onwards, retrospectively claimed that:

> In the education of girls ... we rarely spoke about "motherhood". Rather, we educated the girls in their own interest and that of the nation, preparing them to lead wholesome lives, to take an active role in the world of work and society. But first and foremost, what we wanted was to educate them to have a bright and cheery life as young girls.[34]

However, this statement is not consistent with the documentary evidence. There is nothing in the written documents and pamphlets of the BDM that indicates that the aim of the movement was simply 'to educate them to have a bright and cheery life as young girls'. Rüdiger also talked of forming 'politically aware' girls. By this, she meant not girls who would 'debate and discuss in parliament', but girls and women who would know about the necessity of the life of the German *Volk* and act in accordance with this. The aims of the BDM to create 'the German woman and mother' ruled out political engagement.

The training of girls entailed a variety of components, including physical fitness, health, hygiene, dress codes and sexual attitudes. The body itself no longer remained in the private sphere of the individual, but was subordinated to the national interest.[35] Physical training was very closely linked to health and to racial-biological ideas. To this extent, sport was not an end in itself, but a means of training German youth in accordance with National Socialist ideals.[36] Its goal was inner discipline. Consequently, no free or spontaneous sport or dance was allowed. Any expression of individualistic movement that went against the National Socialist sense of order was proscribed. Instead, regulation and discipline were emphasized. Many dance and exercise routines were structured within a certain form, such as a circle, a square or simply in rows.[37] Girls were to keep their bodies firm and healthy by means of exercise, in order to be able to reproduce for the nation in the future. They were instilled with the sense that they were responsible for the preservation of the nation.[38] Girls had to pass a special fitness test in order to enter the *Jungmädel* (JM).[39] This meant they were all able to meet a certain required standard of physical fitness. Fit girls would develop into healthy women, bear healthy children, and therefore preserve the health of the nation in the future. Notwithstanding the Nazi ideological imperatives behind physical training, the sporting activities were very popular with BDM girls, and games and competitions generated interest and enthusiasm for the organization.

In 1934, in order to promote the idea of unity of body, soul and spirit, Baldur von Schirach, the leader of the National Socialist youth movement, introduced an achievement badge for physical prowess.[40] By 1940, 60,000 such badges had been awarded.[41]

But the objective of sport was not personal achievement. Sports prizes were not awarded for the sake of individual merit per se, but as part of the overall attempt of the regime to create an entire generation of healthy girls, within the framework of its racial programme. Physical training was important for health and for the 'pure' preservation of the race. Indeed, this was so central to Nazi beliefs, that the BDM broke down the old taboo that girls ought not to take part in sporting activities in public, by organizing sports festivals in villages and towns, as well as hikes and camping trips. Schirach recognized the fact that this was rather revolutionary.[42] Sports galas and competitions, such as the National Sports Gala, held for the first time in Bamberg in 1938, became important occasions. They opened with songs, a speech and flag-raising. Gymnastic displays and races formed the main part of such events, which closed with formation dancing and a parade of all the participants.[43]

Special training manuals elaborated on physical training for the *Jungmädel* (JM), girls aged between 10 and 14.[44] JM members had to take part in a wide variety of physical activities including running and swimming. The full range was illustrated in the manual, including ball-throwing games, gymnastics and floor exercises. There was also formation dancing, for example, in concentric circles, with an accompanying musical score. A similar book was designed for the physical training of girls in the BDM.[45] This manual illustrated sports activities and formation dances. It stressed that there could be no ideological education without physical education, for physical training was the most important and effective means in the educational programme of the Nazi youth groups. Sport was considered to be important because it strengthened the will, created camaraderie and exercised each part of the body. Such books dedicated to physical education illustrate the great importance attached to sport by the regime and its youth groups. They had the clear intention of creating a whole generation of healthy and fit German girls. Schirach continually emphasized the need for a 'synthesis between body and spirit' as the aim of the BDM.[46]

Health education was considered to be especially important for girls, as they would become the bearers of the next generation. 'You have the duty to be healthy' was the motto for the BDM in 1939.[47] To the BDM, beauty was nothing other than the expression of physical and spiritual health, the harmony of body, soul and spirit. BDM leaders had to care for the health of their members by ensuring the correct nutrition, clothing, way of life, physical exercise, leisure and relaxation. Health was of paramount concern, for as natural selection showed, the sick and unfit perished. This could not be allowed to happen to the German *Volk*, for only healthy nations could survive and a successful nation needed to be 'pure' and 'fit'. Hence, the National Socialist state had to promote and strive for health and fitness, in order to secure the future stock of the race. The German nation had to be healthy, capable of achievement and able to cope with life.

The BDM educated its members about how the health of the nation was to be achieved. For example, the sending away of children to the countryside served the aims of the health of the nation. Each year, hundreds of thousands of children were sent into the countryside, pale and weak. They returned home healthy, tanned and strong. Whilst away, they learned to appreciate the beauty of the German homeland. The BDM also taught girls the importance of the measures and laws introduced by the National Socialist government to preserve and protect the hereditary health of the German *Volk*, such as the Marriage Health Law and the Law for the Prevention of Hereditarily Diseased Offspring.[48] This highlighted to the BDM girls their personal responsibility for their health, as their own health was an integral part of that of the whole nation. Therefore, they had the duty to protect their own health and to refrain from associating with the 'inferior', in order that future generations would be strong and fit. It was repeatedly stressed that 'to be healthy and to remain healthy is not our private concern, but our duty!'[49]

Each BDM girl was to be 'the founder and protector of a healthy, fit German family'.[50] BDM girls were to be 'the expression of the harmony of health and beauty'. Care of the body, skin, hair and nails were of great importance, as was dental care. Directions for such care were given in great detail. Sufficient sleep was also important – at least ten hours per night – and the value of sleep for overall health was to be enhanced by sleeping in an airy room with the window open. Care for clothes was also significant, as were living conditions, with the right amount of air, light and heat. Correct nourishment was necessary too, not just for personal health, but for the health of the nation. Girls had to eat regularly and to have the right balance of vitamins and minerals in their diet. In addition, the use of alcohol and nicotine was strongly rejected.

Dress was another important aspect of girls' training in the BDM. Girls were expected to wear their BDM uniform on all national holidays, on Party days, and on all special family and school festival days.[51] The uniform, which consisted of a white blouse and a dark-blue skirt, was practical and simple. Wearing the uniform, with its distinctive kerchief and knot, was, of course, an outward sign of being part of the rank and file of the movement. The uniform had to be washed and ironed properly, and was to be worn 'with pride'.[52] It was not to be embellished with jewellery or accessories. Cleanliness and an orderly appearance were part of the requirement too. Simplicity and orderliness were criteria that applied to ordinary clothes as well as to the uniform. There was much antagonism towards international fashion.[53] There was a call for the introduction of a German fashion, quite separate from French, British or American styles. German fashion was to be based on simple lines and forms, with the added advantage of using new materials such as the synthetic silk and spun rayon being produced by the German textile industry in the mid-1930s.[54] Nazi fashion excoriated the former styles of the 'vamp', who wore bright nail polish and plenty of make-up; the 'sweetheart', who was petite and blonde, with a 'warbling little voice'; and the 'boyish girl', who had very short hair, wore men's clothes, smoked, drank and told jokes.[55] Indeed, all these stereotypes – even the 'blue stocking' for her intellectualism – were viewed with 'unmitigated contempt'.[56] They did not match up to the ideal type – the BDM girl. Girls and young women were to be clean and tastefully dressed, without having to owe their good appearance to cosmetics or jewellery.[57] This sense of Nazi fashion held some popular appeal and there was a certain amount of desire to belong to the BDM in order to be able to wear the uniform, which was practical, yet not unattractive. Stargardt has cited the example of a Berlin girl who 'bitterly rued her parents' refusal to buy her an outfit when her whole class at school was admitted to the *Jungmädelbund*.[58]

The attitude towards sexual behaviour in the BDM paralleled that in the rest of society. Essentially, sexual life had its main task in serving the preservation of the race and nation. By and large, the National Socialists' 'new morality' reduced sex to its biological function of reproduction. The ideal, primary aim for BDM girls was childbirth and motherhood within marriage. Early marriage, in particular, was seen as a way of both discouraging promiscuity and encouraging large numbers of legitimate children.[59] Marriage was considered to be a dutiful, moral obligation by the youth group leaders. The demand that sexual activity should be carried out within a marriage remained the overall belief in the BDM. Its leaders were convinced that 'the family should be the only place for children to grow up in and that the destruction of monogamy must be prevented by women'.[60] Hence, the desire in the BDM was not to encourage a child 'at any price', but rather to promote very specific norms of motherhood, in line with the regime's aims of 'selection' of the 'desirable' and 'elimination' of the 'undesirable'.[61] Apart from these attitudes, sexuality was not an issue that was discussed in the BDM. Both the BDM and HJ were essentially non-sexual in their orientation. Hitler Youth boys were expected to treat BDM girls as comrades and to be chivalrous towards them. Non-sexual camaraderie and friendship were the general expectations about behaviour with fellow members of the youth movement.[62] However, 'there was very probably a good deal of flirting during youth group activities, especially when boys and girls were working together'.[63] Lust and desire were not acceptable, and physical training and diversion were partly designed to pre-empt or substitute them. The satisfaction of sexual urges was regarded as shameful, reprehensible and biologically and medically unnecessary. 'Fresh, clean, clear German air' was the alternative to sexual education.[64] To this extent, sexuality was mysticized and was almost completely a taboo area, although girls were warned about the dangers of sexual disease. Whilst clear guidelines were given about punishment for homosexual activities in the HJ, it appears that the issue of lesbianism was not raised at all in the official guidelines of the BDM.[65]

Expectations about sexual behaviour did not always correspond to reality, as exemplified by cases of girls having sexual relationships with soldiers and SS men, and of their having illegitimate babies in order to present the Führer with children. The lack of explanation about sexual behaviour partly explains this phenomenon. Some girls also had relationships with 'racially inferior' men from the eastern occupied territories, which was partly a response to the allure of the exotic, but was, of course, anathema to the regime. Hence, there was some conflict between the emphasis on moral purity within the BDM and the popular perception of the organization. Promiscuous behaviour on the part of BDM girls became even more pronounced during the war. Popular jokes included the following interpretations of the initials BDM: *Bubi Drück Mich* ('squeeze me, laddie'); *Bedarfsartikel Deutscher Männer* ('requisite for German men'); *Brauch Deutsche Mädel* ('make use of German girls'); *Bald Deutscher Mütter* ('German mothers to be'); *Bund Deutscher Milchkühe* ('League of German Milk Cows').[66] Such jokes clearly reveal the popular response to the BDM, suggesting both doubts about standards of morality within the organization and some displeasure at its emphasis on procreation.

The most important vehicles for socialization in the BDM were the weekly *Heimabend* and the summer camps. The main purpose of the *Heimabend* was ideological education or training in the National Socialist *Weltanschauung*. Punctuality played a part in the overall creation of discipline, so that girls who arrived late were obliged to pay a small fine.[67] The girls sang old Germanic songs and learned new ones. They received instruction on a number of subjects, such as National Socialism, the work of the BDM, German history and race.[68] Instruction often took the form of stories, for example about loyalty, honour, courage and obedience, and such sentiments were underlined with appropriate songs.[69] The girls then did handicrafts or watched a puppet show, and the activities ended with a final song. The *Heimabend* lasted two hours. It took place in the afternoon for JM girls and in the evening for BDM girls.

The content of *Mädelschaft*, which was a series of guidelines for BDM leaders on the structuring of the *Heimabend*, gives a clear indication of the type of activities and training involved in these sessions, and especially the themes taught. For example, the April 1938 edition was a special issue on Bismarck.[70] After considering Bismarck and his achievements, a number of pages were dedicated to Hitler and his creation of a new great German empire.[71] This was followed by a large section showing BDM leaders the types of activities they might use for the *Heimabend*, such as speeches by Hitler and songs. The May 1938 edition took the First World War as its main theme, including the sense of camaraderie among the soldiers and a number of soldiers' letters which showed their unity, determination and love for their fatherland.[72] After the Anschluß of March 1938, the June 1938 issue was designed to teach BDM girls about Austria, by means of a combination of history, poems, short stories and illustrations. The November 1938 issue was dedicated to the rise of the National Socialist Party, its 'time of struggle' and its heroes, such as Horst Wessel and Herbert Norkus.[73] The April 1939 edition was on the theme of 'The Struggle against Bolshevism'. It showed the evils and perils of Bolshevism, for example how it destroyed marriage and the family, and explored Germany's role as a bulwark against the spread of Bolshevism.[74] This edition also had a section entitled 'You have the Duty to be Healthy!', which underlined the importance of regular exercise, sufficient sleep and care of the body. It also stated that girls who sat in stuffy and crowded cinemas or overcrowded and smoky bars were behaving irresponsibly and not living the lifestyle that was expected of them in order to fulfil their duties as future mothers of the German nation.[75]

The June 1939 special edition for the BDM summer camp placed an emphasis on nature and the struggle for survival, underlining that only the healthy survived, whilst the weak and the sick perished.[76] The final part of it summarizes activities in the summer camp and gives a clear indication of the socialization of girls in the BDM.[77] This starts with a section on the orderliness and cleanliness of the camp. It was the responsibility of the camp-leader to ensure this from the start, for example, by confiscating anything the girls left lying around and only returning such items after the collection of a fine. The camp-leaders then had to arrange the times for flag-raising, meals and training, and to ensure the punctuality of the girls for each of these activities. Each morning, on waking, after cleaning their teeth and brushing their hair, the girls would either go on a march or sing a song. The method of flag-raising and procedures for meal times were given in minute detail. Set speeches were included that were to be used at flag-raising and meal times. One of the main functions of the summer camps was to give systematic instruction on contemporary political events. The participants were to acquire an under-standing of the political life of the German *Volk* and its 'living space'. It was the task of the camp-leader to clearly and simply explain the political situation to the participants. The themes and topics included the shame inflicted upon Germany by the Treaty of Versailles, Hitler's foreign policy successes and the struggle of the German nation for its 'living space'. Camp-leaders were instructed about what songs to sing in the camp and when to sing them. For example, it was optimal to use songs when marching through a village or town, when the girls were tired, in order to raise their spirits, on rainy days when the girls had to remain in the camp, or on evenings in the village squares to en-courage local people to join in the singing. The guidelines included ten compulsory songs that had to be used in the summer camp. These could be supplemented with oth-ers, but had to be the main ones sung. Instruction was given about what entertainment to use for the 'children's afternoon' and the 'village evening', such as songs and plays. Books for the summer camp were also recommended. Finally, instructions were given on how to end the camp. This was to be done by discussing a particular theme – such as the glory of nature – and then summing up the purpose of the camp, a greeting to Hitler and a final song. Hence, the whole camp was very carefully orchestrated and planned out, from start to finish, with the clear objective of the political socialization of its participants.[78]

The JM *Heimabend* and camps had similar imperatives, as can be seen from the guide-lines for leaders.[79] In 1936, for example, the themes covered included the life of Adolf Hitler, nature, the *Winterhilfswerk* (Winter Relief Agency), motherhood and heredity. In 1937, the Four Year Plan, the 'Jewish Question', Hitler's achievements and the homeland featured as important topics for education. Much instruction was carried out by means of short stories.[80] The girls in the JM were encouraged to be brave, devoted, comradely, obedient and honourable.[81] Camaraderie was the foremost quality expected from the JM. She was asked: 'Can you make personal sacrifices in order to help a comrade? And if you can, do you then ask for thanks or public recognition? Is your camaraderie still there when there is no one to observe it?' JM honour was also highly valued. There was no room in the organization for dishonesty, deceit, scandal or envy.

In January 1938, a new BDM agency, the *Glaube und Schönheit* (Faith and Beauty), was formed for 17- to 21- year-old girls, under the leadership of Clementine zu Castell.[82] By February 1939, the organization had some 500,000 members. Physical and ideological training formed the core of its work. Its members took part in activities for two to three hours per week. For the purpose of training, the young women were formed into working groups for different themes or subjects including sport, gymnastics, national tradition, plays and culture, handicrafts, music, foreign news, health, and household and agricultural competence. There were also groups on fashion design and anti–air raid protection. This arrangement enabled girls to take part in activities in which they were particularly interested.[83] Physical education was at the forefront of *Glaube und Schönheit* training, for 'a healthy and beautiful body' was considered to be the prerequisite of 'a healthy and beautiful spirit'.[84] Beyond this, the main task of the *Glaube und Schönheit* was to form 'self-assured young women', rooted in the National Socialist spirit and capable of taking their part in the creation and maintenance of their *Volk*.[85] The *Glaube und Schönheit* organization allowed girls to take part in the elite sports of tennis, fencing and horseriding, as well as home design. In 1943, 'the ideal of the lovely, beautiful and proud girl' of the *Glaube und Schönheit* was considered to be an elite type of woman. By the time she reached the age of 28, she would take the title of *Hohe Frau*, according to Himmler, the ultimate expression of the racially pure, physically fit and accomplished German woman.[86]

An important factor in girls' socialization in the BDM was the creation of a new ethos regarding their working or professional life. National Socialist ideology certainly attached value to work, as service to the 'national community', and as a 'moral duty' for both males and females. Manual labour, in particular, was considered important, as it would ensure that the nation would comprise physically fit, healthy and hardy individuals, who would transmit these attributes to future generations. For boys, all the physical training and drills in the HJ would serve them in the future as workers in heavy industry, on the land or, ultimately, in the armed forces. For girls, physical education would prepare them for their work placements and, of course, ultimately to become mothers.[87] It was generally accepted that girls would give up their jobs once they were married, in order to take care of their households.[88] The work ethos, and therefore the training given to girls, was to be understood in this sense. Household instruction had been of prime significance in girls' training since the genesis of the BDM. Even then, Adolf Lenk, the founder of the National Socialist youth movement, had claimed that members of the girls' groups had the task of becoming good German housewives.[89] Subsequent measures carried through by the youth leadership of the regime aimed to give girls a broader knowledge of household skills and abilities. Indeed, they were part of a wider attempt at the rationalization of housework under National Socialism, bound up with the Nazi policy of autarky and the duty of women to support the Nazi economy through their household economy.[90]

Whilst boys' training in the HJ took on a more militant nature between 1937 and 1939, with a greater emphasis on pre-military preparation, in the BDM a development towards preparation for 'female' activities was evident in this period. As early as 1936, the first BDM 'household school' had been set up, in which girls could gain experience and training in household activities. Specific training in household management and child care was given in the BDM household schools.[91] Here, a one-year course provided its participants with everything they would need to know as future mothers. The teaching plan at the household schools involved four main areas of work: practical teaching, which included cookery, baking, gardening and needlework; theoretical training, which consisted of lessons about nutrition, health, care for infants and for the sick; studies about the 'national community', which dealt with issues of nation, race and the national economy; and sport, which included hiking as well as activities such as singing and dancing.

A further development in this respect was the *Pflichtjahr*. This was a one-year compulsory work placement for girls which came into effect from 1 January 1939.[92] The rationale behind the *Pflichtjahr* was twofold – to give girls necessary experience and training and to help mothers of *kinderreich* families and farmers' wives.[93] It was deemed especially important that those girls who had spent their whole lives in towns and cities should serve in the countryside, so that for at least a year they could do farm work and get to know about rural life. This measure was intended to create a sense of connection and closeness to the homeland. Agricultural service had started out as a voluntary task. In 1934, 7,000 girls had begun farm work and by 1937, 43,000 girls had taken part in the scheme, mainly working on farms in Silesia, East Prussia and Pomerania.[94] Most of the girls doing agricultural service lived in a camp with their leader and from there went to help on individual farms, starting their work at 6 am each day. Other girls stayed on a farm with the farmer's family. Farm work was considered to prepare girls for marriage and motherhood. Those doing their *Pflichtjahr* in towns were required to help in the households of *kinderreich* families, with housework, washing, cooking and shopping. Work was a preparation for the tasks and requirements of motherhood. Apart from agricultural labour and household work, jobs in the 'caring professions' were deemed suitable, especially because skills could be acquired – such as looking after newborn babies – that were directly applicable to family life.[95] Hence, whether in connection with familial or professional situations, girls in the BDM had to learn that the state allocated specific obligations to them, and demanded self-discipline and duty fulfilment from them.[96] By 1940, there were 157,728 girls working in agriculture and 178,244 in domestic service for their *Pflichtjahr*.[97] Kater describes this as 'a ruthless exploitation of unpaid menial labour'.[98]

THE BDM IN WARTIME

During the war, the term 'domestic training' was applied more widely, ultimately changing its meaning to a total preparation to serve in any manner required by the state. Short training courses were run, teaching girls to make 'new out of old' and to help soldiers with washing and mending clothes.[99] BDM members were faced with new duties and obligations.[100] In the first year of the war, over nine million girls were mobilized, especially for agricultural work.[101] Youth mobilization involved a wide variety of activities, including the distribution of propaganda material for the Party, the distribution of food ration cards, the harvesting of crops, the collection of money for the War Winter Relief Agency, looking after the wounded, caring for children, and gathering herbs and wild fruit. Kater estimates that in 1939–40, 'over a million BDM members spent 6.5 million work hours on the collection of various herbs and tea'.[102] BDM girls were to be proud to help German soldiers, for example by setting up washing and mending centres for soldiers' clothes.[103] They sewed slippers for soldiers out of woollen blankets or plaited them out of straw.[104] They did agricultural work, looked after children, helped out in kindergartens and schools, and were also involved in active war service, for example as employees in armaments factories. BDM girls were also required to work as tram conductors and postal workers in the towns and cities during the war. They helped civilians at train stations, handing out food and drinks to passengers, as well as assisting the victims of air raids. They worked in kitchens to prepare sandwiches and soup for people who had been rendered homeless by the Allied bombing campaigns and collected and distributed everyday items such as toothpaste, toothbrushes and hairbrushes to them. The BDM girls became increasingly involved in first-aid duties for both soldiers and civilians. They assisted in nursing the wounded in hospitals. Towards the end of the war, in the bleakest and most hopeless days, many girls continued to show a willingness to make sacrifices for their nation, even when their lives were in danger.[105]

Hence, the scope and range of duties expanded considerably throughout the duration of the Third Reich and especially during the war. The BDM girls became involved in *Osteinsatz* (Eastern Service). From mid-1940 onwards, in conjunction with the SS, BDM girls were sent into the eastern occupied territories to clean and prepare the houses for German settlers, once the SS had removed the former inhabitants. Some BDM girls assisted the SS in evicting Poles from their homes.[106] After their initial duties in the eastern territories, which lasted approximately four to six weeks, many BDM girls had to remain in these territories for up to one year, in order to help the newcomers to settle there, offering assistance in the homes and schools. The BDM girls were sometimes shocked and appalled at the demeanour and lack of hygiene of the 'ethnic Germans'.[107] The reality they were presented with was somewhat different from their expectations. Nevertheless, the BDM girls carried out their tasks, going into the villages where they sang German songs and played German games with the children, so that they could learn German, as well as showing them maps of greater Germany and teaching children the basics of how to write and read German.[108] *Osteinsatz* had become an increasingly large part of BDM activities as the war progressed.[109] The carefree days of rambling and camping had long gone.

The BDM was an integral part of a blood-binding community, whose members were called upon to serve their nation and take responsibility for the future of their race under

National Socialism.[110] The BDM played a significant role in the Nazi process of social-izing and training German girls. In doing so, it borrowed much from the traditions of the earlier *Wandervögel* movement, but it added its own National Socialist ideals and ethos. As noted above, after 1933, many young girls were obliged to become members of the BDM, once other youth organizations had been dissolved or merged into the Nazi youth movement. However, it must be noted that the swell in the BDM membership between 1933 and 1936 was also the result of voluntary entry into the organization. Many girls were initially attracted to the BDM for a variety of reasons, such as to gain independence from their parents and to take part in activities previously inaccessible to them. They were attracted by the sport, singing and handicraft activities on offer to them in the organization. They could go on adventurous trips and have opportuni-ties for careers as youth group leaders that broke the limits of their social, regional or family boundaries, but they were not free or independent in reality. Parental authority was simply replaced by state force and discipline. BDM members, and even leaders, were individually unimportant, as part of a larger formation. The BDM did not aim at the individual development and independent thought of its members, but instead at making them true believers in the National Socialist system. Once membership became compulsory and ideological training became more pronounced, the allure of the BDM waned. Girls became increasingly subordinated to the organization and limited by the restrictions it placed upon them.

Motherhood was important both ideologically and in practice. The type of train-ing the girls underwent within the BDM was aimed at future motherhood. As BDM leaders were told, the purpose of BDM activities was 'to create a generation of girls that will become a generation of healthy women and mothers'.[111] Hence, the emphasis upon physical education was not for its own sake, but had the purpose of creating fit bodies to reproduce healthy, strong offspring.[112] As future mothers, BDM girls were to become protectors and preservers of the German race. The centrality of motherhood and race to the organization and to the state is plainly evident from the literary output of the BDM. Yet, at the same time, in practice there were modernizing effects resulting from BDM ac-tivities. These were functional and were a product of the circumstances of the war and the necessity of using BDM girls in roles related to it. Measures that appeared modernizing were simply pragmatic attempts on the part of the regime to prevent the collapse of the agricultural workforce and to meet the requirements of state efficiency. But reactionary ideology continued to underpin the regime's intentions, even though it could not adhere to this as rigidly as its leaders would have wished. This ideology should not be ignored or negated. The ideological education and training of girls remained central to the aims of the Nazi regime. Hence, pragmatic concerns that created a tendency towards modernity and a concurrent conventionalization of girls' pursuits corresponding with the regime's ideology were both evident in the BDM. Girls were obliged to fulfil their roles in the Nazi state until its demise. Ultimately, Hilde Seffert, a former BDM member claims, 'we were cheated of our youth'; whilst another former BDM girl, Gudrun Pausewang, talks of the hurt 'having to admit to oneself that one had believed in a false ideal, that the whole thing had been a lie and that one had been abused'.[113]

NOTES

1. The most important contributions on the subject include: D. Reese, 'Bund Deutscher Mädel – Zur Geschichte der weiblichen deutschen Jugend im Dritten Reich', in Frauengruppe Faschismusforschung (ed.), *Mutterkreuz und Arbeitsbuch: Zur Geschichte der Frauen in der Weimarer Republik und im Nationalsozialismus* (Frankfurt am Main, 1981); D. Reese, *'Straff, aber nicht Stramm – Herb, aber nicht derb'. Zur Vergesellschaftung der Mädchen durch den Bund Deutscher Mädel im Sozialkulturellen Vergleich zweier Milieus* (Weinheim and Basel, 1989); Klaus, *Mädchen in der Hitlerjugend*; Klaus, *Mädchen im Dritten Reich*; G. Kinz, *Der Bund Deutscher Mädel. Ein Beitrag zur Außerschulischen Mädchenerziehung im Nationalsozialismus* (Frankfurt am Main, 1990); B. Jürgens, *Zur Geschichte des BDM (Bund Deutscher Mädel) von 1923 bis 1939* (Frankfurt am Main, 1994); G. Miller-Kipp (ed.), *'Auch du gehörst dem Führer': Die Geschichte des Bundes Deutscher Mädel (BDM) in Quellen und Dokumenten* (Munich, 2002). See also A. Böltken, *Führerinnen im 'Führerstaat'* (Pfannenweiler, 1995); F. Niederdalhoff, *'Im Sinne des Systems einsatzbereit…': Mädchenarbeit im 'Bund Deutscher Mädel' (BDM) und in der 'Freien Deutschen Jugend' (FDJ) – Ein Vergleich* (Münster, 1997); R. Strien, *Mädchenerziehung und -sozialisation in der Zeit des Nationalsozialismus und ihre lebensgeschichtliche Bedeutung* (Opladen, 2000), pp. 80–89.
2. For example, see M. Maschmann, *Account Rendered: A Dossier on My Former Self* (London, 1964); R. Finckh, *Mit uns zieht die neue Zeit* (Baden-Baden, 1979); M. Hannsmann, *Der helle Tag bricht an – Ein Kind wird Nazi* (Hamburg, 1982); G. Herr, *Inhaltsreiche Jahre – aus dem Leben einer BdM-Führerin 1930–1945* (Lausanne, 1985).
3. D. Reese, 'Mädchen im Bund Deutscher Mädel', in E. Kleinau and C. Opitz (eds), *Geschichte der Mädchen- und Frauenbildung*, Vol. 2 (Frankfurt am Main, 1996), pp. 271–82.
4. D. Reese, *Growing up Female in Nazi Germany* (Ann Arbor, 2006), p. 4.
5. D. Peukert, *The Weimar Republic: The Crisis of Classical Modernity* (London, 1991), p. 93.
6. M. de Ras, *Body, Femininity and Nationalism: Girls in the German Youth Movement 1900–1934* (New York and London, 2008), pp. 6–7.
7. Ibid., p. 41.
8. Ibid., p. 193.
9. Ibid.
10. Ibid., pp. 187–9.
11. Reese, *Growing up Female*, p. 31.
12. Hannsmann, *Der helle Tag bricht an – Ein Kind wird Nazi*, p. 34.
13. Finckh, *Mit uns zieht die neue Zeit*, p. 81.
14. Reese, *Growing up Female*, p. 7.
15. C. Leitsch, 'Drei BDM-Biographinnen', *Dokumentationsstelle zur NS-Sozialpolitik: Mitteilungen*, April 1986, p. 77.
16. Maschmann, *Account Rendered*, pp. 10 and 12.
17. D. Reese, 'Emanzipation oder Vergesellschaftung: Mädchen im "Bund Deutscher Mädel"', in H.-U. Otto and H. Sünker (eds), *Politische Formierung und soziale Erziehung im Nationalsozialismus* (Frankfurt am Main, 1991), p. 212.
18. Reese, *Growing up Female*, p. 8.
19. See Reese, *Growing up Female*, which uses case studies of Minden in Westphalia and Wedding in Berlin to show the different attitudes towards the BDM, pp. 102–57 and pp. 158–246.

20. Reese, 'Mädchen im Bund Deutscher Mädel', p. 280.

21. Cited in L. Becker, 'Der Bund Deutscher Mädel', in R. Benze and G. Gräfer (eds), *Erziehungsmächte und Erziehungshoheit im Grossdeutschen Reich als gestaltende Kräfte im Leben des Deutschen* (Leipzig, 1940), p. 95.

22. Maschmann, *Account Rendered*, p. 61.

23. Kinz, *Der Bund Deutscher Mädel*, pp. 126–7.

24. S. Roberts, *The House That Hitler Built* (London, 1937), p. 208. On the impact of the BDM upon its members, see Miller-Kipp (ed.), *'Auch du gehörst dem Führer'*, pp. 303–23.

25. J. Rüdiger, 'Der Bund Deutscher Mädel in der Hitler Jugend', in P. Meier-Benneckenstein (ed.), *Das Dritte Reich im Aufbau* (Berlin, 1939), Vol. 2, p. 398. On discipline in the BDM, see also IfZ Db 44.92, *Die Dienstform des BDM* (1941).

26. S. Rogge, '"Mädel, komm zum BDM!"', in *Hart und Zart. Frauenleben, 1920–1970* (Berlin, 1990), p. 154.

27. This difference in socialization was also noticeable in Mussolini's Italian Fascist youth groups. On this, see T. Koon, *Believe, Obey, Fight: Political Socialization of Youth in Fascist Italy, 1922–1943* (Chapel Hill and London, 1985), pp. 97–8.

28. On this, BA NSD 43/151-5, 'Du hast die Pflicht, gesund zu sein!'

29. Cited in Knopp, *Hitler's Children*, p. 99.

30. On what follows, see H. Rahn, 'Artgemäße Mädchenerziehung und Rasse', *Nationalsozialistische Mädchenerziehung*, 12, 1940, p. 224.

31. A. Klönne, *Hitlerjugend. Die Jugend und ihre Organisation im Dritten Reich* (Hanover and Frankfurt am Main, 1955), p. 69.

32. 'Eltern, schenkt nur gute Bücher', *Das Deutsche Mädel*, November 1936, pp. 22–3.

33. IfZ Db 44.102, 'BDM-Werk Glaube und Schönheit. Schulungsdienst', October 1941, pp. 65–8.

34. Cited in Reese, *Growing Up Female*, pp. 43–4.

35. Klaus, *Mädchen im Dritten Reich*, p. 48.

36. On this, see G. Pfister and D. Reese, 'Gender, Body Culture, and Body Politics in National Socialism', *Sport History*, No. 1 (1995), pp. 91–121.

37. See *Das Deutsche Mädel*, March 1938, pp. 4–5.

38. See E. Zill, 'Die körperliche Schulung im BDM', in H. Munske (ed.), *Mädel im Dritten Reich* (Berlin, 1935), p. 27.

39. Reese, *Growing Up Female*, pp. 71–2.

40. See Klaus, *Mädchen im Dritten Reich*, p. 49.

41. IfZ Db 44.65/2, *Mädel im Dienst. BDM-Sport* (Potsdam, 1940), p. 14.

42. B. von Schirach, *Die Hitler-Jugend, Idee und Gestalt* (Leipzig, 1934), p. 101.

43. IfZ Db 44.65/2, *Mädel im Dienst. BDM-Sport* (Potsdam, 1940), pp. 13–14 and 17.

44. IfZ Db 44.65/4, *Mädel im Dienst. Jungmädel-Sport* (Potsdam, 1942).

45. IfZ Db 44.65/2, *Mädel im Dienst. BDM-Sport* (Potsdam, 1940).

46. IfZ Db 44.32/8, 'Dienstvorschrift der Hitler-Jugend', p. 3.

47. IfZ Db 44.43, *Die Mädelschaft. Blätter für Heimabendgestaltung im BDM*, May 1939, p. 2.

48. Ibid., pp. 6–8.

49. Ibid., p. 8.

50. On what follows, see ibid., pp. 10–24.

51. BA NS 28/83, 'Richtlinien für den Bund deutscher Mädel in der Hitlerjugend', no date.

52. *Das Deutsche Mädel*, April 1939, p. 22.

53. See, for example, *Das Deutsche Mädel*, August 1937, p. 30, which talks about the foolishness of fashion.

54. *Das Deutsche Mädel*, January 1937, p. 11.

55. *Das Deutsche Mädel*, January 1938, pp. 29–32.
56. C. Kirkpatrick, *Nazi Germany. Its Women and Family Life* (Indianapolis and New York, 1938), p. 103.
57. BA NSD 47/6-1933, 'Schönheitspflege?!', *Amtliche Frauenkorrespondenz*, p. 8.
58. Stargardt, *Witnesses of War*, p. 33.
59. BA NSD 47/19, *Jugend und Elternhaus. Beiträge zur Jugenderziehung unserer Zeit* (1944), pp. 40–41.
60. Maschmann, *Account Rendered*, p. 150.
61. Reese, 'Straff, aber nicht Stramm – Herb, aber nicht Derb', p. 44.
62. Rüdiger, 'Der Bund Deutscher Mädel', p. 397.
63. Maschmann, *Account Rendered*, p. 150.
64. Klaus, *Mädchen in der Hitlerjugend*, p. 109. On attitudes towards sexual education, see also BA NSD 47/19, *Jugend und Elternhaus*, pp. 17–28.
65. Klaus, *Mädchen im Dritten Reich*, pp. 56–7. On Nazi policy towards lesbianism, see C. Schoppmann, *Nationalsozialistische Sexualpolitik und weibliche Homosexualität* (Pfannenweiler, 1997) and C. Schoppmann, 'National Socialist Policies towards Female Homosexuality', in L. Abrams and E. Harvey (eds), *Gender Relations in German History: Power, Agency and Experience from the Sixteenth Century to the Twentieth Century* (London, 1996), pp. 177–87.
66. On this, see H. Bleuel, *Strength through Joy: Sex and Society in Nazi Germany* (London, 1973), p. 136, and Klaus, *Mädchen in der Hitlerjugend*, p. 104.
67. IfZ Db 44.17, *Mädel im Dienst. Ein Handbuch* (Potsdam, 1934), p. 219.
68. Ibid., p. 220.
69. See IfZ Db 44.28, 'Sommerlager- und Heimabendmaterial für die Schulungs- und Kulturarbeit, Sommer 1941, Jungmädel', as an example of this.
70. IfZ Db 44.43, *Die Mädelschaft. Blätter für Heimabendgestaltung im BDM*, April 1938.
71. Ibid., pp. 29–32.
72. IfZ Db 44.43, *Die Mädelschaft. Blätter für Heimabendgestaltung im BDM*, May 1938.
73. IfZ Db 44.43, *Die Mädelschaft. Blätter für Heimabendgestaltung im BDM*, June 1938 and November 1938.
74. IfZ Db 44.43, *Die Mädelschaft. Blätter für Heimabendgestaltung im BDM*, April 1939, pp. 19 and 25–8.
75. Ibid., p. 46.
76. IfZ Db 44.43(a), *Die Mädelschaft. Sonderausgabe für die Sommerlager*, June 1939, pp. 23–8.
77. On what follows, see ibid., pp. 51–79.
78. For another example of instruction for a three-week summer camp plan, see IfZ Db 44.17, *Mädel im Dienst. Ein Handbuch* (Potsdam, 1934), pp. 284–90.
79. On what follows, see IfZ Db 44.41, *Die Jungmädelschaft. Blätter für Heimabendgestaltung der Jungmädel*.
80. For example, IfZ Db 44.41, *Die Jungmädelschaft. Blätter für Heimabendgestaltung der Jungmädel*, June 1936, includes the story of 'Das Mädchen Helge', whose moral was 'to be brave is good', pp. 6–8.
81. On what follows, see IfZ Db 44.28, 'Sommerlager- und Heimabendmaterial für die Schulungs- und Kulturarbeit, Sommer 1941, Jungmädel', pp. 6–7.
82. On this, see S. Hering and K. Schilde, *Das BDM-Werk 'Glaube und Schönheit': Die Organisation junger Frauen im Nationalsozialismus* (Berlin, 2000).
83. On this, see IfZ Db 44.43, *Die Mädelschaft. Sonderausgabe für die Schulung zur Berufswahl*, August 1939, pp. 38–42.
84. IfZ Db 44.07, *Das Deutsche Mädel*, June 1938, p. 5.
85. Ibid., p. 7.

86. On this, see Kater, *Hitler Youth*, pp. 96–7.

87. On this, see *Das Deutsche Mädel*, November 1940, p. 7.

88. *Das Deutsche Mädel*, February 1938, p. 7.

89. D. Reese, 'Bund Deutscher Mädel', p. 166.

90. See Pine, *Nazi Family Policy, 1933–1945*, pp. 81–6. See also, J. Stephenson, 'Propaganda, Autarky and the German Housewife', in D. Welch (ed.), *Nazi Propaganda: The Power and the Limitations* (London, 1983), pp. 136–8.

91. On what follows, see *Das Deutsche Mädel*, January 1937, p. 9.

92. On this, see BA NSD 47/16-1, I. Berghaus, 'Das Pflichtjahr. Wegweiser und Ratgeber für Mädel, Eltern und Hausfrau'.

93. On what follows, see IfZ Db 44.43, *Die Mädelschaft. Sonderausgabe für die Schulung zur Berufswahl*, August 1939, pp. 6–9.

94. Kater, *Hitler Youth*, p. 84.

95. See Rüdiger, 'Der Bund Deutscher Mädel', p. 401.

96. See Schirach, *Die Hitler-Jugend, Idee und Gestalt*, p. 97.

97. Kater, *Hitler Youth*, p. 85.

98. Ibid.

99. BA NS 26/358, 'Mädelerziehung im Kriege', pp. 116–17.

100. See IfZ Db 44.61, *Wir schaffen. Jahrbuch des BDM* (1941), pp. 157–77. On the activities of the BDM during the war, see also Reese, 'Bund Deutscher Mädel', pp. 174–80.

101. BA NS 26/358, quoted in Reese, 'Bund Deutscher Mädel', p. 175.

102. Kater, *Hitler Youth*, p. 91.

103. *Das Deutsche Mädel*, January 1940, p. 6.

104. Stargardt, *Witnesses of War*, p. 33.

105. See Knopp, *Hitler's Children*, p. 110.

106. Stargardt, *Witnesses of War*, p. 120.

107. Kater, *Hitler Youth*, p. 89.

108. *Das Deutsche Mädel*, April 1940, pp. 10–11.

109. For an autobiographical account of *Osteinsatz*, see H. Fritsch, *Land mein Land: Bauerntum und Landdienst BDM-Osteinsatz Siedlungsgeschichte im Osten* (Preußisch Oldendorf, 1986).

110. Special BDM pamphlets were issued on questions of race and racial obligations. For example, see IfZ Db 44.104, *Mädel voran!*, pp. 193 ff.

111. IfZ Db 44.17, *Mädel im Dienst. Ein Handbuch* (Potsdam, 1934), p. 9.

112. Ibid., p. 8.

113. Cited in Knopp, *Hitler's Children*, pp. 112–13.

CONCLUSION

The education and socialization of youth by the Nazi regime to become the ideal future generation of Germans in line with its ideology are central to our wider understanding of the Third Reich. The Nazi government attempted to achieve both complete social control and a 'total education' of German youth. This incorporated a root and branch reshaping of values. Education under National Socialism was used to disseminate the key components of Nazi ideology – in particular the creation of national identity and racial awareness. Both formal education in schools and socialization in youth groups formed very significant aspects of this process.

There were significant historical links between the *Kaiserreich*, the Weimar Republic and the Third Reich in terms of education. It is important to treat the Third Reich in the context of earlier administrations and to consider both similarities and differences. The extreme nationalism and authoritarianism that characterized the end of the nineteenth century was never fully eliminated during the Weimar years despite attempts at introducing progressive educational policies. In certain ways, the Nazi regime built upon the foundations from previous eras, but it often added a more radical direction to educational policy. Nazi education policy consciously donned an irrational character, based upon the power of suggestion and emotional impact rather than upon the power of reason. The educational philosophy of National Socialism was fundamentally irrational. It echoed earlier ideals, such as pan-German nationalism from the days of the *Kaiserreich*, and pushed irrationalism to its most extreme limit. However, the Nazis had to take into account the realities of the need to develop a high level of technology and industry in order to prepare for war, and hence had to temper this irrationalism. In addition, the war itself occasioned changes to the essence and direction of Nazi educational policy.

Both the nature of Nazi policy-making and the tensions that existed between modernization and reaction in the Third Reich led to inconsistencies and ambiguities in education policy. Nazi policy-making was such that initiatives came from a number of different arenas. Hitler's fundamental beliefs about education provided the backdrop to Nazi education policy and its ethos. They were a strange blend of concepts taken from dominant contemporaneous ideas, as well as resulting from Hitler's own educational experience. Educational policy-making should have been the responsibility of the Ministry of Education, led by Bernhard Rust. However, Rust encountered intervention and challenges to his authority from a number of Nazi leaders, notably Baldur von Schirach,

Martin Bormann, Robert Ley, Alfred Rosenberg, Philip Bouhler and Heinrich Himmler. Furthermore, even civil servants from his own Ministry flouted his authority. This was quite typical of the way in which the Third Reich functioned. This chaotic nature of government, as emphasized by 'structuralist' and 'functionalist' historians, meant that there was much competition between different individuals and agencies and sometimes contradictions in policy-making.

Overall, the Nazi leadership disliked and distrusted the *Gymnasium* with its humanist tradition, its emphasis on classical education and its academic snobbery. Historically, the *Gymnasium* emerged in the tradition of classical humanism. It subsequently became quite strongly nationalist, but, nevertheless, under National Socialism, it was to lose its academic and elite status. The Nazi government aimed both to decrease the significance of the *Gymnasium* and to reduce the influence of the Churches in German education. It claimed that these policies were designed to rationalize and modernize the education system. However, the truth of the matter was that the regime despised the traditional *Gymnasien* because they were too academic, whilst it closed down the Church schools because it regarded them as a threat. Hence, the promises and claims made by the Nazi government to 'modernize' education remained unfulfilled in reality. Nazi anti-liberalism and anti-intellectualism in education produced a series of measures that failed to modernize the German educational system.

The Nazi education system had a short lifespan lasting just twelve years, half of them during wartime conditions. The brevity of the period was significant in terms of the capacity of the regime to push through the changes it desired, and the outbreak of the war engendered changes in its priorities. The years 1933–8 were spent mainly in the process of 'coordinating' teachers and trying to ensure their loyalty to the regime. The NSLB provided reports on the political reliability of teachers for appointments and promotions and attempted to achieve the ideological indoctrination of teachers. The main alterations to the school system and to the curriculum came in the years 1938 and 1939. New curricular changes found form in the publication of new textbooks between 1939 and 1942. The introduction and use of new school textbooks greatly assisted the Nazi regime in its aim of inculcating pupils with Nazi ideology. The spirit of *völkisch* ideology was conveyed through children's books. Specific subjects such as biology, history, geography, mathematics and German were all utilized to this end and the new subject of *Rassenkunde* was added to the curriculum. Through school textbooks, Nazi pedagogues sought to develop in children a sense of identity with the nation, the Nazi regime and its policies. The Third Reich did not have a clear and coherent concept of education beyond indoctrination. Political attitudes played a central role in the shaping of Nazi education policy. Education was linked with racial values. Anti-Semitism and racism in the curriculum represented a unique contribution of the Nazi regime to the history of education in Germany.

The Nazi elite educational institutions performed a special function within the Third Reich and within the Nazi education system. Certainly they challenged the traditional

Gymnasien in terms of status. They entailed a new kind of ideological elitism. The three main types of educational institutions to train the future elite of German society – the Napolas, the Adolf Hitler Schools and the *Ordensburgen* – represented a microcosm of the Nazi *Weltanschauung* by fostering the leadership principle, promoting competitiveness and emphasizing life as a struggle and as survival of the 'fittest'. They encouraged physical prowess, excoriated the 'enemies of the Reich', in particular the Jews, Communists and Socialists, emphasized racial purity, glorified war and fostered militarism. They underlined the necessity for *Lebensraum* and had a significant part to play in the achievement of a 'greater German empire'. They were typically National Socialist institutions aimed at the ideological training of a new elite.

In the Hitler Youth and the League of German Girls, the Nazis created comprehensive youth organizations that were unparalleled in the history of German youth movements. Nevertheless, the Nazi youth organization in many ways did follow in the footsteps of the earlier German youth movement, which encapsulated elements of German romanticism and folklore, Nietzschean philosophy and traditional concepts such as *Heimat*. The Nazi youth groups deviated from earlier traditions and developed their own distinctive ideology. The pedagogic activities of the Nazi youth groups strove towards the creation of the 'national community' and they encouraged their members to be willing to make sacrifices for the state. Furthermore, through its anti-intellectual stance and its taking up so much of the free time of its members, the Hitler Youth contributed to the reduction in academic standards in the Third Reich. This led to tensions between the youth organizations and the schools. In particular more conservative teachers of an older generation found the youth groups problematic. Children and young people were encouraged to challenge conventional figures of authority, such as schoolteachers, priests and even their parents, enhancing the role of the youth groups, whilst simultaneously creating an anti-intellectual climate and eroding many of the traditional socialization functions of the family.

Under the circumstances of 'total war', the Nazi regime was unable to make all the educational changes it had hoped to introduce. Education had come to a virtual standstill by the end of the war. The Allied bombing raids had resulted in the mass evacuation of schoolchildren from the cities to the countryside in the *Kinderlandverschickung* scheme. Older children were conscripted as auxiliaries. Universities were emptied of male students in 1944 following the order for the creation of the *Volkssturm*. In May 1945, the Allies faced a grave problem in Germany, a country in disarray. As far as education was concerned, a variety of difficulties presented themselves. The existing textbooks were all unsuitable. There was a severe shortage of trained teachers and a lack of school buildings. Many schools had been destroyed or were being used to accommodate displaced persons. Most significantly, there was a need for a comprehensive 'denazification' and 're-education' of Germany's citizens. The regime and its ideology were discredited. The atrocities committed in the name of the German population became more widely known as the public was confronted with the full truth about the concentration camps and the death camps.

An understanding of education in the Third Reich illustrates the dangers of political ideology determining which subjects are taught in schools and how they are taught. In a system in which Party organizations determined what was to be taught, 'national political' education had been prioritized under National Socialism. Furthermore, the sophistication and complexity of the whole system made it even more dangerous in its impact. In both the schools and the youth groups, National Socialism tapped into the deep-rooted desire of many young Germans to be part of a larger group and to belong. Nazi ideology defined and underlined all pedagogic activity – knowledge of the Party and its leader, the 'national community' and racial awareness formed the core of education in the Third Reich. Educational content in the Third Reich largely comprised Party propaganda. Nazi 'total' education in the schools and youth groups together aimed to create a new young generation of Germans committed to Nazi ideology and able to carry out their obligations to the state. Ultimately, of course, this entailed a willingness to lay down their lives for it.

GLOSSARY OF ABBREVIATIONS AND TERMS

AHS – *Adolf Hitler Schule* (Adolf Hitler School)

BDM – *Bund Deutscher Mädel* (League of German Girls)

Blut und Boden – blood and soil

DAF – *Deutsche Arbeitsfront* (German Labour Front)

Führer – leader

Führerprinzip – leadership principle

Gau – region; the largest unit of the NSDAP's territorial organization

Gauleiter – regional leader

Gleichschaltung – coordination or streamlining

Herrenvolk – master race

HJ – *Hitlerjugend* (Hitler Youth)

Kaiserreich – Second German Empire

KdF – *Kraft durch Freude* (Strength through Joy)

kinderreich – literally 'rich in children'; term used to describe 'valuable' families with four or more children

KLV – *Kinderlandverschickung* (sending children to the countryside)

KPD – Kommunistische Partei Deutschland (German Communist Party)

Kreis – district; the second largest unit of the NSDAP's territorial organization

Kreisleiter – district leaders

Lebensraum – living space

Machtergreifung – seizure of power

Napola – *Nationalpolitische Erziehungsanstalten* (National Political Educational Institute)

NSDAP – *Nationalsozialistische Deutsche Arbeiterpartei* (National Socialist German Workers' Party)

NS-Deutscher Studentenbund – National Socialist German Students' Association

NSF – *NS-Frauenschaft* (National Socialist Womanhood)

NSLB – *Nationalsozialistischer Lehrerbund* (National Socialist Teachers' Association)

NSV – *Nationalsozialistiche Volkswohlfahrt* (National Socialist People's Welfare)

Ordensburg – Order Castle (Nazi elite educational institution)

Ort – local branch; the smallest unit of the NSDAP's territorial organization

Osteinsatz – Eastern Service

RM – *Reichsmark* (unit of currency)

SA – *Sturmabteilungen* (Stormtroopers)

SS – *Schutzstaffeln* (Nazi elite formation led by Heinrich Himmler)

Volk – nation; people

völkisch – nationalistic

Volksgemeinschaft – national community; people's community

Wehrmacht – armed forces

Weltanschauung – world view

WHW – *Winterhilfswerk* (Winter Relief Agency)

BIBLIOGRAPHY

PRIMARY SOURCES

Unpublished

Bundesarchiv, Berlin (BA)

NS 12 Hauptamt für Erzieher/ NS-Lehrerbund

NS 15 Der Beauftragte des Führers für die Überwachung der gesamten geistigen und weltanschaulichen Schulung und Erziehung der NSDAP

NS 22 Reichsorganisationsleiter der NSDAP

NS 26 Hauptarchiv der NSDAP

NS 28 Hitler-Jugend

NSD Drucksachen der NSDAP, ihrer Gliederungen, angeschlossenen Verbände und betreuten Organisationen

R 49 Reichskommissar für die Festigung deutschen Volkstums

R 89 Reichsversicherungsamt

R 4901 Reichsministerium für Wissenschaft, Erziehung und Volksbildung

Institut für Zeitgeschichte, Munich (IfZ)

Db 44.07, Db 44.17, Db 44.28, Db 44.32, Db 44.41, Db 44.43, Db 44.61, Db 44.65, Db 44.92, Db 44.102, Db 44.104

Published

Bäumler, A., *Männerbund und Wissenschaft* (Berlin, 1934).

Bäumler, A., *Politik und Erziehung* (Berlin, 1937).

Becker, C. H., *Vom Wesen der deutschen Universität* (Berlin, 1925).

Belling, C. and Schütze, A., *Der Film in der Hitlerjugend* (Berlin, 1937).

Benze, R. and Gräfer, G. (eds), *Erziehungsmächte und Erziehungshoheit im Grossdeutschen Reich als gestaltende Kräfte im Leben des Deutschen* (Leipzig, 1940).

Boelitz, O., *Der Aufbau des preussischen Bildungswesens nach der Staatsumwälzung* (Berlin, 1925).

Frick, W., *Kampfziel der deutschen Schule* (Langensalza, 1933).

Froebel, F., *The Education of Man*, translated by W. Hailmann (New York, 1887).

Hitler, A., *Mein Kampf*, translated by R. Mannheim, with an introduction by D. C. Watt (London, 1992).

Hitler's Table Talk 1941–1944: His Private Conversations, with an introduction by H. R. Trevor-Roper (New York, 1976).

Krieck, E., *Nationalpolitische Erziehung* (Leipzig, 1941).

Lange, F., *Reines Deutschtum* (Berlin, 1898).

Ley, R., *Schmiede des Schwertes* (Munich, 1942).

Meier-Benneckenstein, P. (ed.), *Das Dritte Reich im Aufbau* (Berlin, 1939).

Munske, H. (ed.), *Mädel im Dritten Reich* (Berlin, 1935).

Rauschning, H., *Hitler Speaks: A Series of Political Conversations with Adolf Hitler on his Real Aims* (London, 1939).

Rosenberg, A., *Der Mythos des 20. Jahrhunderts: Eine Wertung der seelisch-geistigen Gestaltenkämpfe unserer Zeit* (Munich, 1934).

von Schirach, B., *Die Hitler-Jugend, Idee und Gestalt* (Leipzig, 1934).

Wyneken, G., *Der Gedankenkreis der freien Schulgemeinde* (Leipzig, 1913).

School Curricula and Textbooks

Allgemeinbildender Grundlehrgang, 1. Teil (Breslau and Leipzig, 1941).

Bei uns In Nürnberg. Erstes Lesebuch (Nuremberg, 1934).

Brohmer, P., *Biologischer Unterricht und völkischer Erziehung* (Frankfurt am Main, 1933).

Deutsches Lesebuch für Volksschulen II (Frankfurt am Main, 1936).

Deutsches Lesebuch für Volksschulen, 2. Band, 3. und 4. Schuljahren (Kiel, 1937).

Deutsches Lesebuch für Volksschulen, 3. und 4. Schuljahr (Berlin, 1937).

Dreyer, H. *et al.* (eds), *Deutsches Lesebuch für Mittelschulen. Klasse 1* (Frankfurt am Main, 1942).

Eckhardt, H., *Die Körperanlage des Kindes und ihre Entwicklung. Ziel und Weg einer biologische Körpererziehung* (Stuttgart, 1935).

Erziehung und Unterricht in der höheren Schule. Amtliche Ausgabe des Reichs- und Preußischen Ministeriums für Wissenschaft, Erziehung und Volksbildung (Berlin, 1938).

Fibel für die Volksschulen Württembergs (Stuttgart, 1937).

Fibel für Niedersachsen (Hanover, 1939).

Fink, F., *Die Judenfrage im Unterricht* (Nuremberg, 1937).

Fischer, J., *Volks- und Staatskunde, 1. Teil* (Selbstverlag, 1938).

Frank, E., *Fröhlicher Anfang. Ausgabe für Thüringen* (Frankfurt am Main, 1943).

Gehl, W., *Geschichte für höhere Schulen Mittelstufe, Heft 4* (Breslau, 1936).

Graff, J. (ed.), *Vererbungslehre, Rassenkunde und Erbgesundheitspflege: Einführung nach methodischen Grundsätzen* (Munich, 1933).

Günther, E. (ed.), *Wehrphysik – Ein Handbuch für Lehrer* (Frankfurt am Main, 1936).

Günther, H., *Rassenkunde des deutschen Volkes* (Berlin, 1938).

Hand ins Hand fürs Vaterland. Eine deutsche Fibel von Otto Zimmermann (Braunschweig, 1943).

Hayn, F., *Politische Sippenkunde in der Schule* (Leipzig, 1936).

Hiemer, E., *Der Giftpilz* (Nuremberg, 1938).

Hiemer, E., *Der Pudelmopsdackelpinscher und andere Erzählungen* (Nuremberg, 1940).

Höfner, A., *Der Schulgarten in der Unterrichtspraxis* (Munich, 1937).

Hohmann, W., *Volk und Reich. Der deutschen Geschichtbuch für Oberschulen und Gymnasien, Klasse 8. Von Bismarck bis zur Gegenwart* (Frankfurt am Main, 1941).

Jantzen, W., *Die Geographie im Dienste der nationalpolitischen Erziehung* (Breslau, 1936).

Kahnmeyer, L. and Schulze, H., *Realienbuch enthaltend Geschichte, Erdkunde, Naturgeschichte, Physik, Chemie und Mineralogie* (Bielefeld, 1938).

Kamps Neues Realienbuch für Schule und Haus (Bochum in Westfalen, 1937).

Kickler, H. *et al.* (eds), *Dich ruft Dein Volk. Deutsches Lesebuch für Mittelschulen, 4. Band, Klasse 5 und 6* (Bielefeld, 1942).

Klagen, D. (ed.), *Volk und Führer: Deutsche Geschichte für Schulen* (Frankfurt am Main, 1943).

Klagges, D., *Geschichtsunterricht als nationalpolitische Erziehung* (Frankfurt am Main, 1936).

Kumsteller, B., *Werden und Wachsen. Ein Geschichtsatlas auf völkischer Grundlage* (Braunschweig, 1938).

Lebensgut. Ein deutsches Lesebuch für höhere Schulen. Dritter Teil (Frankfurt am Main, 1937).

von Leers, J., *Für das Reich: Deutsche Geschichte in Geschichtserzählungen* (Leipzig, 1940).

Maaken, N. *et al.* (eds), *Ewiges Deutschland. Schroedels Lesebuch für Mittelschulen für den Gau Schleswig-Holstein, 3. Band, Klasse 3–6* (Halle an der Saale, c. 1942).

Mahnkopf, J., *Von der Uhrzeit zum Grossdeutschen Reich* (Leipzig, 1941).

Mein erstes Buch (Dortmund, 1935).

Mühlenfibel. Erstes Lesebuch für schleswig-holsteinisches Kinder (Braunschweig/Berlin/Hamburg, 1935).

Olbricht, K. and Kärgel, H., *Deutschland als Ganze. Der Erdkunde Unterricht in der Volks- und Mittelschule* (Berlin, 1938).

Petersen, P., *Landvolk und Landarbeit. Lehrbuch für ländliche Berufsschulen. Erstes Berufsschuljahr* (Breslau, 1939).

Sotke, F., *Deutsches Volk und deutscher Staat. Staatsbürgerkunde für junge Deutsche* (Leipzig, 1936).

Vogel, A., *Erblehre und Rassenkunde für die Grund- und Hauptschule* (Baden, 1937).

Von Drinnen und Draussen. Heimatfibel für die deutsche Jugend (Frankfurt am Main, 1942).

Von neuen Deutschlands. Ergänzungshefte zu deutschen Lesebuchern. Heft 1, 3–5. Schuljahr (Frankfurt am Main, 1935).

Waetzig, A., *Volk, Nation, Staat. Ein Beitrag zur staatspoliticshen Schulung unserer jungen Volksgenossen* (Stuttgart, 1937).

Warneck, H. and Matschke, W., *Geschichte für Volksschulen* (Leipzig, 1942).

Newspapers and Journals
Der Biologe
The Daily Herald
Das Deutsche Mädel
The Listener
The Manchester Guardian
Nationalsozialistische Mädchenerziehung
Unterrichtsblätter für Mathematik und Naturwissenschaften
Völkischer Beobachter
Zeitschrift für neusprachlichen Unterricht

SECONDARY SOURCES

Abrams, L. and Harvey, E. (eds), *Gender Relations in German History: Power, Agency and Experience from the Sixteenth Century to the Twentieth Century* (London, 1996).

Albisetti, J., *Secondary School Reform in Imperial Germany* (Princeton, 1983).

Albisetti, J., *Schooling German Girls and Women: Secondary and Higher Education in the Nineteenth Century* (Princeton, 1988).

Allen, A. T., *Feminism and Motherhood in Germany, 1890–1914* (New Brunswick, 1991).

Allen, A. T., 'Children between Public and Private Worlds: The Kindergarten and Public Policy in Germany, 1840–Present', in Wollons, R. (ed.), *Kindergartens and Cultures: The Global Diffusion of an Idea* (New Haven, 2000), pp. 16–41.

Arntz, H., *Ordensburg Vogelsang 1934–1945: Erziehung zur politischen Führung im Dritten Reich* (Euskirchen, 1986).

Ash, M. (ed.), *German Universities Past and Future: Crisis or Renewal?* (Oxford, 1997).

Aumüller-Roske, U., 'Weibliche Elite für die Diktatur? Zur Rolle der nationalpolitischen Erziehungsanstalten für Mädchen im Dritten Reich', in Aumüller-Roske, U. (ed.), *Frauenleben-Frauenbilder-Frauengeschichte* (Pfaffenweiler, 1988), pp. 17–44.

Aumüller-Roske, U., 'Die Nationalpolitischen Erziehungsanstalten für Mädchen im Grossdeutschen Reich: Kleine Karriere für Frauen?', in Gravenhorst, L. and Tatschmurat, C. (eds), *Töchter-Fragen: NS-Frauen Geschichte* (Freiburg, 1990).

Barnett, C., 'The Education of Military Elites', *Journal of Contemporary History*, Vol. 2, No. 3 (1967), pp. 15–35.

Bäumer, Ä., *NS-Biologie* (Stuttgart, 1990).

Bäumer-Schleinkofer, Ä., *Nazi Biology and Schools* (Frankfurt am Main, 1995).

Baumeister, S., *NS-Führungskader. Rekrutierung und Ausbildung bis zum Beginn des Zweiten Weltkriegs 1933–1939* (Konstanz, 1997).

Beevor, A., *Berlin: The Downfall 1945* (London, 2002).

Bessel, R., *Nazism and War* (London, 2004).

Blackburn, G., *Education in the Third Reich: A Study of Race and History in Nazi Textbooks* (Albany, 1985).

Bleuel, H., *Strength through Joy: Sex and Society in Nazi Germany* (London, 1973).

Boberach, H., *Jugend unter Hitler* (Dusseldorf, 1982).

Boesten, E., *Jugendwiderstand im Faschismus* (Cologne, 1983).

Böltken, A., *Führerinnen im 'Führerstaat'* (Pfannenweiler, 1995).

Bowen, J., *Soviet Education: Anton Makarenko and the Years of Experiment* (Madison, 1962).

Brämer, R. and Kremer, A., *Physikunterricht im Dritten Reich* (Marburg, 1980).

Brauner, G., *The Education of a Gentleman. Theories of Gentlemanly Education in England 1660–1775* (New Haven, 1959).

vom Bruch, R., 'A Slow Farewell to Humboldt? Stages in the History of German Universities, 1810–1945', in Ash, M. (ed.), *German Universities Past and Future: Crisis or Renewal?* (Oxford, 1997), pp. 3–27.

Burleigh, M. and Wippermann, W., *The Racial State: Germany 1933–1945* (Cambridge, 1991).

Craig, G., *The Politics of the Prussian Army 1640–1945* (Oxford, 1955).

Demeter, K., *The German Officer-Corps in Society and State 1650–1945* (London, 1965).

Dithmar, R. (ed.), *Schule und Unterricht im Dritten Reich* (Neuwied, 1989).

Eilers, R., *Die nationalsozialistische Schulpolitik. Eine Studie zur Funktion der Erziehung im totalitären Staat* (Cologne, 1963).

Evans, R., *The Coming of the Third Reich* (London, 2004).

Evans, R., *The Third Reich in Power* (London, 2006).

Feiten, W., *Der Nationalsozialistische Lehrerbund. Entwicklung und Organisation* (Weinheim and Basel, 1981).

Feller, B. and Feller, W., *Die Adolf-Hitler-Schulen. Pädagogische Provinz versus Ideologische Zuchtanstalt* (Weinheim and Munich, 2001).

Finckh, R., *Mit uns zieht die neue Zeit* (Baden-Baden, 1979).

Flessau, K.-I., *Schule der Diktatur. Lehrpläne und Schulbücher des Nationalsozialismus* (Frankfurt am Main, 1979).

Flessau, K.-I., *et al.* (eds), *Erziehung im Nationalsozialismus* (Cologne, 1987).

Fricke-Finkelnburg, R., *Nationalsozialismus und Schule* (Opladen, 1989).

Fritsch, H., *Land mein Land: Bauerntum und Landdienst BDM-Osteinsatz Siedlungsgeschichte im Osten* (Preußisch Oldendorf, 1986).

Gallin, A., *Midwives to Nazism: University Professors in Weimar Germany 1925–1933* (Macon, 1986).

Genschel, H., 'Geschichtsdidaktik und Geschichtsunterricht im nationalsozialistischen Deutschland', in Schneider, G. and Bergmann, K. (eds), *Gesellschaft, Staat und Geschichtsunterricht* (Dusseldorf, 1982).

Giles, G., 'The Rise of the National Socialist Students' Association and the Failure of Political Education in the Third Reich', in Stachura, P. (ed.), *The Shaping of the Nazi State* (London, 1978).

Giles, G., *Students and National Socialism in Germany* (Princeton, 1985).

Gölz, K. and Jansen, W., 'Der Chemieunterricht im NS-Staat. Ein Beitrag zur Geschichte der Chemiedidaktik', *Gesellschaft Deutscher Chemiker, Fachgruppe Geschichte der Chemie* Mitteilung, Vol. 4 (1990).

Goodman, W., *Anton Simeonovitch Makarenko: Russian Teacher* (London, 1949).

von der Grün, M., *Wie war das eigentlich?: Kindheit und Jugend im Dritten Reich* (Darmstadt, 1979).

Grüttner, M., *Studenten im Dritten Reich* (Paderborn, 1995).

Hahn, H.-J., *Education and Society in Germany* (Oxford, 1998).

Hannsmann, M., *Der helle Tag bricht an – Ein Kind wird Nazi* (Hamburg, 1982).

Hasubek, P., *Das deutsche Lesebuch in der Zeit des Nationalsozialismus. Ein Beitrag zur Literaturpädagogik zwischen 1933 und 1945* (Hanover, 1972).

Hatheway, J., *In Perfect Formation: SS Ideology and the Junkerschule-Tölz* (Atglen, 1999).

Hearst, E., 'Ordensburgen: Finishing Schools for Nazi Leaders', *Wiener Library Bulletin*, Vol. XIX, No. 3, p. 38.

Heiber, H., *Universität unterm Hakenkreuz: Teil 1* (Munich, 1991).

Heiber, H., *Universität unterm Hakenkreuz: Teil 2* (Munich, 1992).

Heinemann, M. (ed.), *Erziehung und Schulung im Dritten Reich* (Stuttgart, 1980).

von Hellfeld, M. *Edelweißpiraten in Köln* (Cologne, 1983).

Herbst, J., *Requiem for a German Past: A Boyhood among the Nazis* (Madison, 1999).

Herf, J., *Reactionary Modernism: Technology, Culture and Politics in Weimar and the Third Reich* (Cambridge, 1984).

Hering, S. and Schilde, K., *Das BDM-Werk 'Glaube und Schönheit': Die Organisation junger Frauen im Nationalsozialismus* (Berlin, 2000).

Herr, G., *Inhaltsreiche Jahre – aus dem Leben einer BdM-Führerin 1930–1945* (Lausanne, 1985).

Herrlitz, H.- G. et al., *Deutsche Schulgeschichte von 1800 bis zum Gegenwart* (Weinheim and Munich, 1993).

Heske, H., '… und morgen die ganze Welt'. Erdkundeunterricht im Nationalsozialismus* (Gießen, 1990).

Holmes, B. and Keele, A. (eds), *When Truth was Treason: German Youth against Hitler* (Urbana and Chicago, 1995).

Honey, J., *Tom Brown's Universe: The Development of the Victorian Public School* (London, 1977).

Huber, K., *Jugend unterm Hakenkreuz* (Berlin, 1982).

Isaacs, N., 'Froebel's Educational Philosophy', in Laurence, E. (ed.), *Friedrich Froebel and English Education* (London, 1969).

Jarausch, K., *Students, Society and Politics in Imperial Germany: The Rise of Academic Illiberalism* (Princeton, 1982).

Jens, I. (ed.), *At the Heart of the White Rose: Letters and Diaries of Hans and Sophie Scholl* (New York, 1987).

Jürgens, B., *Zur Geschichte des BDM (Bund Deutscher Mädel) von 1923 bis 1939* (Frankfurt am Main, 1994).

Kamenetsky, C., *Children's Literature in Hitler's Germany: The Cultural Policy of National Socialism* (Athens, Ohio, 1984).

Kanz, H. (ed.), *Der Nationalsozialismus als pädagogisches Problem: Deutsche Erziehungsgeschichte 1933–1945* (Frankfurt am Main, 1984).

Kater, M., *Hitler Youth* (Cambridge, Mass. and London, 2004).

Keim, W., *Erziehung unter der Nazi-Diktatur* (Darmstadt, 1997).

Kinz, G., *Der Bund Deutscher Mädel: Ein Beitrag zur Außerschulischen Mädchenerziehung im Nationalsozialismus* (Frankfurt am Main, 1990).

Kirkpatrick, C., *Nazi Germany. Its Women and Family Life* (Indianapolis and New York, 1938).

Klaus, M., *Mädchen in der Hitlerjugend. Die Erziehung zur 'deutschen Frau'* (Cologne, 1980).

Klaus, M., *Mädchen im Dritten Reich. Der Bund Deutscher Mädel (BDM)* (Cologne, 1983).

Klönne, A., *Hitlerjugend. Die Jugend und ihre Organisation im Dritten Reich* (Hanover and Frankfurt am Main, 1955).

Klönne, A., *Jugend im Dritten Reich: Die Hitler-Jugend und Ihre Gegner* (Cologne, 1982).

Knopp, G., *Hitler's Children* (Stroud, 2002).

Koch, H., *The Hitler Youth: Origins and Development 1922–1945* (London, 1975).

Kocka, J., 'German History before Hitler: The Debate about the German *Sonderweg*', *Journal of Contemporary History*, Vol. 23 (1988), pp. 3–16.

Kogon, E., *Der SS Staat* (Stockholm, 1947).

Koon, T., *Believe, Obey, Fight: Political Socialisation of Youth in Fascist Italy, 1922–1943* (Chapel Hill and London, 1985).

Kühnel, F., *Hans Schemm. Gauleiter und Kultusminister (1891–1935)* (Nuremberg, 1985).

Lamberti, M., 'German Schoolteachers, National Socialism, and the Politics of Culture at the End of the Weimar Republic', *Central European History*, Vol. 34, No. 1 (2001), pp. 53–82.

Lamberti, M., *The Politics of Education: Teachers and School Reform in Weimar Germany* (New York and Oxford, 2002).

Laqueur, W., *Young Germany: A History of the German Youth Movement* (London, 1981).

Leeb, J. (ed.), *'Wir waren Hitlers Eliteschüler': Ehemalige Zöglinge der NS-Ausleseschulen brechen ihr Schweigen* (Hamburg, 1998).

Leitsch, C., 'Drei BDM-Biographinnen', *Dokumentationsstelle zur NS-Sozialpolitik: Mitteilungen*, April (1986).

McCulloch, G., *Philosophers and Kings: Education for Leadership in Modern England* (Cambridge, 1991).

Mann, E., *School for Barbarians: Education under the Nazis* (London, 1939).

Maschmann, M., *Account Rendered: A Dossier on My Former Self* (London, 1964).

Miller-Kipp, G. (ed.), *'Auch du gehörst dem Führer': Die Geschichte des Bundes Deutscher Mädel (BDM) in Quellen und Dokumenten* (Munich, 2002).

Moll, C., 'Acts of Resistance: The White Rose in the Light of New Archival Evidence', in Geyer, M. and Boyer, J. (eds), *Resistance against the Third Reich 1933–1990* (Chicago, 1994).

Mosse, G. (ed.), *Nazi Culture: Intellectual, Cultural and Social Life in the Third Reich* (London, 1966).

Mouton, M., *From Nurturing the Nation to Purifying the Volk: Weimar and Nazi Family Policy, 1918–1945* (Cambridge, 2007).

Neumann, P., *Other Men's Graves* (London, 1958).

Niederdalhoff, F., *'Im Sinne des Systems einsatzbereit…': Mädchenarbeit im 'Bund Deutscher Mädel' (BDM) und in der 'Freien Deutschen Jugend' (FDJ) – Ein Vergleich* (Münster, 1997).

Noakes, J. (ed.), *Nazism 1919–1945: A Documentary Reader*, Vol. 4 (Exeter, 1998).

Noakes, J. and Pridham, G. (eds), *Nazism 1919–1945: A Documentary Reader*, Vol. 2 (Exeter, 1984).

Orlow, D., 'Die Adolf-Hitler-Schulen', *Vierteljahrshefte für Zeitgeschichte,* Vol. 13 (1965), pp. 272–84.

Orme, N., *From Childhood to Chivalry: The Education of the English Kings and Aristocracy 1066–1530* (London, 1984).

Ortmeyer, B., *Schulzeit unterm Hitlerbild* (Frankfurt am Main, 1996).

Otto, H.-U. and Sünker, H. (eds), *Politische Formierung und soziale Erziehung im Nationalsozialismus* (Frankfurt am Main, 1991).

Overy, R., *The Dictators: Hitler's Germany and Stalin's Russia* (London, 2004).

Peukert, D., *Die Edelweißpiraten. Protestbewegung jugendlciher Arbeiter im Dritten Reich. Eine Dokumentation* (Cologne, 1980).

Peukert, D., *Inside Nazi Germany: Conformity, Opposition and Racism in Everyday Life* (London, 1987).

Peukert, D., *The Weimar Republic: The Crisis of Classical Modernity* (London, 1991).

Pfister, G. and Reese, D., 'Gender, Body Culture, and Body Politics in National Socialism', *Sport History*, No. 1 (1995), pp. 91–121.

Pine, L., 'The Dissemination of Nazi Ideology and Family Values through School Textbooks', *History of Education*, Vol. 25, No. 1 (1996), pp. 91–109.

Pine, L., *Nazi Family Policy, 1933–1945* (Oxford, 1997).

Pine, L., *Hitler's 'National Community': Society and Culture in Nazi Germany* (London, 2007).

Piper, E., *Alfred Rosenberg: Hitlers Chefideologe* (Munich, 2005).

de Ras, M., *Body, Femininity and Nationalism: Girls in the German Youth Movement 1900–1934* (New York and London, 2008).

Reese, D., 'Bund Deutscher Mädel – Zur Geschichte der weiblichen deutschen Jugend im Dritten Reich', in Frauengruppe Faschismusforschung (ed.), *Mutterkreuz und Arbeitsbuch: Zur Geschichte der Frauen in der Weimarer Republik und im Nationalsozialismus* (Frankfurt am Main, 1981).

Reese, D., *'Straff, aber nicht Stramm – Herb, aber nicht Derb'. Zur Vergesellschaftung der Mädchen durch den Bund Deutscher Mädel im Sozialkulturellen Vergleich zweier Milieus* (Weinheim, 1989).

Reese, D., 'Mädchen im Bund Deutscher Mädel', in Kleinau, E. and Opitz, C. (eds), *Geschichte der Mädchen- und Frauenbildung*, Vol. 2 (Frankfurt am Main, 1996), pp. 271–82.

Reese, D., *Growing up Female in Nazi Germany* (Ann Arbor, 2006).

Ringer, F., *The Decline of the German Mandarins: The German Academic Community, 1890–1933* (Cambridge, Mass., 1969).

Roberts, S., *The House That Hitler Built* (London, 1937).

Rogge, S., '"Mädel, komm zum BDM!"', in *Hart und Zart. Frauenleben, 1920–1970* (Berlin, 1990).

Samuel, R. and Hinton Thomas, R., *Education and Society in Modern Germany* (London, 1949).

Schneider, C., Stillke, C. and Leineweber, B., *Das Erbe der Napola: Versuch einer Generationengeschichte des Nationalsozialismus* (Hamburg, 1996).

Schiedeck, J. and Stahlmann, M., 'Totalizing of Experience: Educational Camps', in Sünker, H. and Otto, H.-U. (eds), *Education and Fascism: Political Identity and Social Education in Nazi Society* (London, 1997), pp. 54–80.

Schnurr, S., 'Vom Wolfahrtsstaat zum Erziehungsstaat: Sozialpolitik und soziale Arbeit in der Weimarer Republik und im Nationalsozialismus', *Widersprüche*, Vol. 8 (1988), pp. 47–64.

Scholtz, H., 'Die "NS-Ordensburgen"', *Vierteljahrshefte für Zeitgeschichte*, Vol. 15 (1967), pp. 269–98.

Scholtz, H., *NS-Ausleseschulen. Internatsschulen als Herrschaftsmittel des Führerstaates* (Göttingen, 1973).

Schoppmann, C., *Nationalsozialistische Sexualpolitik und weibliche Homosexualität* (Pfannenweiler, 1997).

Schulze-Kossens, R., *Militärischer Führernachwuchs der Waffen SS: Die Junkerschulen* (Osnabruck, 1982).

Siefken, H. (ed.), *The White Rose: Student Resistance to National Socialism 1942–1943* (Nottingham, 1991).

Simon, B. and Bradley, I. (eds), *The Victorian Public School: Studies in the Development of an Educational Institution* (Dublin, 1975).

Stachura, P. (ed.), *The Shaping of the Nazi State* (London, 1978).

Stachura, P., *The German Youth Movement 1900–1945: An Interpretative and Documentary History* (London, 1981).

Stargardt, N., *Witnesses of War: Children's Lives under the Nazis* (London, 2005).

Strien, R., *Mädchenerziehung und – sozialisation in der Zeit des Nationalsozialismus und ihre lebensgeschichtliche Bedeutung* (Opladen, 2000).

Sünker, H. and Otto, H.-U. (eds), *Education and Fascism: Political Identity and Social Education in Nazi Germany* (London, 1997).

Ueberhorst, H. (ed.), *Elite für die Diktatur. Die Nationalpolitischen Erziehungsanstalten 1933–1945. Ein Dokumentarbericht* (Düsseldorf, 1969).

Vorländer, H., *Die NSV. Darstellung und Dokumentation einer nationalsozialistischen Organisation* (Boppard, 1988).

Walk, J., *Jüdische Schule und Erziehung im Dritten Reich* (Frankfurt am Main, 1991).

Wegner, G., 'Schooling for a New Mythos: Race, Anti-Semitism and the Curriculum Materials of a Nazi Race Educator', *Paedagogica Historica*, Vol. XXVII (1992), pp. 189–213.

Wegner, G., *Anti-Semitism and Schooling under the Third Reich* (New York and London, 2002).

Wegner, G., 'Mothers of the Race: The Elite Schools for German Girls under the Nazi Dictatorship', *Journal of Curriculum and Supervision*, Vol. 19, No. 2 (2004), pp. 169–88.

Wehler, H., *Aus der Geschichte Lernen?* (Munich, 1988).

Weinberg, I., *The English Public Schools: The Sociology of Elite Education* (New York, 1967).

Welch, D., 'Educational Film Propaganda and the Nazi Youth', in Welch, D. (ed.), *Nazi Propaganda: The Power and the Limitations* (London, 1983), pp. 65–87.

Welch, D. (ed.), *Nazi Propaganda: The Power and the Limitations* (London, 1983).

Wilkinson, R. (ed.), *Governing Elites: Studies in Training and Selection* (Oxford, 1969).

Wortmann, M., *Baldur von Schirach: Hitlers Jugendführer* (Cologne, 1982).

INDEX

Abitur (school-leaving certificate), 7
Adolf Hitler Schulen (Adolf Hitler Schools)
  (AHS), 5, 72, 79–83, 139
agricultural work, girls, 130
Allgemeiner Deutscher Frauenverein (General
  German Women's Association), 9
anti-Semitism, 43–4, 49, 51, 56, 57–8
  see also Jews
Aufbauschule (feeder school), 28
Ausleseschulen (selection schools), 71
Axmann, Artur, 98, 99, 107

Bach, Johann Sebastian, 59
Bartholomäi, Hans-Georg, 77
Bauer, Elvira, 57
Bäumer, Gertrud, 9
Bäumler, Alfred, 60
Becker, Carl Heinrich, 10, 33
Beier, Ilse, 46
biology, curriculum, 42–4
Blasen (Bubbles), 108
'blood and soil' (*Blut und Boden*), 3, 42, 49,
  54, 59, 82
boarding schools, 30–1
Boelitz, Otto, 10
Bormann, Martin, 21, 138
Bouhler, Philip, 21, 41, 138
boys, youth groups, 95–113
Britain, elite education, 73–5
Brohmer, Paul, 42
Buchholz, Hans, 90
Bund Deutscher Mädel (League of German
  Girls) (BDM), 5–6, 102, 117–33, 139
  agricultural service, 130
  camps, 127–8

health education, 124–5
Heimabend, 127
  origins, 117–19
  sexual activity, 126–7
  uniform, 125–6
  war duties, 130–3
Bündische Jugend, 96
Burschenschaft, 32–3

camps
  Bund Deutscher Mädel (BDM), 127–8
  Hitler Youth, 101, 105
  teacher training, 15–19
Castell, Clementine zu, 129
Catholic youth groups, 100
chemistry, curriculum, 46–8
Communist Youth Association of Germany
  (KJVD), 100
Cornberg, Jobst-Christian von, 104
Crössinsee Ordensburg, 83, 88
curriculum, 4–5, 41–66, 138

Dehmlaw, Friedrich, 53
denominational schools, 28–9
Deutscher Schulverlag, 42
Deutsches Jungvolk (DJ), 102
Diesterweg, Adolf, 7
Döbereiner, Johann Wolfgang, 47
domestic advice, 60–1, 130
Drexler, Anton, 96

Eckart, Dietrich, 53–4
Edelweiss Pirates, 108, 109
Einstein, Albert, 34, 46
Eintopf ('one-pot dish') campaign, 55

Eisenecker, Maria, 122
elite schools, 5, 71–90, 138–9
England, public schools, 73–5
eugenics, 29, 42–3

family, ideology, 55–6, 59–60
films, propaganda, 65–6, 106
Fink, Fritz, 57
First World War, 9, 54
folklore, 53, 88
Franck, Walther, 46
Frauenschulen, 11
Freischar Junger Nation (Free Band of the
    Young Nation), 118
Frick, Wilhelm, 22
Friedrich, Artur, 45
Froebel, Friedrich, 23
Führerprinzip (leadership principle), 5, 89

geography, curriculum, 48–9
German, curriculum, 52–6
German Socialist Youth Association (SAP), 100
girls
    elite education, 78–9
    Hitler Youth, 102
    Kaiserreich education policy, 9
    Nazi education policy, 28, 60–1
    physical education, 64–5
    Weimar education policy, 11
    youth groups, 117–33
    see also women
Glaube und Schönheit (Faith and Beauty), 129
Gleichschaltung (streamlining), 14–15, 100,
    119
Goebbels, Josef, 42
Göllnitz, Willy, 45
Greater German Youth Movement, 97
Großdeutscher Bund (Greater German League),
    118
Gruber, Kurt, 97
Grundmann, Harald, 82
Günther, Erich, 45
Gymnasium, 7, 8–9, 11, 28, 81, 138
'Gypsies', 30

Habenicht, Hans Jürgen, 104
Häffner, Gerd, 112
Hanitzsch, Werner, 104
'harvest kindergartens', 25
health education, 124–5
Heißmeyer, August, 75, 77, 79
Heidegger, Martin, 34
Herbart, Johann Friedrich, 7
Herbst, Jurgen, 102, 105, 110, 112
'hereditary health', 42–3, 59–60, 81, 125
Hiemer, Ernst, 58
Hiemke, Rudolf, 104
hiking, 64, 65
Himmler, Heinrich, 21, 78, 89, 138
history, curriculum, 49–51
Hitler, Adolf
    education views, 13, 137
    and Hitler Youth, 99–100
    physical education views, 61–2
Hitlerjugend (Hitler Youth) (HJ), 5, 21–2,
    95–113, 139
    camps, 101, 105
    films, 106
    Heimabend, 101, 104–5
    Jungvolk, 98, 101
    leaders, 107
    military training, 105–6
    origins, 95–9
    Streifendienst (Patrol Service), 109
    uniform, 104
    war duties, 110–13
Hochschule der NSDAP (High School of the
    Party), 88
Hübener group, 110
Humboldt, Wilhelm von, 7, 32

intellectualism, Hitler's view of, 13

Jantzen, Walter, 49
Jews
    exclusion from school, 30
    teachers, 15, 27
    see also anti-Semitism
Jumbo Band, 108

Jungmädel (JM), 102, 123, 124
Jungnationaler Bund (Young-National League), 118
Junkers, 85–6

Kaiserreich, education policy, 2, 8–9, 12, 61, 137
Kärgel, Hermann, 49
Karsen, Fritz, 9–10
Kehlenbeck, Paul, 113
Kerschensteiner, Georg, 8
kindergartens, 23–5
Kinderlandverschickung (KLV), 31, 102, 139
Klagges, Dieter, 51
Krieck, Ernst, 4, 41

Lagarde, Paul de, 8, 22
land service, 102–3, 130
Landsmannschaften, 32–3
Langbehn, Julius, 8, 22
Lange, Friedrich, 9
Lange, Helene, 9
leaders
    education of, 82–3, 83–7
    Hitler Youth, 107
League of German Girls *see Bund Deutscher Mädel*
League of Radical School Reformers, 10
Lebensraum ('living space'), 5, 42, 48–9, 139
Leers, Johann von, 51
Lenard, Philipp, 46
Lenk, Adolf, 96–7, 119, 129
Leonhardt, Walter, 47
Ley, Robert, 21, 72, 79–80, 83, 86, 138
Linde, Carl von, 47
Loest, Erich, 103, 107
Loschmidt, Josef, 47

Mahnkopf, Johannes, 51
Makarenko, Anton, 73
Marienburg Ordensburg, 83
Maschmann, Melita, 120, 121
mathematics, curriculum, 51–2
Matschke, Willi, 51

Max von Baden, Prince, 10
Mein Kampf, 16
Meuten (Packs), 108
military physics, 44–5
Ministry of Education, policy-making, 2, 21–3
Mittelschule, 11
Mohr, Trude, 121
Müncheberg, Hans, 76
Musische Gymnasien (Musical Grammar Schools), 30–1

Nationalpolitische Erziehungsanstalten (National Political Educational Institutions) (Napolas), 5, 71–2, 75–9, 89, 139
Nationalsozialistiche Volkswohlfahrt (National Socialist People's Welfare) (NSV), kindergartens, 24–5
Nationalsozialistische Deutsche Arbeiterpartei (National Socialist German Workers' Party) (NSDAP), 14, 29, 86–7
    youth group, 96–7
Nationalsozialistischer Lehrerbund (National Socialist Teachers' League) (NSLB), 14–21, 102, 138
Neumann, Peter, 76–7, 83, 85
Nietzsche, Friedrich, 86
NS-Deutscher Studentenbund (National Socialist German Students' Association), 33–4
nutritional advice, 60

Oberlyzeum, 11
Oberrealschule, 9, 11
Oberschule, 11, 28
Oestreich, Paul, 10
Olbricht, Konrad, 49
Ordensburgen (Order Castles), 5, 72, 83–8, 139
Osteinsatz (Eastern Service), 131

Pausewang, Gudrun, 132–3
Pflichtjahr, 130
physical education, 61–5, 82

physics, curriculum, 44–6
policy-making, 2, 21–3
propaganda, 2, 18, 65–6, 106
protest groups, 108–10
Prussian State Boarding Schools, 12

racial studies, 4–5, 42–4, 56–60
radio, propaganda, 65–6
Rassenkunde (racial studies), 57, 138
Rauschning, Hermann, 86
Realgymnasium, 9, 11
religious education, 28–9
Rosenberg, Alfred, 21, 41, 50, 78, 88, 138
Rüdiger, Jutta, 123
Rust, Bernhard, 3, 18, 21–2, 42, 65, 72, 76,
   78, 80, 137–8

Scheel, Gustav Adolf, 34
Schemm, Hans, 14–15, 20, 43, 50
Schirach, Baldur von, 21, 33, 72, 79–80,
   97–8, 100, 107, 119, 123, 137
Scholl, Hans and Sophie, 109–10
school gardens, 44
schools
   elite schools, 5, 71–90, 138–9
   Nazi policies, 26–31
Schulstreit (school dispute), 8
Schultze, Walter, 34–5
Seffert, Hilde, 132
Seifert, Alwin, 83
sexual activity, 126
Silesia, teacher training, 15–16
Social Democratic Socialist Working Youth
   (SAJ), 100
Sommer, Theo, 76
Sonderweg (special path), 2, 8
Sonthofen Ordensburg, 83, 84, 87, 88
special schools, 29
Spengler, Oswald, 22
sport
   curriculum, 63–4
   girls, 123–4
Spranger, Eduard, 23
SS (Schutzstaffeln), 1, 77–8, 89

SS-Junkerschulen (Junker Schools), 85–6,
   88–9
Stark, Johannes, 46
Strasser, Gregor, 119
Strothmann, Dietrich, 111–12
student groups, 32–3
Studentenorden, 32
Der Stürmer, 57–8
Swing Youth, 108

teachers
   Hitler's view of, 13
   training, 14–21, 30, 138
Tempel, Wilhelm, 33
textbooks, 41–2, 54–5, 138
Treitschke, Heinrich von, 22, 32

universities
   Nazi policies, 31–6
   women's enrollment, 28
University of Berlin, 31–2
USSR, elite education, 73

Vogel, Alfred, 43–4
Vogelsang Ordensburg, 83–5
Volksbildung (national education), 7
Volksgemeinschaft (national community), 2,
   77, 852
Volksschule (elementary school), 7, 28–9
Volkstum (national traditions), 28, 42, 98

Waechtler, Fritz, 20
Wandervogel movement (birds of passage),
   95–6, 98, 118, 119, 122, 132
Warneck, Hans, 51
weapons training, 44–5
Wehrmacht, 105, 111
Weimar Republic
   education policy, 2, 9–12, 61, 137
   youth groups, 96
Weischedel, G., 27
Weltanschauung (Nazi world view), 2, 5, 72,
   77, 82, 139
Wessel, Horst, 54

White Rose movement, 109–10
Wilhelm II, Kaiser, 8
Winterhilfswerk (Winter Relief Agency), 55,
    99, 128, 131
women
    motherhood ideal, 55–6, 130, 132

training courses, 88
university students, 28
see also girls
Wyneken, Gustav, 95–6

youth groups, 4, 95–113, 117–33, 139